LANGUAGE AND LITERACY

LANGUAGE AND LITERACY: THE SELECTED WRITINGS OF KENNETH S. GOODMAN

Volume I
Process, Theory, Research

Edited and introduced by
Frederick V. Gollasch

Routledge & Kegan Paul
Boston, London and Henley

First published in 1982
by Routledge & Kegan Paul Ltd
9 Park Street,
Boston, Mass. 02108, USA,
39 Store Street,
London WC1E 7DD and
Broadway House,
Newtown Road,
Henley-on-Thames,
Oxon RG9 1EN
Printed in the United States of America

Library of Congress Cataloging in Publication Data

Goodman, Kenneth S.
Language and literacy.
Bibliography: p.
Includes index.
Contents: v. 1. Process, theory, research -
1. Reading, Psychology of. 2. Psycholinguistics. I. Title.
BF456.R2G63 153.6 81-11848

ISBN 0-7100-0875-9 (v. 1) AACR2

CONTENTS

FOREWORD

In the early 1960s, as a doctoral student at UCLA, I became interested in looking at reading. My interest grew from two sources. One was my concern as a graduate student to familiarize myself as fully as possible with research and theory relating to reading. The other was my curiosity about the implications for education of the explosion of activity in the field of linguistics.

The more I read the more convinced I became that linguistics had to have the key to some of the unanswered questions in reading. As I pushed that idea I also realized that there were many significant questions linguistics generates about reading that had not even been asked before.

But an extensive survey of the literature in reading and linguistics showed only a handful of writings in this field. That left me with a dilemma. Either I was moving down a blind alley others had already abandoned or I was out at the frontier of the field. Events of the next few years made clear that the latter was the case. One can not now pick up a text or journal dealing with reading without finding applications of linguistics.

I started with a few key assumptions:

Reading is language.
Readers are users of language.
Linguistic concepts and methods can explain reading.
Nothing readers do is accidental. It all results from interaction with text.

As my work progressed, I came to realize that reading is a psycholinguistic process, one in which thought and language interact. I realized that readers seek meaning, that as they read they are engaging in *comprehending*, constructing meaning through interaction with print.

The vehicle I chose to examine reading was simple: have subjects read orally whole, real, language texts they hadn't seen before and then analyze what they did as they read. What readers did was produce miscues; not everything matched what was expected; some of the responses were unexpected. But the unexpected responses showed the reader at work. Through these miscues we could see reading *in process*.

The analysis of these miscues led to my conclusion that reading could be characterized as a 'psycholinguistic guessing game.' The reader makes minimal use of cues, engages in tentative information processing, predicts, samples, confirms or disconfirms and reprocesses or corrects when necessary. The reader is actively seeking to make sense of written language.

These concepts are the core of the theory of reading that I have developed. This reading theory and the model that represents it have been continuously developed in interaction with the analysis of miscues of real readers reading different texts. The model is a macro model, that is, it attempts to deal with the whole of the reading process.

As linguists, psycholinguists, and cognitive psychologists began to turn their attention to reading, they brought to some of the phenomena of reading new terminology which has been applied by others to my theory. It has been characterized as an analysis-by-synthesis view, and inside-out view, and a top-down view. None of these are terms that I have used myself. While each, depending on whose definition you use, has some applicability, none captures the essential meaning - seeking, interactive essence of the theory.

I was, and have remained through all my work, an educationist and a teacher educator. This volume focusses mainly on theory and research. But the reader should understand that my constant motivation has been to understand reading and other language processes in order to contribute to the improvement of teaching and learning.

That may explain why I can not be satisfied with limited research designs or perspectives with leaps from laboratory experiments to methods and materials. It may explain my insistence on a reality base for assertions about reading and learning to read.

A primary motivation for bringing this volume together is to make my work more accessible to the field. Perhaps because my work has been widely quoted in recent years, many references and treatments of my ideas are now being based on secondary sources rather than my own statements. It is hoped that greater accessibility will make it possible for readers to check out representations and characterizations of my beliefs and convictions themselves.

Publication, like all language activity, involves risk-taking. Every author must wonder, as I have, whether some day he or she will regret having made public statements he or she no longer believes. But it is only through public interchange of ideas that growth in any field or in the individuals involved takes place. In my own case, the response to my published work has done a great deal to shape and encourage it. As I read through the papers included in this volume, there were certainly times when I encountered statements I would no longer make in the same way today. Usually that was due to development and refinement of my position. Sometimes, however, an early exploration has given way to a view that is quite different. Just for example:

1 My early uncertainty about the need to go from print to sound in reading has given way to a deep conviction that reading and listening are parallel processes with no necessary recoding.
2 My early belief that dialect divergence contributes barriers to reading comprehension has been disproven by my own research.
3 It has taken me a long time to fully purge from my view of reading the preoccupation with words which I feel still pervades the field.

Fred Gollasch was of inestimable help to me in selecting these articles. He brought an outside perspective which we hope has made it possible to avoid unnecessary overlap and to make the delicate decisions of which works are sufficiently obsolete that they might cause confusion if included.

A colleague recently shared with me a statement from William James cited by Abraham Kaplan, which in some sense seems to parallel closely some of the reactions to my work over the years. At the risk of seeming immodest, I offer it here:

> The three classic stages of a theory's career. First a new theory is attacked as absurd; then it is admitted to be true, but obvious and insignificant; finally it is seen as so important that its adversaries claim that they themselves discovered it.

Kenneth S. Goodman
Tucson, Arizona
February, 1979

ACKNOWLEDGMENTS

Chapter 1, The Reading Process, is from Kenneth S. and Yetta M. Goodman, 'Reading of American Children Whose Language Is a Stable Rural Dialect of English or a Language Other Than English,' Tucson, Arizona, August 1978. This chapter is part of a report of a project funded by the National Institute of Education, US Department of Health, Education and Welfare. However, the opinions herein expressed do not necessarily reflect the position or policy of the NIE.

Chapter 2, The Reading Process: Theory and Practice, is from 'Language and Learning to Read: What Teachers Should Know about Language,' edited by Richard E. Hodges and E. Hugh Rudorf. Copyright © 1972 by Houghton Mifflin Company. Reprinted by permission of the publisher.

Chapter 3, Reading: A Psycholinguistic Guessing Game, first appeared in 'The Journal of the Reading Specialist,' vol. 6, no. 4, May 1967, pp. 126-35. Copyright © 1967 by the College Reading Association. Reprinted by permission of the College Reading Association.

Chapter 4, The Linguistics of Reading, first appeared in the 'Elementary School Journal,' vol. 64, no. 8, April 1964. Copyright 1964 by the University of Chicago. Reprinted by permission of the University of Chicago Press.

Chapter 5, Decoding: From Code to What?, first appeared in 'Journal of Reading,' April 1971. Reprinted by permission of the International Reading Association.

Chapter 6, Psycholinguistic Universals in the Reading Process, is from 'Journal of Typographic Research' (now called 'Visible Language'), vol. IV, no. 2, Spring 1970, pp. 103-10, reprinted by permission of 'Visible Language.'

Chapter 7, What Is Universal About the Reading Process, first appeared in Proceedings of the 20th Annual Convention of the Japan Reading Association, 1976, pp. 69-79. Reprinted by permission.

Chapter 8, What We Know About Reading, is from P. D. Allen and Dorothy Watson, 'Findings of Research in Miscue Analysis: Classroom Implications,' ERIC, 1976, pp. 57-69. Copyright © 1976 by the National Council of Teachers of English. Reprinted with permission.

Chapter 9, Miscues: Windows on the Reading Process, is from Kenneth S. Goodman (ed.), 'Miscue Analysis: Applications to Reading Instruction,' ERIC, 1973. Copyright © 1973 by the National Council of Teachers of English. Reprinted with permission.

Chapter 10, Miscue Analysis: Theory and Reality in Reading, first appeared in John E. Merritt (ed.), 'New Horizons in Reading,' Proceedings of the Fifth IRA World Congress on Reading, 1976. Reprinted by permission of the International Reading Association.

Chapter 11, A Linguistic Study of Cues and Miscues in Reading, is from 'Elementary English,' vol. 42, no. 6, October 1965. Copyright © 1965 by the National Council of Teachers of English. Reprinted with permission.

Chapter 12, Analysis of Oral Reading Miscues: Applied Psycholinguistics, first appeared in 'Reading Research Quarterly,' Fall 1969, pp. 9-30. Reprinted by permission of the International Reading Association.

Chapter 13 first appeared as Influences of the Visual Peripheral Field in Reading in 'Research in the Teaching of English,' Fall 1975. Copyright © 1975 by the National Council of Teachers of English. Reprinted by permission.

Chapter 14, Kenneth S. and Yetta M. Goodman, Learning About Psycholinguistic Processes by Analyzing Oral Reading, is from 'Harvard Educational Review,' vol. 40, no. 3, 1977, pp. 317-33. Reprinted by permission of 'Harvard Educational Review.'

Chapter 15, Linguistically Sound Research in Reading, first appeared in Roger Farr, Samuel Weintraub and Bruce Tone (eds), 'Improving Reading Research,' 1976, pp. 89-100. Reprinted by permission of the International Reading Association.

Chapter 16, by Brian Cambourne, first appeared as Getting to Goodman: An Analysis of the Goodman Model of Reading with Some Suggestions for Evaluation, in 'Reading Research Quarterly,' vol. XII, no. 4, 1976-7, pp. 605-36. Reprinted with the permission of Brian Cambourne and the International Reading Association.

The Appendix, The Goodman Taxonomy of Reading Miscues, is from P. D. Allen and Dorothy Watson, 'Findings of Research in Miscue Analysis: Classroom Implications,' ERIC, 1976, pp. 157-244. Copyright © 1976 by the National Council of Teachers of English. Reprinted with permission.

INTRODUCTION
Psycholinguistics and Reading: The Work of Kenneth Goodman

Kenneth Goodman has now been investigating the oral reading behavior of children for over a decade and a half, and there can be little doubt that his work has had a powerful impact on the field of reading and on education in general. His interest in reading was first sparked during the early 1960s by the contradiction he saw between the lip service being paid to the importance of comprehension by the authorities of the day and the lack of consideration for comprehension in their reading programs. From his first sample study of children reading in 1963,[1] through the subsequent tens of thousands of miscues analyzed from a wide range of readers of differing ages and backgrounds, his insights have made significant contributions to our understanding of the reading process.

The development of the technique of miscue analysis as a research tool and as a diagnostic instrument has been important, but there can be little doubt that Goodman's greatest contribution has been his development of a coherent, unified model of the reading process. This model grew directly from observations of children reading and has had considerable influence on traditional views of reading and of readers. The impact of this work is evident in any review of the literature in reading as well as in a wide spectrum of subjects relevant to language and to language education.

This impact will continue to grow because of a number of principles and attitudes that underlie the Goodman work and that set it apart from most traditional research. Features of his work include:

1 The utilization of a broad range of scientific knowledge from various disciplines in the formulation of a theory of reading.
2 The utilization of descriptive research that observes what the reader is doing in as natural a setting as possible.
3 The insistence on integrating research and theory. Goodman sees theory *not* as being simply the end product of research, but the operational base from which research evolves. The research then in turn adds to and modifies the theory.
4 The use of whole stories, in an attempt to eliminate some of the problems of using short or fragmented text.
5 Detailed and complex data recording which allows a broad holistic view of the ongoing process in context, as well as a flexibility of focus.

6 A positive view of all children as competent language learners that focusses on their strengths and accomplishments rather than their weaknesses and failures.

These principles and attitudes are positive factors that have contributed to the relevance and accuracy of Goodman's research findings. These findings are being verified by continuing research in many countries, across ages and languages, providing mounting evidence that there is one reading process as described by the Goodman model.

There can be little doubt that the contribution of the work of Kenneth Goodman to the field of reading research and theory is a great one, but the full importance of his work will only be able to be fully assessed some time in the future.

This review of his work is an attempt to present, in one chapter, an overview of his understanding of the reading process; what led to the development of that understanding; and the implications of his work for education. First, however, it will be helpful to take a brief look at the development of psycholinguistics which is the framework through which Goodman operates.

THE DEVELOPMENT OF PSYCHOLINGUISTICS

Psycholinguistics (a blend of the terms psychology and linguistics) is a discipline concerned basically with the interaction between thought and language. During the mid-1950s, there was a revival of interest in language by psychologists who came to see that human language is very closely linked to understanding, and thus to cognitive processes. Some linguists welcomed this interest in the belief that psychology may contribute something to their study of language processes. This marked the humble beginnings of psycholinguistics.

Psycholinguistics has led to new insights into the reading process through new perspectives. These new insights have come largely from a careful application of the systematized knowledge about language provided by the science of linguistics. Up until recently, this systematized knowledge was not available and could not be used to understand reading.

Psycholinguists make a powerful claim for their position. They claim that in order to understanding reading, one must view it from a psycholinguistic vantage point because reading is a psycholinguistic process, one in which there is an interaction between thought and language, and therefore, all the central questions involved in reading are really psycholinguistic ones (Goodman, 1976, p.6).

THE GOODMAN ORIENTATION

It is important to understand that Goodman's psycholinguistic orientation is not only different from traditional views of the reading process, but it is the prime base - together with his 'naturalistic' approach to research - from which stem the insights that have made possible his significant contributions to the field of reading. Goodman observed children reading in a situation that eliminated the unnatural as much as possible. His claim is that 'we worked with real kids reading real books in real schools ... everything we know we have learned from kids' (Goodman, 1973, p.3).

Unlike many experimental researchers who undertake a narrow study of some process of instruction, Goodman collected data that was concerned with what children were doing when reading. He collected the 'whole' data that was embedded in a meaningful language context and studied that data in order to gain insight into the reading process. He then utilized the insights gained to develop a model of the reading process. His view, then, is a very broad one that attempts to encompass the whole of the complex reading process.

This approach makes his position somewhat more vulnerable than that of empirical researchers whose studies are narrow and supposedly 'neat,' and leaves him open to much criticism. He welcomes constructive criticism (Goodman, 1970, p.135) because he knows that it will lead to better understanding, but his work has often been criticized as being unscientific. Goodman disagrees. He responds, 'All scientific investigation must start with direct observation of available aspects of what is being studied. What distinguishes scientific from other forms of investigation is a constant striving to get beneath and beyond what is superficially observable' (Goodman, 1975, p.20).

Goodman has used the observation of oral reading as his source of data, believing it to be a valid means of getting to the reading process, by comparing the oral reading to the written text. His rationale is that the oral response is generated while meaning is being constructed, and therefore, provides a powerful means of examining process and underlying competence (Goodman and Goodman, 1977, p.318).

However, Goodman believes that very little can be learned from such observation if a naively empirical position is maintained:

> As the chemist must peer into the molecular structure, as the astronomer must ponder the effects of heavenly bodies on each other, as the ecologist must pursue the intricate web of interrelationships in a biological community, so the scientist in dealing with reading must look beyond behavior to process. Understanding reading requires depth analysis and a constant search for the insights which will let us infer the workings of the mind as print is processed and

meaning created. (Goodman, 1975, p.20)

The depth is provided by the tool that Goodman has devised - miscue analysis.

MISCUE ANALYSIS

A miscue is defined as 'an actual observed response in oral reading which does not match the expected response' (Goodman, 1973, p.5), and has often been described as a window on the reading process. Goodman does not consider miscues to be errors because they reveal more about the learner's strengths than his weaknesses. He believes that 'they are the best possible indicators of how efficiently and effectively the reader is using the reading process' (Goodman, 1974, p.7).

In miscue analysis readers' observed responses (oral readings) are compared to the expected responses (the written material) to provide a continuous basis of comparison that gives insights into 'the reader's development of meaning and the reading process as a whole' (Goodman and Goodman, 1977, p.320). The necessary requirements for conducting miscue analysis are outlined by Goodman:

> The written material must be new to the readers and complete with a beginning, middle, and end. The text needs to be long and difficult enough to produce a sufficient number of miscues. In addition, readers must receive no help, probe, or intrusion from the researcher. At most, if readers hesitate for more than thirty seconds, they are urged to guess, and only if hesitation continues are they told to keep reading even if it means skipping a word or phrase. Miscue analysis, in short, requires as natural a reading situation as possible. (Goodman and Goodman, 1977, p.320)

Miscue analysis was first used in 1963 (Goodman, 1965). Goodman was attempting to understand the reading process by giving subjects stories to read orally, and two things very quickly became clear:

> First, it was obvious that oral reading is not the accurate rendition of the text that it had been assumed to be. Readers, even good ones, make errors. Second, it was clear that linguistic insights, scientific views of language, were very much appropriate to describing reading behavior. The things the readers did were linguistic things - they were not random. (Goodman, 1973, p.5)

What was happening was that readers were showing their natural competence as language users.

Since those first discoveries, Goodman has always viewed

reading as a language process. He sees it as the receptive aspect of written language and thus the parallel process to listening. He regards the reader as a user of language, one who constructs meaning from written language (Goodman, 1976, p.1). He believes that in literate societies there are four language processes: speaking, writing, listening and reading. 'Two are productive; two are receptive. Reading is no less a receptive language process than listening is' (Goodman, 1975a, p.627). After a decade and a half of research, Goodman's claim is that everything he and his co-workers have observed among readers of all levels of proficiency supports the validity of that assumption (Goodman and Goodman, 1977, p.317), and because reading is language[2] he believes that 'the teaching of reading must be based on the best available knowledge of language' (Goodman, 1964, p.355).

Because Goodman believes that reading is an active process in which the reader is interacting with the writer through print, he sees miscues not simply as errors, but as observable responses that are caused by and reflect the psycholinguistic process in which he is engaged (Goodman, 1974, pp.6-7). This position has two important implications. It separates Goodman from those who hold the simplistic view that reading must be accurate, and it changes the view from a negative one where errors are seen as undesirable, to a positive view of miscues as by-products of the reading process (Goodman, 1976, p.2).

In his early studies of miscues Goodman's search and discovery are best described in his own words:

> I naively looked for easily identified cause-effect relationships. For each miscue I looked for some one cue. In this I was operating as others had done in research on error analysis. The difference was that I was using scientific linguistics to categorize the phenomena. So when I found myself saying a miscue had a graphic cause, I found myself aware that there also were grammatical relationships involved: 'lad' and 'lady' look quite a bit alike but they are also both nouns and they have related meanings. Both are kinds of people. So if a reader substitutes 'lady' for 'lad' which of these factors is the cause? I was led then to the development of an analytic taxonomy which considers the relationships between the expected response (ER) and the observed response (OR) from all possible angles. (Goodman, 1973, p.6)

Goodman had come to the point of understanding that it was necessary to look at the whole process of reading if one wanted worthwhile answers. The problem was, however, that the reading process and children's miscues were so complex as to demand a theoretically based framework by which the phenomena might be intelligibly described (Goodman and Burke, 1970, p.121).

THE TAXONOMY

Since 1965 Goodman has developed and is continuing to refine a taxonomy on the basis of his descriptive studies. Each miscue is examined carefully by asking a number of questions about the relationships of the expected to the observed response. The structure of the taxonomy is necessarily complex, relying on answers to approximately twenty one questions for each miscue, the reason being that it is not possible to explain complex processes with simplistic descriptions.[3]

Miscue analysis using this taxonomy is most suited to depth research on small numbers of subjects and what emerges for each subject is valuable information on the 'patterns of how the cuing systems are used in on-going reading' (Goodman, 1976, p.4). A simplified form of miscue analysis called the Reading Miscue Inventory (RMI) has been developed by Yetta M. Goodman and Carolyn Burke, utilizing the most significant questions from the taxonomy. This is gaining wider acceptance among classroom teachers and clinicians as a diagnostic tool, but is also a very valuable means of gaining insights into the reading process of individuals. For this reason it is proving helpful in teacher education. Other more simplified forms of miscue analysis have been developed by a number of people, but it is important to realize that there is a direct relationship between the simplification of the form and the loss of information about the subject's reading strategies.

INSIGHTS FROM MISCUE ANALYSIS

A decade and a half of miscue analysis across many age, dialect and language groups in many parts of the world has contributed many important educational insights. One of the most important is the respect that all educators need to have for the language learning ability of children.

A young child's ability to handle spoken language, to understand others and be able to generate sentences that he or she has never heard before is impressive. Goodman explains it in these words:

> Each child creates language for himself, moving toward the language forms of his community, as he strives for effective communication. His success is so obvious that it is taken for granted by most adults. By the time a child is five or six, regardless of the culture into which he is born, he is fully competent to use his mother tongue to meet his own needs in communication, thought and learning. And he has the ability to continue developing language as he grows and learns and as his needs become more complex. (Goodman, 1969, p.1)

Because of the child's natural ability to handle language, some linguists believe that the child's language ability is innate. Goodman believes that human infants are born with the capability for language and the need to communicate (Goodman, 1969a, p.137).

Many examples of young children's miscues contained in the Goodman writings reveal the complex processes that are being handled by young readers indicating that they are indeed competent language users. There are important implications here for the teaching of reading. Goodman says, 'We know a lot about a kid's ability to use language now but it all adds up to one thing. If you're going to teach kids to read you're going to have to show a healthy respect for the prodigious language achievements and language learning ability of the human young' (Goodman, 1974, p.3).

THE GOODMAN MODEL OF READING

The insights gained from miscue analysis have been used by Goodman to develop a model of reading commonly referred to as the Goodman Model of Reading. Goodman defines reading as 'a psycholinguistic process by which the reader, a language user, reconstructs, as best he can, a message which has been encoded by a writer as a graphic display' (Goodman, 1970, p.135). On a number of occasions, he has described the reading process as 'a psycholinguistic guessing game,' a brief but apt summary of his theory of reading which, like the reading process itself, is complex and involved.

Goodman believes that three sources of information are available to the reader: 'One kind, the graphic information, reaches the reader visually. The other two, syntactic and semantic information, are supplied by the reader as he begins to process the visual input' (Goodman, 1973, p.9).

If he is to be successful, the reader must comprehend, 'he must be actively involved in the reconstruction of a message' (Goodman, 1976, p.5). The task, Goodman says, 'is not to hear the word or recognize the word or name it. The task is to get the underlying structure, to get at the meaning, and to constantly keep the meaning in mind' (Goodman, 1971, p.7). Because the reader's aim is meaning, he uses as much or as little of each of the three kinds of information as is necessary to get the meaning (Goodman, 1973, p.9). Miscue analysis has revealed that 'all three systems are used in an integrated fashion' (Goodman and Goodman, 1977, p.331). This 'dynamic interaction between the reader and the written language' (Goodman and Goodman, 1977, p.322), is best described in Goodman's own words:

> He makes predictions of the grammatical structure, using the control over language structure he learned when he learned oral language. He supplies semantic concepts to get the mean-

> ing from the structure. In turn, his sense of syntactic structure and meaning make it possible to predict the graphic input so he is highly selective, sampling the print to confirm his prediction. (Goodman, 1973, p.9)

Thus prediction and confirmation (according to Goodman) are two basic processes involved in reading. A third is the process of correction. If the prediction or hypothesis that was made during reading was not confirmed, and the reading did not make sense semantically and/or syntactically, then it is likely that the reader would regress to correct the prediction in order to get to meaning by reprocessing the available cues. Throughout the reading process, the efficient reader is constantly sampling the print, using a minimum of information to get to meaning. Therefore, apart from the obvious stages of initiating and terminating the reading task, there are four main processes visualized in the Goodman model, those of sampling, predicting, confirming and correcting. The integrated picture is well described in the following passage:

> Readers develop sampling strategies to pick only the most useful and necessary graphic cues. They develop prediction strategies to get to the underlying grammatical structure and to anticipate what they are likely to find in the print. They develop confirmation strategies to check on the validity of their predictions. And they have correction strategies to use when their predictions do not work out and they need to reprocess the graphic, syntactic and semantic cues to get to the meaning. (Goodman, 1973, p.9)

Goodman also believes that reading can be usefully represented by a series of cycles - optical, perceptual, syntactic and meaning cycles which are employed more or less sequentially throughout a story or text, but they may be telescoped if the reader is able to leap ahead to meaning (Goodman, 1975, p.23).

Most of Goodman's research is reported in three large studies conducted for the US Department of Health, Education and Welfare published in 1968, 1973 and 1978. However, his conceptual writings are supported by and punctuated with miscue research data. Although space does not permit the inclusion of data here, the following is a description of some of the processes involved in one girl's reading miscues, which will illuminate what has been said thus far:

> Peggy's performance allows us to see a language user as a functional psycholinguist. Peggy's example is not unusual; what she does is also done by other readers. *She processes graphic information*: many of her miscues show a graphic relationship between the expected and observed response. *She processes syntactic information*: she substitutes noun for noun, verb for verb, noun phrase for noun phrase, verb

> phrase for verb phrase. She transforms; she omits an intensifier, changes a dependent clause to an independent clause, shifts a 'wh-' question sentence to a declarative sentence. *She draws on her conceptual background and struggles toward meaning, repeating, correcting and reprocessing as necessary.* She predicts grammar and meaning and monitors her own success. She builds and uses psycholinguistic strategies as she reads. In short, her miscues are far from random. (Goodman, 1977, p.319; emphasis added)

In summary, then, reading is seen by Goodman as a process in which three types of information (graphophonic, syntactic, and semantic) are dealt with in an integrated way through the processes of sampling, predicting, confirming and correcting with the primary aim of getting to meaning. The reader is seen as a user of language, seeking meaning, interacting with the graphic input as he 'concentrates his total prior experience and learning on the task, drawing on his experiences and the concepts he has attained as well as the language competence he has achieved' (Goodman, 1969b, p.15).

PREMISES

There are a number of important related premises that need to be dealt with in this discussion of Goodman's work. Some of them have been touched on already, but it will be helpful to list them here:

Premise 1 *Reading is a language process.*
Goodman believes that there are four language processes: writing, reading, speaking, and listening. He argues that reading 'is no less a receptive language process than listening is' (1975, p.627). The traditional view (very much influenced by some linguists) is that written language is really a secondary, more abstract representation of 'real' language which is oral language.

Recent evidence suggests that young children are learning to read from exposure to print in the environment long before their parents or teachers are aware that they are becoming literate, and they are learning in much the same way that they are learning to speak (Goodman and Goodman, 1976, p.2).

Premise 2 *Reading is a psycholinguistic process.*
If one accepts that reading is a language process, it is logical to argue that reading is an interaction between language and thought, and it follows that adequate answers to important questions will not be found if we do not view reading in this light.

Premise 3 *Children have a natural competence to acquire and develop language.*
It is widely accepted that children display amazing ability to understand and acquire oral language. A decade and a half of miscue analysis research indicates that this also applies to written language and that children's oral language ability is an important source that can be utilized in efficient reading.

Premise 4 *Language is learned from whole to part and its acquisition is facilitated in a purposeful, meaningful, communicative context.*
Michael Halliday (1975, 1977) has shown that in the development of language, function precedes form, that children acquire and develop language because language has a purpose. They learn to communicate first, and the more they communicate, the better they learn the accepted forms of language. Many years of research with a broad sample of readers of all ages has shown that reading development is greatly enhanced by the use of meaningful, relevant materials.

Premise 5 *Reading research, in order to be valid and reliable, must involve itself with whole, relevant, meaningful language.*
This is a logical outcome of premises 3 and 4. Much reading research in the past has been preoccupied with fragments of language.

Premise 6 *Both expected and unexpected oral responses to printed texts are produced through the same process* (Goodman and Goodman, 1977, p.320).

Premise 7 *Oral reading is a valid means of gaining insight into the silent reading process.*

Premise 8 *The types of inferences made about the reading process in the taxonomy questions are relevant to the 'real life' situation* (Cambourne, 1977, p.624).

The premises 6-8 are crucial to the validity of miscue analysis. If, for example, it can be shown that miscues are not caused by the same process that produces expected responses, then miscue analysis becomes invalid as an instrument for gaining insight into the reading process. Similar arguments apply to premises 7 and 8.

Premise 9 *There is a single reading process for fluent and beginning readers of which the primary aim is comprehension.*
This premise is an important outcome of the theory of psycholinguistics. Of all the premises underlying Goodman's work, this is probably the most difficult to defend. There is little doubt that it has caused the greatest controversy, because many will not accept that it is possible for children to learn to

read without teaching sub-skills (e.g. phonics skills).

Premise 10 *Attempts to understand the complex reading process will not be very successful with traditional narrow 'experimental' approaches. The problem demands broader theory based methods.* Goodman's argument for an underlying theory is strong:

> Behavior...is the end product of a process. The external behavior is observable and serves as an indicator of the underlying competence. Behavior can be observed, but it can not be understood without some theory of how it is produced. Seemingly identical behaviors may result from very different processing. Very different behaviors may prove closely related if they are seen within a theoretical framework. (1976, p.7)

Premise 11 *Depth analysis of a few subjects will be more rewarding than narrow statistical studies involving many subjects over a short period of time.*
Goodman strongly criticizes reliance on the experimental model as a basic tool in reading research (in Farr, et al., 1976, pp.92-3) concluding with these words:

> At best, it can only 'prove' or 'disprove' a small set of hypotheses already believed to be true. It plows no new ground, provides no new insights...
>
> Manipulation of data - however rigorously it's conducted - can never make up for the original poor quality of the data itself. Sound data can only come from a base of knowledge, sound assumptions, and a theoretical framework that gives the data value.
>
> Of what value is it to prove everyone does something if understanding *how* one person does it is what we really need to know?

Premise 12 *Miscue analysis methodology is no less scientific than more traditional experimental methods.*
Often people assume that if something isn't traditional it must be wrong. Miscue analysis is a comprehensive and consistent attempt, based on the latest knowledge of language and children, to get 'beneath and beyond the superficial' (Goodman, 1975, p.20).

THE TEACHING OF READING

Goodman sees himself in an applied, rather than a basic, field of research and has had much to say about the teaching of reading. In comparison to traditional views of reading and reading instruction, his concepts are considered by some to be somewhat controversial.

He does not believe that there is a hierarchy of sub-skills involved in learning to read; that the teaching of reading should begin, 'not with letters or sounds but with whole real relevant natural language' (Goodman, 1976, p.18).

Again he emphasizes that reading is a language process:

> Children learn first to speak in a situation in which they are surrounded by the sounds of speech in action. In this setting, language is learned from whole to part, from general to specific. Learning to read follows the same pattern. (Goodman and Menosky, 1971, p.1)

Closely allied to this belief is the concept that beginning readers use the same process as fluent readers. On the basis of research with readers at all levels of proficiency, Goodman concluded that 'there is only one reading process. Readers may differ in the control of this process but not in the process they use' (Goodman and Goodman, 1976, p.18).

Goodman has been critical of the strong emphasis on phonics in teaching reading. He is concerned that the literature dealing with the reading process is cluttered with outmoded beliefs based on pre-existing, naive, 'common sense' notions that are interfering with the application of modern scientific concepts of language and thought (Goodman, 1967, p.1). He claims that phonic approaches to reading are preoccupied with precise letter identification that is based on the false idea that 'reading is a precise process. It involves exact, detailed, sequential perception and identification of letters, words, spelling patterns and larger language units' (Goodman, 1967, p.1). In other words this view of reading has dominated the literature when, in fact, it does not have a sound research base, but has simply been assumed to be true.

Goodman does not believe (as a number of his critics have claimed) that phonics plays no part in the reading process. He simply believes that phonics is far less important than is reflected in many traditional reading programs. Continuing evidence from his extensive research has convinced him of this.

Goodman's criticism of narrowly based phonics programs is closely allied to his most outspoken criticism which applies to a much wider audience:

> Language may be dissected and pulled apart into pieces to better understand its workings, but because it is a process, these pieces, sounds, words, phrases, cease to be language apart from whole language in use. Language is not encountered by the learner except as it is used when he learns to talk - yet he does learn to talk. Because we have not properly respected language, *we have tended to think we facilitated learning to read by breaking written language into bite-size pieces for learners. Instead, we turned it from easy-to-learn language into hard-to-learn abstractions.* (Good-

man, 1973, p.12; emphasis added)

A quick survey of beginning reading programs and reading research indicates that this criticism has very wide application. Goodman is concerned that we are doing more harm than good by fragmenting language. His main argument is that we do not and can not read letter by letter or word by word. A good reader 'is one so efficient in sampling and predicting that he uses the least (not the most) available (surface) information necessary. All the information must be available for the process to operate in the reader and for the sampling strategies it requires to develop in the beginner' (Goodman, 1969b, p.17). Goodman's research has indicated that it is harder to read words in isolation than in context (Goodman, 1965, pp.639-43), and he makes a number of suggestions for helping to move the teaching of reading away from the emphasis on individual words:

> Essentially they involve shifting focus to comprehension; the goal of reading instruction becomes more effective reading for more complete comprehension. Instead of word attack skills, sight vocabularies, and word perception the program must be designed to build comprehension strategies.... Children learning to read should see words always as units of larger, meaningful units. In that way they can use the correspondences between oral and written English within the semantic and syntactic contexts. As children include these correspondences they will develop the strategies for using them in actual reading. (Goodman, 1969c, p.15)

Goodman is adamant that teachers must make the fullest possible use of the language competence and the total experiential background that children bring to school with them, by providing reading material that is whole and meaningful, that 'deals with familiar situations and ideas and ... is written in a language which is like his [the child's] own oral language' (Goodman, 1969a, p.142). Then and only then can the child 'bring all of his language strength to bear on the task' (Goodman, 1969a, p.142). Any instruction (the Goodman argument continues) that does not build on the process of natural language learning is at cross purposes with the child's natural tendencies and will blunt their natural language strengths and may even become counterproductive (Goodman and Goodman, 1976, p.3). What seems to happen often in the classroom is that literacy is presented as something new and unlike language as the child has known and used it and it cannot become a natural continuation of the child's growing competence (Goodman, 1971a, p.48).

Goodman believes 'that children learn to read and write in the same way and for the same reason that they learn to speak and listen' (Goodman and Goodman, 1976, p.3). Children learn to speak because they see the need and they have the capacity to learn it naturally. Many problems associated with learning to read would disappear (according to Goodman) if teachers and parents would encourage the child to see the need for literacy, and would build on the child's natural strengths.

Many traditional reading programs assume that accuracy is an essential part of reading. Successful readers (Goodman says) are those who are effective and efficient. In other words, 'they can construct a message which substantially agrees with the one the writer began with ... [and] ... they use the least amount of effort to achieve that end' (Goodman, 1974a, p.826). Years of research have shown that readers who strive for accuracy are often inefficient in getting to meaning. They are like over-cautious drivers in cars, unable to sort out from the mass of realities assaulting their senses those that are needed to make effective decisions (Goodman, 1974a, p.826).

For Goodman there is only one prime objective in reading. That is comprehension. Everything else 'is either a skill to be used in achieving comprehension (for example, selecting key graphic cues), a subcategory of comprehension (for example critical reading) or a use to be made of comprehension (for example appreciation of literature)' (Goodman and Niles, 1970, pp.28-9). Goodman is convinced that 'each instructional activity should, in fact, be screened on the basis of whether it contributes to comprehension' (Goodman, 1970a, p.19). He points out that meaning is as important for the beginning reader as it is for the proficient reader and, therefore, the selection of materials at all levels is also of utmost importance. All reading materials must be relevant to the individual reader, they must 'make it possible for him to build on his strengths, not put him at a disadvantage by focussing on his weaknesses' (Goodman and Niles, 1970, p.28).

Goodman has long been campaigning for schools to take more positive attitudes to groups that contain high proportions of children with reading problems, such as the poor, the black, the bilingual and the culturally divergent. He claims that many schools for too long have been inflexible; have not had relevant instructional programs for all learners; have tried to force 'standard English' on the kids; and have looked in the wrong places (such as the use of archaic phonics programs, tracking exercises, etc.) for remedies (Goodman, 1968, pp.1-2).

One of the major problems has been that many educators have taken the view that any child that speaks differently is deficient in language ability. On this issue Goodman emphasizes that 'linguistic study reveals that all dialects are fully functioning language variants each with systematic phonology, grammatical structure, and vocabulary' (Goodman, 1971b, p.93). 'Science,' he says, 'has brought us to the understanding the poets always had: all language has system, utility, and beauty' (Goodman, 1972, p.4). The basis of the problem is that any child 'who is made to accept another dialect for learning must accept the view that his own language is inferior....In a very real sense, since this is the language of his parents, his family, his community, he must reject his own culture and himself, as he is, in order to become something else' (Goodman, 1965a, p.859).

Again, Goodman's solution to this problem stems from his research. As with all learners he suggests that we build on their strengths. The solution involves accepting the dialect of the child and building on it while eliminating the imposed disadvantages.[4] Among others these include positive measures such as using language experience materials from the child's own language and allowing them to read standard materials in their own dialect (Goodman, 1971c, p.74).

He believes that 'dialect-involved miscues do not interfere with the reading process or the construction of meaning, since they move to the reader's own language' (Goodman, 1973a, p.6). The essence of his message is that we must accept and honour children's language, because by doing this we are 'encouraging divergent speakers to use their language competence, both receptive and productive, and accepting their dialect-based miscues, we minimize the effect of dialect differences. In rejecting their dialects we maximize the effects' (Goodman, 1973a, pp.6-7). After all, the real aim of language is to 'dig and be dug in return' (L. Hughes in Goodman, 1965a, p.860).

Goodman has been critical of our language curricula because like so many other educational practices it is based on faulty foundations:

> So predominant in our research is our snobbery that large bodies of research are virtually worthless. Most studies of child language development lumped immaturity and dialect difference together, compounding an already faulty language model. In fact, studies have been presented by researchers who apparently think one can study language, language acquisition and language performance without knowing anything about language....The whole language curriculum is built on a base of linguistic misconceptions. (Goodman, 1969f, p.9)

Goodman has labeled the model of school language development that tries to force the child's language into the narrow channel labeled correct, proper or standard, the 'Uptight Model', and has used the term 'Expansion Model' to describe the attempt to build on the competence the child already possesses, helping him to develop outwardly (Goodman, 1969d, p.9). An essential feature of the latter model would be the opportunity for children to use language in school as often as possible. As Goodman says, 'if we follow the old adage that children should be seen but not heard we are going to have linguistically crippled children' (Goodman, 1972a, p.28).

Although much of Goodman's work has been applied to beginning readers and readers who are still in the process of developing fluency, there are applications for readers at all stages of development. Goodman submits that the concept of working with whole natural language in reading is of utmost importance for the child who suffers from learning difficulties. It is he 'who will suffer most from our attempts to structure his learning' (Goodman, 1969e, p.7). He also believes that the fluent reader needs to develop independence in the use of techniques and strategies (they will not always follow the same sequence as publishers suggest); they need a wide range of reading experiences requiring flexibility in uses of strategies; they need to understand the importance and the pleasure of reading; they need to develop the ability to read critically (Goodman and Niles, 1970, pp.33-6).

It is obvious in all that has been said thus far that the teacher's role is vital. Goodman believes that in order to be effective teachers of reading, teachers must integrate the best knowledge from many disciplines such as child development, classroom practice, psychology and, of course, psycholinguistics (Goodman, 1968a, p.313), and they must understand the real relevance of the theory and research if they are to understand and see reading materials in their true perspective (Goodman, 1971d, p.181). In fact, Goodman says if teachers want more effective and relevant materials and methods, they must not only be enlightened, but must 'work in direct contact with the readers for whom the curriculum must be relevant' (Goodman, 1969g, p.4).

There can be no doubt that the teacher's attitude to the child is crucial. The positive attitude that is required towards the child's language is clearly described by Goodman in the following passage:

> One of the things we have to do with any child when he comes to school is to build his pride and his confidence in his linguistic achievement. He should be proud of the language that he has. He should be elated that he has such a marvelous tool, and he should feel quite confident that he can use his language to communicate about things that are important to him. That means that the teacher has to take some pains to listen and to understand what he says....We have to encourage him to express through language his thoughts and reactions to the world, and accept rather than correct his expressions and refrain from trying to teach him a proper way of expressing them. At such moments we introduce shame and confusion in the place of pride and confidence. If we accept his expressions, he has been successful; if we do not understand them, then the child has not effectively communicated. That is the point at which we can assist. (Goodman, 1972a, p.24)

A teacher with a negative attitude to a child's use of language can not only inhibit communication, but can disrupt the learning process (Goodman, 1969a, p.138). Rather the teacher must take on the role of 'helper, facilitator and stimulator...[and] learn to interpret the kinds of errors her youngsters make as they spiral forward in their movement toward independence in reading' (Goodman, 1970a, p.9). Teachers must work with children, helping them to build strategies for comprehension, if they want to help them become efficient and effective readers (Goodman, 1973b, p.9).

READING TESTS

One of the important contributions Goodman has made to the field of education is his emphasis on the need for a distinction between competence and performance.[5] This distinction has wide application, but is particularly relevant to language and reading, and even more so at this time when behavioural objectives are being thrust upon us. Goodman says that what we are really aiming to build in education is not the outward performance (or behavior) but the underlying competence (Goodman, 1970, p.27).

Goodman has taken considerable space to detail the inadequacies of present-day reading tests and the logic behind them (1971e, 1973c, 1974b), and one of his strongest criticisms is that they do not make the distinction between competence and performance. He says:

> We may use tests, or oral reading, or other performances as evidence of this competence, but we are never justified in saying that the performance we can observe and measure is the competence itself....Only with a thorough understanding of the reading process and how it is used can one interpret behavior in reading to get insight into the strength of the reading process as it is being used. (Goodman, 1974a, p.827)

He describes reading tests as 'anchors against progress' (Goodman, 1974a, p.828), and indicates that future tests will need to move away from the counting of errors to an analysis of performance. He believes that they will need to deal with comprehension in a range of reading situations, to avoid irrelevance and get at the reader's ability to use written language effectively. However, the greatest need is to improve their use. Furthermore, Goodman indicates that not even the very best of tests 'can substitute for the insights which professional teachers can get from working closely with children' (Goodman, 1973c, p.11).

CONCLUSION

In summary, then, Goodman's view is a broad one, because reading is a very complex process and cannot be understood or explained from a narrow simplistic stance. His theory of reading instruction is based (as he says it must be) 'on an articulated theory of the reading process' (Goodman, 1972b, p.1), which in turn is rooted in research with children of different ages and levels of proficiency and draws on knowledge from many disciplines.

His approach is a new one that has brought with it considerable insight. Goodman says, 'We know now how reading works; we know how it is learned; we understand its uses and limitations better' (Goodman, 1974a, p.828), but he is quick to add:

> There is no simple breakthrough in reading just around the corner which will change instruction to a foolproof science. As more is understood about reading and learning to read, it becomes ever clearer how complex these processes are. No simple antitoxin can be injected in nonreaders to make them readers. But progress will come as misconceptions disappear in favor of sound understanding. (Goodman and Niles, 1970, p.37)

Goodman has clearly indicated that he has not provided a new method of teaching reading, that psycholinguistics is not a method and neither is miscue analysis. One can use psycholinguistics as the basis for a sound methodology just as miscue analysis can be used as a basis for sound instruction. But what has been provided is a new perspective, and this perspective 'is process-centered, language-centered, meaning-centered. It requires a new respect for language, a new respect for the learner, and a new respect for the reading teacher' (Goodman, 1973, p.11).

F.V. Gollasch
Tucson, Arizona
November, 1979

NOTES

1 Chapter 11 in this volume.
2 The commonly held view that reading is not language but simply the use of language tends to diminish the importance of the reader in the process. Reading is seen here as one of four language processes. It is not like language, or a process that uses language. It is language. The reader is actively involved in producing language during reading.
3 The number of questions asked in the taxonomy has varied from time to time. The twenty one referred to here are

taken from the original version of the 1976 paper, Miscue Analysis: Theory and Reality in Reading - Chapter 10 in this volume. The full taxonomy is contained in the Appendix.

4 Goodman lists six positive measures in Urban Dialects and Reading Instruction, 1971c, p.74.

5 This distinction was first emphasized by the linguist Chomsky, although Goodman and Chomsky would differ somewhat in their interpretation of these terms.

REFERENCES

Cambourne, Brian (1977), Getting to Goodman: an Analysis of the Goodman Model of Reading with some Suggestions for Evaluation, 'Reading Research Quarterly', vol.XII, no.4, pp.605-36.

Farr, R., S. Weintraub, and B. Tone (1976), 'Improving Reading Research', IRA, Newark, Delaware.

Goodman, Kenneth S. (1964), The Linguistics of Reading, 'Elementary School Journal', vol.64, no.8, April.

Goodman, K.S. (1965), A Linguistic Study of Cues and Miscues in Reading, 'Elementary English', vol.42, no.6, October.

Goodman, K.S. (1965a), Dialect Barriers to Reading Comprehension, 'Elementary English', vol.42, no.8, December, pp.852-60.

Goodman, K.S. (1967), Reading: A Psycholinguistic Guessing Game, 'Journal of the Reading Specialist', May.

Goodman, K.S. (1968), Reading Disability: A Challenge, 'The Michigan English Teacher', October-November.

Goodman, K.S. (1968a), Linguistic Insights Teachers May Apply, 'Education', vol.88, no.4, April-May, pp.313-16.

Goodman, K.S. (1969), On Valuing Diversity in Language: Overview, 'Childhood Education', December.

Goodman, K.S. (1969a), The Language Children Bring to School: How to Build on It, 'The Grade Teacher', March.

Goodman, K.S. (1969b), Analysis of Oral Reading Miscues: Applied Psycholinguistics, 'Reading Research Quarterly', vol.5, pp.9-30.

Goodman, K.S. (1969c), Words and Morphemes in Reading, in Goodman, 'Psycholinguistics and the Teaching of Reading', IRA, Newark, Delaware.

Goodman, K.S. (1969d), Let's Dump the Up-Tight Model in English, 'Elementary School Journal', October.

Goodman, K.S. (1969e), A Psycholinguistic Approach to Reading. Implications for the Mentally Retarded, 'The Slow Learning Child', (Australia), Summer.

Goodman, K.S. (1969f), Language and the Ethnocentric Researcher, 'SRIS Quarterly', Summer.

Goodman, K.S. (1969g), Linguistics in a Relevant Curriculum, 'Education', April-May, pp.303-7.

Goodman, K.S. (1970), Psycholinguistic Universals in the

Reading Process, 'Journal of Typographic Research', Spring, pp.103-10.
Goodman, K.S. (1970a), Comprehension-Centered Reading Instruction, proceeding of the 1970 Claremont Reading Conference.
Goodman, K.S. and C.L. Burke (1970), When a Child Reads: A Psycholinguistic Analysis, 'Elementary English', January.
Goodman, K.S. and O. Niles (1970), 'Reading: Process and Program', NCTE, Champaign, Ill.
Goodman, K.S. (1971), Decoding - From Code to What? 'Journal of Reading', April.
Goodman, K.S. (1971a), Language and Experience: A Place to Begin, in Helen Robinson (ed.), 'Coordinating Reading Instruction', Scott, Foresman & Co., Glenview, Ill.
Goodman, K.S. (1971b), Who Gave Us the Right? 'The English Record', Spring.
Goodman, K.S. (1971c), Urban Dialects and Reading Instruction, in J.P. Kender (ed.), 'Teaching Reading - Not by Decoding Alone', Interstate, Danville, Va., pp.61-75.
Goodman, K.S. and F. Smith (1971d), On the Psycholinguistic Method of Teaching Reading, 'Elementary School Journal', January.
Goodman, K.S. (1971e), Promises, Promises, 'The Reading Teacher', January.
Goodman, K.S. and D. Menosky (1971), Reading Instruction: Let's Get It All Together, 'Instructor', March, pp.44-5.
Goodman, K.S. (1972), Up-Tight Ain't Right, 'School Library Journal', October.
Goodman, K.S. (1972a), Oral Language Miscues, 'Viewpoints', vol.48, no.1, January, pp.13-28.
Goodman, K.S. (1972b), Orthography in a Theory of Reading Instruction, 'Elementary English', December.
Goodman, K.S. (1973), Miscues: Windows on the Reading Process, in K.S. Goodman (ed.), 'Miscue Analysis, Applications to Reading Instruction', ERIC, Urbana, Ill., pp.3-14.
Goodman, K.S. (1973a), Dialect Barriers to Reading Comprehension Revisited, 'Reading Teacher', October.
Goodman, K.S. (1973b), Strategies for Increasing Comprehension in Reading, in H. Robinson, 'Improving Reading in the Intermediate Years', Scott, Foresman & Co., Glenview, Ill., pp.59-71.
Goodman, K.S. (1973c), Testing in Reading: A General Critique, in R. Ruddell (ed.), 'Accountability and Reading Instruction', NCTE, Urbana.
Goodman, K.S. (1974), Reading: You Can Get Back to Kansas Anytime You're Ready, Dorothy, 'English Journal', November.
Goodman, K.S. (1974a), Effective Teachers of Reading Know Language and Children, 'Elementary English', September.
Goodman, K.S. (1974b), Military-Industrial Thinking Finally Captures the Schools, 'Educational Leadership', February.
Goodman, K.S. (1975), The Reading Process, proceedings of

the 6th Western Learning Symposium on Learning: Language and Reading, Bellingham, Wash.

Goodman, K.S. (1975a), Do You Have to be Smart to Read? Do You Have to Read to be Smart? 'Reading Teacher', April, pp.625-32.

Goodman, K.S. (1976), Miscue Analysis: Theory and Reality in Reading, in J.E. Merritt (ed.), 'New Horizons in Reading', proceedings of Fifth IRA World Congress on Reading, IRA, Newark, Delaware.

Goodman, K.S. and Y.M. Goodman (1976), Learning to Read is Natural, paper presented at Conference on Theory and Practice of Beginning Reading Instruction, Pittsburgh, April 13.

Goodman, K.S. and Y.M. Goodman (1977), Learning about Psycholinguistic Processes by Analyzing Oral Reading, 'Harvard Educational Review', vol.40-3, pp.317-33.

Halliday, M.A.K. (1975), Learning How to Mean: Explorations in the Development of Language, Edward Arnold, London.

Halliday, M.A.K. (1977), How Children Learn Language, in K.D. Watson and R.D. Eigleson (eds), 'English and the Secondary Schools: Today and Tomorrow', English Teachers Association of NSW, Sydney.

US Dept of Health, Education and Welfare (1968), Office of Education, Bureau of Research, Final Report - Project No. S425, Study of Children's Behavior While Reading Orally, March (Director K.S. Goodman).

US Dept of Health, Education and Welfare (1973), Office of Education, Bureau of Research, Final Report - Project No. 9-0375, Theoretically Based Studies of Patterns of Miscues in Oral Reading Performance, April (Director K.S. Goodman).

US Dept of Health, Education and Welfare (1978), National Institute of Education, Final Report - Project NIE-C-00-3-0087, Reading of American Children Whose Language is a Stable Rural Dialect of English or a Language Other Than English, August (Director K.S. Goodman).

The reader will notice that there is some unavoidable overlap of content between articles in this volume. Because of Goodman's perspective, it is difficult to classify his writings into neat, self-contained categories or sections. His writings are a reflection of his approach, one that is always concerned with the total picture. There is a continual integration of theory, practice and content which we would hope the reader would see as a strength.

Our basic intent in this volume has been to begin each section with one or more clear, simple articles that might serve as a good introduction for those with little familiarity with the Goodman writings. It is hoped that the introductory comments prior to each article will not only prepare the reader with valuable prior information, but will facilitate the selection of the most relevant material.

Part One
THE READING PROCESS

Part One comprises eight articles. We have chosen not to present them chronologically, but rather to begin with the Bellingham paper, which is the most comprehensive and recent commentary by Goodman on the reading process. It is paired with a second article showing the relationship between the Goodman model of reading and miscue analysis research. This pattern of beginning a section of complementary articles that present a basic, balanced, up-to-date view of the Goodman position is continued in later sections and is specifically designed to guard against the tendency for readers to focus on an older first paper and assume that the position of that paper is the author's present position. The third and fourth chapters give valuable historical perspective to Goodman's work, and the fifth - Decoding: From Code to What? - is included because of its importance and because it is less technical than the majority of papers in this volume. Chapters 6 and 7 deal with universals in the reading process and the section is nicely rounded and concluded with Goodman's more recent paper, What We Know About Reading (Chapter 8).

We've chosen to begin with a relatively recent presentation of the Goodman Model of Reading. This model is a keystone of Goodman's work: it is both the base for and product of Goodman's research on reading. It is foundational to his views on teaching and learning reading. As the article says, 'The model isn't done yet.' Continuing work, thought, and interaction with others are contributing to continuing expansion and evolution of the model. But that's also true of all theoretical models. Any model must respond to increased knowledge of the reality it seeks to represent.

1 THE READING PROCESS

In a very real sense this paper is a progress report. Some years ago I decided that a major reason for the lack of forward motion in attempts to develop more effective reading instruction was a common failure to examine and articulate a clear view of the reading process itself. Knowledge, I felt, was non-cumulative in improving reading instruction largely because we either ignored the reading process and focussed on the manipulation of teacher and/or pupil behaviors or because we treated reading as an unknowable mystery.

Ironically two opposite views were and still are widely found in the professional literature:

1 Reading is what reading is and everybody knows that; usually this translates to 'reading is matching sounds to letters.'
2 'Nobody knows how reading works.' This view usually leads to a next premise: therefore, in instruction, whatever 'works' is its own justification.

Both views are non-productive at best and at the worst seriously impede progress.

My effort has been to create a model of the reading process powerful enough to explain and predict reading behavior and sound enough to be a base on which to build and examine the effectiveness of reading instruction. This model has been developed using the concepts, scientific methodology, and terminology of psycholinguistics, the interdisciplinary science that is concerned with how thought and language are interrelated. The model has also continuously drawn on and been tested against linguistic reality. This reality has taken the form of close analysis of miscues, unexpected responses in oral reading, produced by readers of widely varied proficiency as they dealt with real printed text materials they were seeing for the first time.

The model isn't done yet. No one yet claims a 'finished' model of any language process. But the model represents a productive usable view of what I believe, at this point in time, about the way the reading process works.

A DEFINITION OF READING

Reading is a receptive language process. It is a psycholinguistic process in that it starts with a linguistic surface representation encoded by a writer and ends with meaning which the reader constructs. There is thus an essential interaction between language and thought in reading. The writer encodes thought as language and the reader decodes language to thought.

Further, proficient readers are both efficient and effective. They are effective in constructing a meaning that they can assimilate or accommodate and which bears some level of agreement with the original meaning of the author. And readers are efficient in using the least amount of effort to achieve effectiveness. To accomplish this efficiency readers maintain constant focus on constructing the meaning throughout the process, always seeking the most direct path to meaning, always using strategies for reducing uncertainty, always being selective about the use of the cues available and drawing deeply on prior conceptual and linguistic competence. Efficient readers minimize dependence on visual detail. Any reader's proficiency is variable depending on the semantic background brought by the reader to any given reading task.

SOURCE FOR THE MODEL

All scientific investigation must start with direct observation of available aspects of what is being studied. What distinguishes scientific from other forms of investigation is a constant striving to get beneath and beyond what is superficially observable. That involves finding new tools for making otherwise unavailable aspects observable. Such a tool is the microscope in all its variations designed to extend observation far beyond the limits of the human eye. Scientists also devise classification systems, taxonomies, paradigms as they constantly seek for essences, structures, interrelationships; they are aware of the distractions the obvious can cause and they are aware of how easy it is to overlook vital characteristics of phenomena they study.

The primary source of data for the view of the reading process presented here is observation of oral reading. But little can be learned from such observation if a naively empirical position is maintained. As the chemist must peer into the molecular structure, as the astronomer must ponder the effects of heavenly bodies on each other, as the ecologist must pursue the intricate web of interrelationships in a biological community, so the scientist in dealing with reading must look beyond behavior to process. Understanding reading requires depth analysis and a constant search for the insights which will let us infer the workings of the mind as print is processed and meaning created.

Oral miscue analysis is the tool I've found most useful in the depth analysis of reading behavior as I've sought to understand the reading process (Goodman, 1969).

Miscue analysis compares observed with expected responses as subjects read a story or other written text orally. It provides a continuous basis of comparison between what the readers overtly do and what they are expected to do. A key assumption is that whatever the readers do is not random but is the result of the reading process, whether successfully used or not. Just as the observed behavior of electrons must result from a complex but limited set of forces and conditions, so what the readers do results from limited but complex information sources and interactive but limited alternatives for their use.

When readers produce responses which match our expectations we can only infer successful use of the reading process. When miscues are produced, however, comparing the mismatches between expectation and observation can illuminate where the readers have deviated and what factors of input and process may have been involved. A simple illustration: there has long been concern over reversals in reading, changes in the sequences of letters, apparently involved in word substitution miscues. If 'was' is substituted for 'saw' there appears to be some kind of visual or perceptual aberration in the reader. Our miscue analysis data, however, tells us two things: (1) Such reversals are far less common in reading continuous texts than in word lists. (2) When such reversals do occur they are in only one direction: 'saw' is replaced by 'was' but virtually never is 'was' replaced by 'saw.' The reversal miscue must be influenced by factors other than the obvious visual or perceptual ones. Frequently, syntactic predictability and the range of semantic possibility clearly are involved.

In this depth miscue analysis several basic insights have emerged which have become foundational both to the research and to the model of the reading process:

* Language, reading included, must be seen in its social context. Readers will show the influence of the dialect(s) they control both productively and receptively as they read. Further, the common experience, concepts, interests, views, and life styles of readers with common social and cultural backgrounds will also be reflected in how and what people read and what they take from their reading.
* Competence, what readers are capable of doing, must be separated from performance, what we observe them to do. It is competence that results in the readers' control of and flexibility in using the reading process. Their performance is simply the observable result of the competence.

  Change in performance, whether through instruction or development is important only to the extent that it reflects improved competence. Researchers may use performance or behavioral indicators of underlying competence but they err seriously in equating what readers do with what they are capable of doing.
* Language must be studied in process. Like a living organism it loses its essence if it is frozen or fragmented. Its parts and systems may be examined apart from their

use but only in the living process may they be understood. Failure to recognize this has led many researchers to draw unwarranted and misconceived conclusions about both reading and reading instruction from controlled research on aspects of reading such as word naming, word identification, skill acquisition, and phonic rule development.

Researchers, particularly, have tended to fall into the unexamined view that reading is recognizing the next words. An example is the study of reading acquisition by Singer, Samuels and Spiroff (1974).

They concluded that words were more easily 'learned' in isolation than in text or with illustration. They drew this conclusion from a study in which four (4) words were taught to a number of learners in three conditions:
(a) in isolation.
(b) in 'context': each word was presented in a three word sentence.
(c) with an illustrative picture.

The key misconception in this study is that reading is a matter of identifying (or knowing) a series of words. It is then assumed that learning to read is learning to identify or know words. Further it is assumed that known words are known under all linguistic conditions. Implicit is the assumption that the task of 'learning' four (4) words is representative of the general task of learning to read.

* Language must be studied in its human context. It is a uniquely but universally human achievement. That's not a humanistic assertion. It's a scientific fact. Human language learning and the general function of language in human learning are not usefully described with learning theories derived from study of rats, pigeons, and other non-language users.

A REVISED MODEL

Three kinds of information are available and used in language, whether productive or receptive. These come from 'the symbol system' which uses sounds in oral languages and graphic shapes in written languages. For literate language users of alphabetic languages there is also a set of relationships between sounds and shapes; 'the language structure' which is the grammar, or set of syntactic relationships that make it possible to express highly complex messages using a very small set of symbols. The same syntax underlies both oral and written language; 'the semantic system' which is the set of meanings as organized in concepts and conceptual structures. Meaning is the end product of receptive language, both listening and reading; but meaning is also the context in which reading takes on reality. Listener/readers bring meaning to any communication and conduct themselves as seekers of meaning.

A model of the reading process must account for these information sources. It must also respond to the following realities:

> Written language is displayed over space in contrast to oral language which is displayed in a time continuum.
>
> Writing systems make arbitrary decisions about direction in using space. The reader must adjust to a left-to-right, right-to-left, top-to-bottom, or other arbitrary characteristic of written language. Reading employs visual input. The eye is the input organ. It has certain characteristics and limitations as an optical instrument. It has a lens which must focus; it requires minimal light; it has a limited field; the area of view includes a small area of sharp detail.
>
> Reading must employ memory; it must hold an image, briefly store information, retain knowledge and understanding.

CYCLES

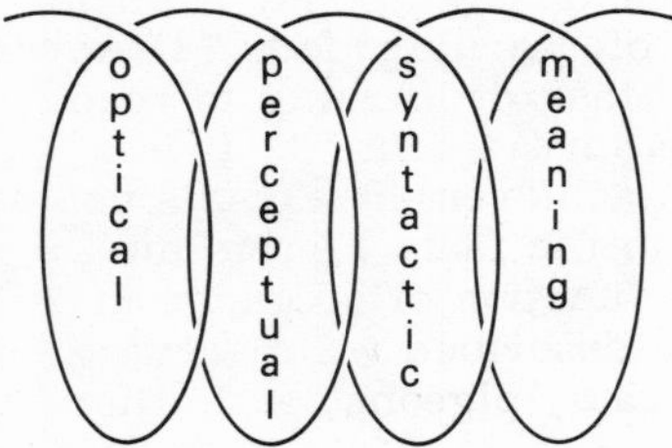

Figure 1.1

Though reading is a process in which information is dealt with and meaning constructed continuously, it can be usefully represented as a series of cycles. Readers employ the cycles more or less sequentially as they move through a story or other text. But the readers' focus, if they are to be productive, is on meaning, so each cycle melts into the next and the readers leap toward meaning. The cycles are telescoped by the readers if they can get to meaning.

PROCESSES

As the readers move through the cycles of reading they employ five processes. The brain is the organ of information processing. It decides what tasks it must handle, what information is available, what strategies it must employ, which input channels

Table 1.1 The revised model

Cycles	Inputs	Output
Start Recognize task as reading known language.	Graphic display Memory: recognition-initiation Activate strategies in memory	Optical scan cycle
1 OPTICAL a) Scan in direction of print display.	Start: Memory: strategies for scanning appropriate to graphic display. Adjust speed of scan to processing speed.	Optical fixation cycle To memory: predict relation of information to direction of display.
b) Fix-focus eyes at point in the print.	Light reflects from graphic display. Visual field includes sharp and fuzzy input. Memory: prior prediction of meaning, structure, graphic redundancy, expectation of locus of key graphic cues.	Perception cycle To memory: cues for image formation.
2 PERCEPTION a) Sample-select. Choose cues from available graphic display.	Fix: cues available in sharp and blurred input. Memory: sampling strategies Prior predictions and decodings to meaning.	To memory: selected cues To feature analysis
b) Feature analysis. Choose features necessary to choose from alternate letters, words, structures.	Sampled features. From memory: Assign allosystem(s) (type style, cursive, etc.). Prior predictions.	Confirm prior prediction. Correct if necessary by return to scan, fix. If no system available, try best approximation or terminate; otherwise proceed to image formation.

Table 1.1 The revised model

Cycles	Inputs	Output
c) Image formation Form image of what is seen, and expected to be seen. Compare with expectations.	From: feature analysis, cues appropriate to allosystem(s) chosen. From memory: graphic, syntactic, semantic constructs Prior predictions Cues from parallel phonological system (optional)	If no image possible, return to feature analysis or prior cycle for more information. Confirm prior predictions. If correction needed return to prior cycle, scan back for source of inconsistency. If image formed, store in memory and go to syntactic cycle.
3 SYNTACTIC CYCLE a) Assign internal surface structure.	From image formation From memory: rules for relating surface display to internal surface structure. Prior predictions and decodings.	If no structure possible, recycle to perception or optical cycles. If inconsistent with predictions, try alternate or correct by recycling and scanning back to point of mismatch. If structure is possible, go to deep structure.
b) Assign deep structure. Seek clauses and their interrelationships	From: internal surface structure. From memory: transformational rules for relating surface and deep structures. Prior predictions and decodings.	If no structure possible try alternative. If still no structure, recycle. If inconsistent with prediction, correct by recycling. If deep structure possible, predict graphic, semantic, syntactic features. Go to meaning. If oral reading, assign appropriate intonation contour. Terminate if no success.

Table 1.1 The revised model

Cycles	Inputs	Output
4 CONSTRUCT MEANING a) Decode	From: deep structure From memory: stored experiences, conceptual constructs, lexicon. Prior predictions.	If meaning not acceptable, recycle to point of inconsistency. If no meaning possible, try alternate deep structure or recycle to seek more information. If still no meaning, hold all information in memory and return to scan. Terminate if no meaning results. If acceptable meaning, go to assimilate/ accommodate.
b) Assimilate/Accommodate If possible, assimilate. If not possible, accommodate prior meaning.	From: decode From memory: prior predictions, prior meaning. Conceptual attitudinal constructs.	If no assimilation possible and no accommodation possible, recycle to correct or obtain more information. If still not possible, hold and return to scan for possible clarification as reading progresses. Accommodations possible; modify meaning of story/text to this point modify predictions of meaning modify concepts modify word definitions restructure attitudes If task complete, terminate. If task incomplete, recycle and scan forward, predict meaning, structure, graphics.

to use, where to seek information. The brain seeks to maximize information it acquires and minimize effort and energy used to acquire it. The five processes it employs in reading are:

I 'Recognition-initiation.' The brain must recognize a graphic display in the visual field as written language and initiate reading. Normally this would occur once in each reading activity, though it's possible for reading to be interrupted by other activities, examining pictures, for example, and then to be reinitiated.

II 'Prediction.' The brain is always anticipating and predicting as it seeks order and significance in sensory inputs.

III 'Confirmation.' If the brain predicts, it must also seek to verify its predictions. So it monitors to confirm or disconfirm with subsequent input what it expected.

IV 'Correction.' The brain reprocesses when it finds inconsistencies or its predictions are disconfirmed.

V 'Termination.' The brain terminates the reading when the reading task is completed, but termination may occur for other reasons: the task is non-productive; little meaning is being constructed, or the meaning is already known, or the story is uninteresting or the reader finds it inappropriate for the particular purpose. At any rate, termination in reading is usually an open option at any point.

These processes have an intrinsic sequence. Prediction precedes confirmation which precedes correction. Yet the same information may be used to confirm a prior prediction and to make a new one.

SHORT CIRCUITS

Any reading that does not end with meaning is a short circuit. Readers may short circuit in a variety of ways for a variety of reasons. In general, readers short circuit when they can't get meaning or lose the structure; when they've been taught or otherwise acquired non-productive reading strategies; when they aren't permitted to terminate non-productive reading. Theoretically, a short circuit can occur at any point in the process. Here is a list of short circuits with successively more complex points:

'Letter Naming': A very old method of reading instruction taught young readers to spell out to themselves any unfamiliar words. This short circuit still occurs but it is not too common.

'Recoding': Since print is a graphic code and speech is also a code, it is possible for readers to concentrate on matching

print to sound with no meaning resulting. Since the readers go from code to code such short circuits may be considered recoding. Recoding may take place on several levels.
'Letter-sound recoding' is the most superficial. Sounds are matched on a one-to-one basis to the print. This sounding-out requires the readers to blend sounds to synthesize words. 'Pattern-matching recoding' involves the readers fitting spelling patterns to sound patterns. Readers focus on features which contrast patterns such as rat-rate, hat-hate, mat-mate. Recoding is often by analogy: since 'bean' looks like 'mean' it must sound like it too. This recoding produces words or word-like utterances without requiring synthesizing.
'Internal surface-structure recoding' involves using the rules needed to relate print to underlying surface structure. Instead of going beyond to deep structure, however, the reader generates an oral surface representation. This recoding can produce words and phrases with approximate intonation patterns.
'Syntactic Nonsense.' The readers may treat print as syntactic nonsense, generating an appropriate deep structure without going beyond to meaning. Even proficient readers resort to this short circuit when conceptual load is too great or when they lack relevant background. With this short circuit the oral reading may be relatively accurate and yet involve little comprehension. Because readers do employ this short circuit we have come to regard the separation of syntactic deep structure from meaning as a useful view.
'Partial structures.' Readers may resort to one or more of these short circuits with alternating periods of productive reading. Furthermore, because the brain is always actively seeking meaning, some comprehension will often 'leak' through even the most non-productive short circuits. It will most likely result in fragments of meaning, a kind of kaleidoscopic view, rather than an integrated understanding.

I suspect that many of these short circuits result from instruction but the studies to demonstrate this remain to be done.

USES AND LIMITATIONS OF THE GOODMAN MODEL

The Goodman model built through miscue analysis is a general model of the reading process based on the premise that there is a single reading process. In that sense it is an unlimited macro model of reading.

It is psycholinguistic, since it deals with how language and thought are interactive. But it operates within a sociolinguistic context. Language is social and it is through language that people mean things to each other. Reading, like all language, operates in a social context that includes readers and writers.

Since reading is a unitary process, several key premises follow: The model deals with reading in the context of written language in the context of language. It focusses on the proficient reader, but is applicable to all stages of development. It has been built through the study of English reading, but it must be applicable to reading in all languages and all orthographies.

Reading comprehension, as the model represents it, must be consistent with language comprehension and general comprehension.

All this means the model may not be inconsistent with any model of a larger context except in factors peculiar to the use and physical aspects of written English. Reading is language, so what's true for language must apply to reading. Reading and listening are both receptive language, so they cannot differ except in the linguistic medium and use. What the model predicts for English reading must also work for any other language except in terms of how specific characteristics of the syntax or orthography are accommodated by the reading process.

The reading model may be criticized for being inconsistent with valid theories of more general processes but it is not responsible for dealing explicitly with more than reading. It can not be attacked for what it need not do.

Similarly, the model must be inclusive of all factors of reading under all conditions, though it need not explicitly or completely stipulate them. It must be applicable to:

1 All characteristics of text, text structure, text length.
2 All characteristics of the reader: linguistic and cognitive background, values and beliefs, motivation, proficiency, physical and mental condition.
3 All characteristics of syntax and grammar.
4 All characteristics of semantic systems: propositional structures, idioms and metaphors, pragmatics, functions, cohesion, inference.
5 All characteristics of memory as they involve language and cognition.
6 All characteristics of perception as it is involved in language and cognition.
7 All characteristics of orthography: symbols, system, features, directionality, relationship to meaning, relationship to phonology.
8 All conditions of reading: purpose, task, setting, third party influences, context.

The model, to be defensible, must be able to include or accommodate detail in any aspect of the reading process or its use without distorting either the model or the detail. It may, of course, offer a reconceptualization of the detail on the basis of the model's internal coherence. Thus, research findings by others that appear inconsistent with the model may be shown to be consistent through reconceptualizing them.

The model can not be criticized for being incomplete, though it can be criticized for being unable to accommodate detailed micro modeling of any factor or aspect.

There are some things the model isn't. It isn't complete in detail in any aspect. It isn't a theory of comprehension, cognition, or perception. And it isn't a theory of reading instruction. That last must be consistent with a model of the reading process. But it must include a learning theory and theories of curriculum and instruction. A theory of reading instruction building on a theory and model of reading is the ultimate bridge to the classroom. The model presented here is not 'something to use on Monday morning.' It is the necessary base for the theory that will generate things to do on Monday and explain why they do or do not help people to read more efficiently and effectively.

REFERENCES

Goodman, K.S. (1969), Analysis of Oral Reading Miscues: Applied Psycholinguistics, 'Reading Research Quarterly,' vol.5, pp.9-30.

Singer, H., S.S. Samuels, and J. Spiroff (1974), The Effects of Pictures and Contextual Conditions on Learning Responses to Printed Words, 'Reading Research Quarterly,' vol.9, pp.555-67.

In this chapter the reading process is discussed from the point of view of its relationship to a potential theory of reading instruction. It indicates Goodman's belief that instruction must have a theoretical base. The article shows the foundation of his model in his research in miscue analysis.

Throughout the article Goodman attempts to relate his views to conventional word-centered views of reading and to indicate the relationship of new terminology to a new conceptualization of reading.

2 THE READING PROCESS: Theory and Practice

Reading instruction is designed to help students use the reading process proficiently. But, reading instruction depends on theories of the reading process for its own theoretical and practical basis; and unfortunately, there are no such theories. All the present ones are too incoherent to be useful. The net result is that tests of reading achievement, methods of teaching reading, materials for reading instruction, and clinical and remedial practices have largely been based on common sense, trial and error, previous practice, and whim.

To be useful, a theory of the reading process must make it possible to explain the full range of reading behavior at all stages of proficiency. It must predict behavior under specific circumstances, in specific students, at specific points of development. It must provide viable answers to all questions relating to the reading process; and it must provide a framework for understanding the relative importance of those questions. In short, a theory of the reading process must make clear how the proficient reader operates and what it is we seek to teach when we teach reading. Such a theory cannot be translated into direct instructional practice. We need a *theory of reading instruction*. This theory must be based on a theory of the reading process that integrates learning theory, research on child development and language learning, and input from all other relevant disciplines.

This instructional theory can, in turn, spawn sound methods and materials which weave the wisdom gleaned by educators from years of teaching children to read into a theoretically sound, articulate, instructional program. There is no dichotomy between theory and practice. Theory must become practical; and practice must achieve theoretical validity.

In this paper, I intend to present the essence of a theory of the reading process and to suggest a few of the elements that a theory of reading instruction must deal with.

THE PSYCHOLINGUISTIC BASE

Whether we define reading in terms of its objectives, in terms of the behavior in which readers engage, or in terms of the inferable process, a reading theory must be built on a psycholinguistic base. The reader starts with a graphic display, printed or handwritten, and if he is successful, he ends with meaning, a reconstruction of the writer's message.

Language, in graphic form, is the code vehicle through which the message is transmitted. *To understand how reading works one must understand how language works.*

To reach his goal of meaning the reader must *use* language, interacting with the graphic display in such a way that he moves from the code to the message. This interaction involves language and thought. Further, since the graphic code itself contains no information which is itself the writer's message, it becomes apparent that the reader supplies a considerable amount of linguistic and conceptual input as he responds to the graphic display. *To understand reading one must understand how language is used.*

A reading theory built on this psycholinguistic base will place many traditional concerns in the study of the reading process in new contexts and suggest reevaluation of the relative importance of such traditional concerns. A key example is the overwhelming concern, in the past, with words and what has been variously labeled 'word recognition,' 'word perception,' 'word attack.' This focus grew out of a common sense view of language as a string of words, and of reading as the ability to cope with that string of words. But language is not a string of words. In any language use, the sum of the whole is in no sense the sum of the parts. And coping with the system or structure of language sequences is vital to successful reading. Old insights about reading based on an overemphasis on words must be carefully reconsidered as the view of words is placed in proper perspective.

At the same time, new concerns are emerging whose significance was previously overlooked or only dimly seen. Grammar, as the system of language, emerges as one such colossal oversight. Whenever any language user attempts to derive meaning from language he must treat it as grammatical sequences, and be aware of grammatical interdependencies. This is true when a reader deals with a simple sequence like 'Tom saw Betty.' He must know that 'Tom' is subject and 'Betty' is object in order to comprehend. In a much more complex sequence, such as 'See Flip run,' he must be aware that the subject 'you' is not present in the surface structure; that 'Flip run' is an embedding of an underlying structure 'Flip runs' in another structure, 'you see (Flip runs)'; and that the clause functions as the object of the verb 'see.' If he cannot process this information, he will not comprehend the message 'See Flip run.' Both examples are three word sentences. The task of reading each sentence depends largely on the processing of grammatical information. Thus, when viewed from a psycholinguistic base, what has appeared to be a word recognition problem is a very different phenomenon.

CONCEPTS AND TERMINOLOGY

A word of caution is necessary. As a theory of the reading process is emerging and the process is revealed more clearly, terminology new to the reading field derived from linguistics and psycholinguistics is also emerging.

New terminology for old ideas is certainly not needed. However, new terms for new concepts are indispensable, and, in many cases, old terms must be redefined as misconceptions are clarified. Reading teachers, and teachers of reading teachers, must resist a tendency to equate new terms with old ones, and to overlook basic but subtle differences in concepts.

THEORY, MODELS, AND REALITY

Earlier, we pointed out a difference between directly interpreting behavior of readers and relating behavior to underlying theoretical views. If we confine our attempt to understand the reading process solely to observable phenomena, we will tend to see the behavior of readers as a kind of direct response to graphic stimuli with no intervening process. In fact, that view has in large measure prevailed. Reading has tended to be treated as a series of sound responses to letter stimuli, or word-name responses to graphic word shapes. The fallacy of this view has always been evident in the behavior of readers; but researchers and text writers have been reluctant to treat reading behavior as an observable indication of underlying competence. To understand the reading process, we must come to see reading behavior as the end product of that process. We must also see reading behavior as a means to understanding the process.

When Galileo dropped his weights from the tower of Pisa or stared through his first crude telescope at Jupiter and saw its moons disappear behind it, he could not serve the ends of his investigation by stopping at a superficial description. It was necessary for him to link these observations to theoretical explanations. Recently, the apparently erratic behavior of our unmanned and manned satellites as they orbited the moon indicated that there was something wrong with the calculations of how they should respond to the moon's gravitational pull. A description of the deviational behavior was not enough. Nor could we blame the phenomena on genetic weaknesses of the vehicles. From the deviations, it was necessary to infer possible flaws in gravitational theory, to reconstruct a theory that could explain that behavior, and then to test the theory against the predicted behavior of new satellites.

Theories make it possible to organize observational data and generate hypotheses. In turn, theories are tested against reality, which confirms them or suggests modification. By means of theoretical models one may relate behavior to the process of which it is the product. Frequently, of course, once a theoretical model is articulated, previously available data take on new significance to the point where we wonder how we could ever have overlooked them.

Theoretical models are necessary whenever a process, whether physical, or psychological, or psycholinguistic, is not directly observable. A model never becomes identical with a process; that would mean that the process was observable. But models are useful to the extent that they can predict the end products of a process. There is now sufficient evidence to construct a model of the reading process. We can infer from the behavior of readers, utilizing linguistic data, and psycholinguistic data about the use of language, what competence underlies the reading behavior and how the reading process works.

One source of knowledge for making such inferences is research in reading miscues, such as our own. By comparing observed oral reading responses with expected responses, we can see how the reader uses available linguistic information and what resources of his own he utilizes. Furthermore, we can see the points at which the process breaks down and the strengths and weaknesses of the reader.

CHARACTERISTICS OF THE READING PROCESS

A strange contradiction exists between actual reading behavior and the widely held common sense view of it. In reading orally materials they haven't seen before, readers do not read in the precisely correct way that they are expected to read. Since, in the common sense view, proficient readers are supposed to read accurately - that is, without errors - when they don't do this, the errors are ignored, explained away, or taken as evidence that they really aren't so proficient after all.

Our research indicates that *all* readers produce the unexpected responses which we call 'miscues.' These miscues occur because the reader is not simply responding to print with accurate word identifications. He is processing information in order to reconstruct the message the writer has sought to convey.

In the sense that the reader uses each graphic cue available to him, reading is not an exact process at all. Instead, the reader engages in a form of information processing in which he uses his knowledge of how language works. As he strives to comprehend, he is highly selective in choosing graphic cues and in predicting language structures.

Figure 2.1 will help to illustrate the essential tasks the reader faces as he moves from a graphic display to meaning. This figure employs the transformational-generative view of language, not because of any commitment to that view, but because it appears to explain the actual behavior of readers.

Meaning cannot be derived directly from the printed page.

The graphic display on the page can however be considered a written surface representation of language. A writer starts with meaning. He then assigns a deep underlying grammatical structure. Using the transformational rules, he then generates a written surface structure. Finally, he utilizes the rules of English orthography (spelling, punctuation) to produce the graphic display. The reader must infer from that graphic display the rules that have produced it and its underlying deep structure. Only then can he reconstruct the writer's message, that is, comprehend the meaning.

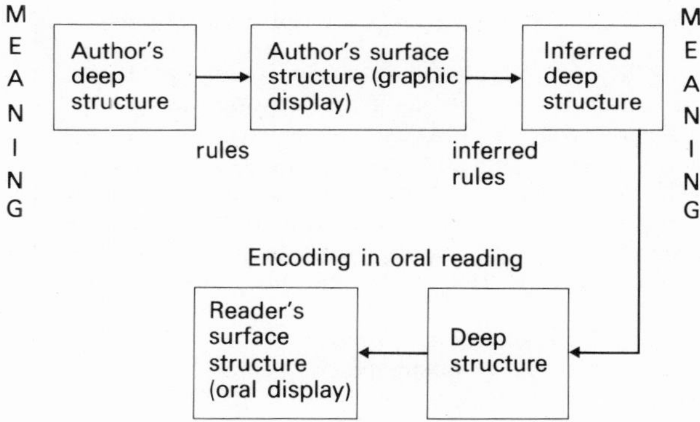

Figure 2.1

If he is reading orally, the reader must then encode the message as oral output producing an oral surface structure. There is no direct connection in this representation between the graphic display and the oral reader's output. In fact, to achieve comprehension, there is no necessary reason to involve oral language in the reading process at all. It is possible, even probable, that some association between oral and written language occurs as the reader moves toward meaning, but that association is not in any sense essential to comprehension. For the proficient reader, two forms of language exist - one written and one spoken. They have the same deep structure, but *after* applying his transformational rules, he may apply either phonological rules or orthographic ones.

Miscues may occur in reading at any point in the process. They will always involve the reader's use of written language; but they will not always interfere with comprehension. Here are some situations which may lead to miscues:

1 *Misperception* At any time, what the reader thinks he sees is partly what he sees and partly what he expects to see. A misperception may result from inadequate selection of visual cues, predictions at variance to the text, or misprocessing of the selected visual cues.

2 *Inability to process* The reader may be unable to deal with the graphic display in any sense that yields language information which he can process. This would be most characteristic of beginning readers lacking in proficiency; but, it is also true in other cases. Reading a text in obscure handwriting or partially obliterated print is an example.

3 *Inference of different deep structures* Readers process language information from the surface structure in such a way that they may predict the deep structure long before they have used all the cues which the surface structure provides. Variant deep structures may be inferred from one text for several reasons:

(a) The reader's language rules may vary somewhat from the writer's. His dialect may be different, hence he may miss or misuse some cues.
(b) There may be a point in the surface structure where an analysis of the surface structure could go either of two ways, each analysis predicting a different deep structure. Thus, the reader can predict a deep structure that is not the one the author used. Notice, for example, these two sentences:
1 He was going to the store.*[1]
2 He was going to go to the store.*
The reader may predict 2 while reading 1.
(c) The surface structure may be ambiguous with two possible deep structures:
1 The doors are closed at 8 pm.
2 Princess Anne will marry whom she pleases.

4 *Lack of, or variation in meaning input* Readers may be unable to produce a deep structure, may produce a variant deep structure, or may be unable to derive meaning, if they lack experiential or conceptual input to bring to the task, or if the concepts they have are at variance with the writer's. Word meanings may be involved as well as idioms and special ways of using phrases. In many cases, however, the reader can handle the language if he has sufficient experience or conceptual background.

5 *Choice of alternate grammatical rules to produce the oral surface structure* In oral reading, the reader encodes meaning as oral output. In doing so, he will tend to shift away from the writer's language choices towards his own.

(a) He may produce an alternate surface structure using optional rules. Example:
1 to make it look new
for
2 to make it look like new
or

1 Freddie didn't mind being compared with his uncle, who was a real chemist.*
for
2 Freddie didn't mind being compared with his uncle. He was a real chemist.*

(b) He may shift to the rules of his own grammar.
1 You are just like Uncle Charles.*
for
2 You're just like Uncle Charles.*

(c) The reader may shift to an alternate but equivalent way of saying the same thing.
1 He was going on nine.*
for
2 He was going to be nine.*

6 *The oral output may involve alternate phonological rules*

(a) These can be rules in the dialect of the reader.
1 breakfases*
for
2 breakfasts*

(b) They can be misarticulations.
1 alunimum
for
2 aluminum.

Listening and reading are the receptive aspects of language use, just as speaking and writing are the generative aspects. Much, therefore, that has been said of the reading process applies to listening as well, at least for literate language users.

Though oral language comes first in the natural history of both the individual and the tribe, when literacy is achieved, oral and written language become parallel alternate forms available to the user. Each has its own functions, strengths, and limitations. The language user chooses the one most appropriate for his communicative need. He may even use them in combination, exploiting the strengths of both, as when a speaker uses written notes.

In languages that use alphabetic writing systems, it may appear that the written language is a secondary representation of the oral language. This is because graphic patterns generally represent oral language patterns rather than each relating to meaning independently. Because of the system of relationships between graphic and phonological patterns, readers may even have the illusion that they are turning print into speech and then processing the aural input as in listening. But, if such were the case, reading would be seriously impeded, because the reader would be required to use graphic information to create sound patterns in a relatively complete sense in order to infer the underlying deep structure and assign meaning. That would make reading a slower and more tedious process than listening, since the listener is able to sample input and move directly to deep structure and meaning.

Written and oral language are alternate surface structures with the same underlying deep structure. In both listening and reading, the language user infers this deep structure from the surface structure without resorting to a shift from oral to written surface structure or vice versa.

In producing language, the user has alternate sets of rules for producing a signal *after* he has conceived his message. Phonological rules produce a signal which is an oral sequence. Orthographic rules produce a signal which is a graphic display. The reader's job is to get from the graphic display to meaning. It is only in the special case of oral reading that the reader is also interested in producing an oral signal and, even then, it appears that proficient readers decode graphic language for meaning and *then* encode (recode) an oral signal.

It is possible with alphabetic writing systems to recode graphic displays as oral sequences without recourse to meaning. Anyone literate in English can do so with 'A marlup was poving his kump.' It is even possible to do so with a language that is foreign to the reader and which he neither speaks nor understands. But this code to code shifting does not yield meaning; in fact, it still leaves the language user with a coded message.

In the recent literature, much has been made of this graphic to oral 'recoding.' It has been mistakenly labeled 'decoding,' which it cannot be, since it does not end with something other than code. Such 'recoding' is not an essential part of the reading process. Even in beginning reading a focus on phonic 'recoding' skills may interfere with the development of strategies for acquiring meaning from written language.

Units of processing in reading

Written language is a display of letters. Letters are composed of straight and curved line segments, and form letter groupings which are separated by white space. But meaning can be derived from written language only when underlying clauses and their interrelationships have been inferred. Thus, the most significant unit in reading is not the letter, word, or sentence, but the *clause*. The reader must be aware of what these clauses are in the deep structure and be able to handle the form in which they are represented in the surface structure. They may be reduced, embedded, combined, branched, conjoined, and subordinated in such a way that the surface structure represents the deep structure in a highly economical, information-loaded manner. A sentence is a clause or a set of interrelated clauses. The surface structure must be sampled to identify the deep structure clauses.

Fortunately, since the grammatical system underlies oral language as well, the reader, even the beginner, has basic control over it.

The native language reader knows the system of his language so well that he predicts its surface structure and infers the deep structure on the basis of small samples of information actually processed. Two interrelated characteristics of language facilitate this prediction and sampling. One is 'sequential constraint.' Given any single language element, the possibilities of which elements may follow are highly constrained: some may follow, some may not, some may but are unlikely. Given a string of elements, the constraints become much greater. Hence, language is highly predictable; particularly with regard to grammatical structures, since there are fewer grammatical structures than possible words that may fit within them.

'Redundancy' is the other factor that facilitates language processing. This term, derived from information theory, means the tendency in language for information to be carried by more than one part of the signal. Language is redundant to the extent that each element carries more than a single bit of information.

In the sentence 'He was watching Mary,' 'watching' has three cues to its function as a verb: its position in the sentence, the use of 'was' with it, and its 'ing' ending. Sequential constraint contributes considerably to redundancy. Since 'q' must always be followed by 'u,' no new information is provided by the 'u.' Redundancy makes it possible to sample without losing information. It also provides a possibility of verification, since multiple cues must be consistent.

Two important principles emerge from these insights: (a) 'the axiom of predictability': a given sequence will be easy to read to the extent that what the reader is most likely to predict actually occurs; uncommon, unusual, or unlikely sequences will be harder to read than common, usual, or likely ones; (b) 'length of passage': since redundancy and sequential constraint build up as the reader progresses in a passage, short passages are harder to read than long ones, other things being equal. The first paragraph of a story will be relatively harder than the first page, for example. Tests composed of questions or short items are considerably harder to read than the more usual reading tasks.

Tentative information processing

Reading at its proficient best is a smooth, rapid, guessing game in which the reader samples from available language cues, using the least amount of available information to achieve his essential task of reconstructing and comprehending the writer's meaning. It can be regarded as a systematic reduction of uncertainty as the reader starts with graphic input and ends with meaning.

Accuracy of identification or perception is not necessary. Rather, the reader needs:

1 *Effective strategies for selecting the most useful cues from the three kinds of information* Some cues carry a lot of informa-

tion; others are either undependable or redundant. Readers must learn to zero-in on the most useful cues while ignoring the others.

2 *Effective strategies for guessing a deep structure so that he may derive meaning.*

3 *Effective strategies for testing guesses* Essentially, the reader must be able to test the fit of his guesses against the grammatical and semantic constraints. He must ask himself whether what he thinks he has read makes sense within the semantic constraints. He also must ask himself whether it sounds like language; that is, whether it is grammatical within the syntactic constraints. These twin contexts are interdependent. There can be no meaning without grammar, though grammar without meaning is possible. Readers dealing with meaning beyond their comprehension can frequently give the illusion of understanding through their ability to manipulate grammatical patterns. Questions can often be answered by transforming them to statements and supplying the unknown elements from the text without knowing the meaning of the answer. The reader, of course, must learn not to be stopped short of comprehension.

4 *Effective strategies for correcting* If the reader realizes he has made a miscue that needs correction, he must be able to recover, to gather and process more information, to reorganize his guesses, find alternate structures, and make sense out of what has eluded him. Regression, moving the eyes back over previously processed text, is often vital to the correction process, since the reader must literally re-view (see again) what he has processed ineffectively.

Figure 2.2 presents our model of the reading process.

TOWARD A THEORY OF READING INSTRUCTION

Eventually, the time will come when reading materials and methods will be solidly based in an articulated theory of reading instruction. This writer would like to present here some of the essentials of such an instructional theory:

1 Meaning must always be the immediate as well as the ultimate goal in reading. *Instruction must be comprehension centered.* This must be foremost in the mind of both the teacher and the learner. Every instructional activity must be organized around a search for meaning.

2 Language systems (phonology, grammar, lexicon) are interdependent and hence language is indivisible. Fractionating language for instructional purposes into words and word parts destroys its essential nature.

3 Language exists only in the process of its use. Instruction must view and deal with language in process. There is *no possible sequencing of skills* in reading instruction since all systems must be used interdependently in the reading process even in the first attempts at learning to read.

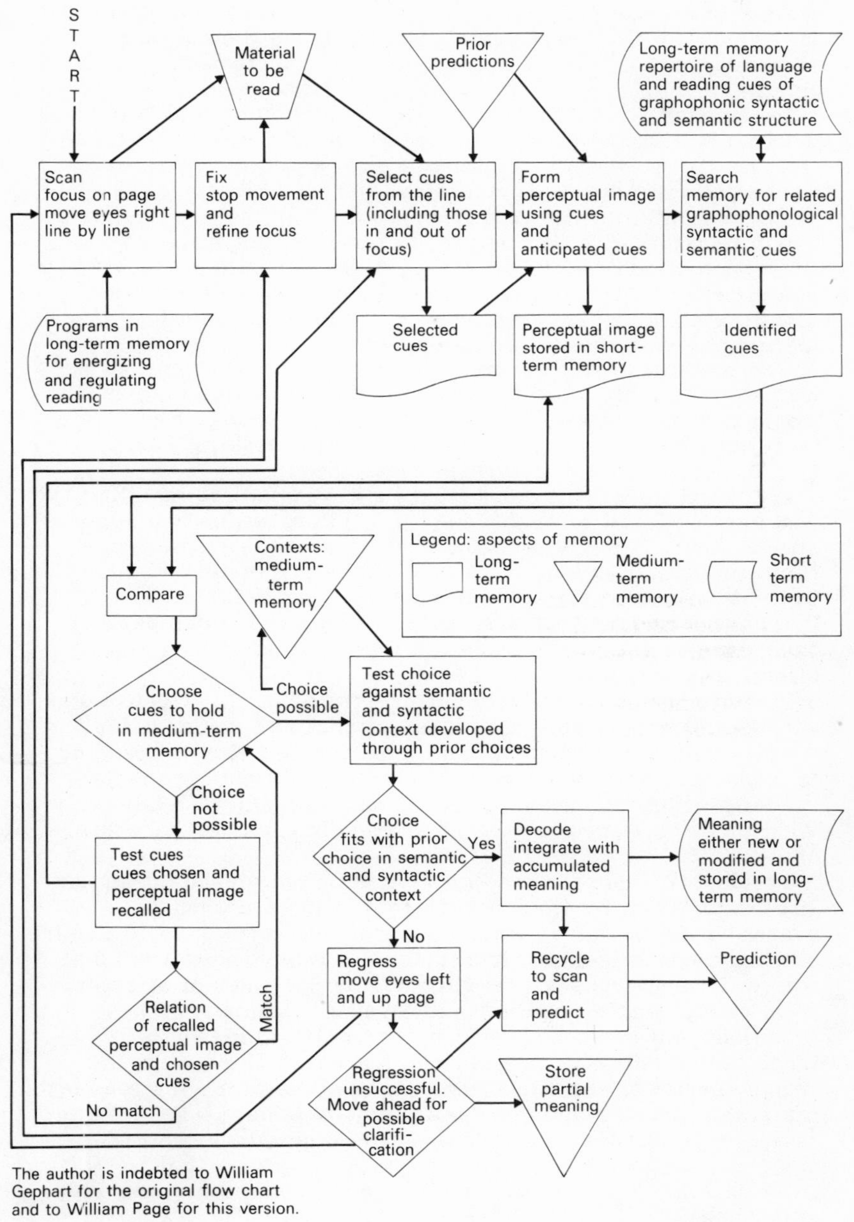

The author is indebted to William Gephart for the original flow chart and to William Page for this version.

Figure 2.2 The Goodman model of reading

4 Children learning to read their native language are competent language users. This competence constitutes their primary resource for learning to read. This is a vital reason why instruction in reading must start 'where the learner is.'
5 Mechanisms which operate in the acquisition of oral language, whether we regard them as learned or innate, are available to the learner as he strives to master literacy. Though those mechanisms are not well understood yet, it is warranted to state that children will find it easiest to learn to read language which is meaningful and natural to them. Perhaps the key motivational factor to be exploited is *communicative need*. Children come to understand language which *they need* to understand. This is no less true in learning to read than it is in learning to understand oral language.
6 The reading process is the psycholinguistic guessing game we have described. Children must learn strategies for predicting, sampling and selecting information, guessing, confirming or rejecting guesses, correcting and reprocessing. Much research must be done on these strategies.
7 Special reading strategies must be developed for handling the reading of special forms of language. Literature is one such special form. It has a special set of constraints; for example, the strong tendency to avoid repetitious use of terms. Such a prohibition makes literary language less predictable. Each language form requires some special strategies which readers must develop to be able to read a broad range of language effectively.
8 Meaning is both input and output in reading. Any selection will be understood only to the extent that the reader brings to it the prerequisite concepts and experiences. Even in reading to learn, the new concepts can only be slightly beyond the reader's prior attainments, and he must be able to relate vicarious experience to real experience in order to make use of it.

Special materials for reading instruction, materials designed and prepared to facilitate learning to read, are perhaps a contradiction in terms, since such materials are likely to distort and fragment language. Eventually, we may come to the point where text materials for reading will be packages of selections with widely ranging content and levels of difficulty. These selections will be accompanied by extensive guidance to teachers on using the materials to increment the developing competence of the learners. In any case, materials for reading instruction must involve natural language; they must be highly predictable on the basis of the learner's language; and they must involve meaning within the learner's grasp; that is, they must be related to the reader's linguistic competence and his experience.

The time will come when we will know enough about the reading process and how it is learned to make the acquisition of literacy a universal extension of language learning.

NOTE

1* Starred examples are taken from Kenneth Goodman and Carolyn Burke (1969), A Study of Oral Reading Miscues That Result in Grammatical Re-Transformations, Final Report, USOE Project No.7-E-219, June.

In April, 1967, Goodman presented this landmark paper at the American Educational Research Association. It grew out of the first five years of Goodman's research and theoretical work on reading and represents the first public presentation of his model. It has been reprinted in eight anthologies and is, perhaps, his most widely cited work. William Gephart drew on the Goodman model in his report to the US Office of Education, which resulted in an ambitious, though short-lived, 'Targeted Research Program in Reading' of USOE. The most important result of that research effort was the stimulation of many others to articulate their own alternate models. This paper then began a decade in the field of reading which saw a pervasive shift from a theoretical to strongly theoretically based research which had to deal with the interdisciplinary psycholinguistic factors Goodman drew on.

3 READING: A Psycholinguistic Guessing Game

As scientific understanding develops in any field of study, preexisting, naive, common sense notions must give way. Such outmoded beliefs clutter the literature dealing with the process of reading. They interfere with the application of modern scientific concepts of language and thought to research in reading. They confuse the attempts at application of such concepts to solution of problems involved in the teaching and learning of reading. The very fact that such naive beliefs are based on common sense explains their persistent and recurrent nature. To the casual and unsophisticated observer they appear to explain, even predict, a set of phenomena in reading. This paper will deal with one such key misconception and offer a more viable scientific alternative.

Simply stated, the common sense notion I seek here to refute is this: 'Reading is a precise process. It involves exact, detailed, sequential perception and identification of letters, words, spelling patterns and large language units.'

In phonic centered approaches to reading, the preoccupation is with precise letter identification. In word centered approaches, the focus is on word identifications. Known words are sight words, precisely named in any setting.

This is not to say that those who have worked diligently in the field of reading are not aware that reading is more than precise, sequential identification. But, the common sense notion, though not adequate, continues to permeate thinking about reading.

Spache (1964) presents a word version of this common sense view: 'Thus, in its simplest form, reading may be considered a series of word perceptions.' The teacher's manual of the Lippincott 'Basic Reading' (McCracken and Walcutt, 1963) incorporates a letter by letter variant in the justification of its reading approach: 'In short, following this program the child learns from the beginning to see words exactly as the most skillful readers see them ... as whole images of complete words with all their letters.'

In place of this misconception, I offer this: Reading is a selective process. It involves partial use of available minimal language cues selected from perceptual input on the basis of the reader's expectation. As this partial information is processed, tentative decisions are made to be confirmed, rejected, or refined as reading progresses.

More simply stated, reading is a psycholinguistic guessing

game. It involves an interaction between thought and language. Efficient reading does not result from precise perception and identification of all elements, but from skill in selecting the fewest, most productive cues necessary to produce guesses which are right the first time. The ability to anticipate that which has not been seen, of course, is vital in reading, just as the ability to anticipate what has not yet been heard is vital in listening.

Consider this actual sample of a relatively proficient child reading orally. The reader is a fourth grade child reading the opening paragraphs of a story from a sixth grade basal reader (Hayes, 1963):

> 'If it bothers you to think of it as baby sitting,' my father said, 'then don't think of it as baby sitting. Think of it as homework. Part of your education. You just happen to do your studying in the room where the baby brother is sleeping, that's all.' He helped my mother with her coat, and then they were gone.

---

hoped © a
So education it was! I ~~opened~~ ~~the~~ dictionary and picked out a

s PH He
word that sound~~ed~~ good. 'Phil/oso/phi/cal!' ~~I~~ yelled. Might

what it means 1.Phizo 2.Phiso/soophical
as well study ~~word meanings first.~~ '~~Philosophical~~: showing calmness

his 1.fort 2.future 3.futshion
and courage in ~~the~~ face of ill fortune.' I mean I really yelled it. I

guess a fellow has to work off steam once in a while.

Figure 3.1

He has not seen the story before. It is, by intention, slightly difficult for him. The insights into his reading process come primarily from his errors, which I choose to call miscues in order to avoid value implications. His expected responses mask the process of their attainment, but his unexpected responses have been achieved through the same process, albeit less successfully applied. The ways that they deviate from the expected reveal this process.

In the common sense view that I am rejecting, all deviations must be treated as errors. Furthermore, it must be assumed in this view that an error either indicates that the reader does not know something or that he has been 'careless' in the application of his knowledge.

For example, his substitution of 'the' for 'your' in the first paragraph of the sample must mean that he was careless, since he has already read 'your' and 'the' correctly in the very same sentence. The implication is that we must teach him to be more careful, that is, to be more precise in identifying each word or letter.

But now let's take the view that I have suggested. What sort of information could have led to tentatively deciding on 'the' in this situation and not rejecting or refining this decision? There obviously is no graphic relationship between 'your' and 'the.' It may be, of course, that he picked up 'the' in the periphery of his visual field. But, there is an important non-graphic relationship between 'the' and 'your.' They both have the same grammatical function: they are, in my terminology, noun markers. Either the reader anticipated a noun marker and supplied one paying no attention to graphic information or he used 'your' as a grammatical signal ignoring its graphic shape. Since the tentative choice 'the' disturbs neither the meaning nor the grammar of the passage, there is no reason to reject and correct it. This explanation appears to be confirmed by two similar miscues in the next paragraph. 'A' and 'his' are both substituted for 'the.' Neither are corrected. Though the substitution of 'his' changes the meaning, the peculiar idiom used in this dictionary definition, 'in the face of ill fortune,' apparently has little meaning to this reader anyway.

The conclusion this time is that he is using noun markers for grammatical, as well as graphic, information in reaching his tentative conclusions. Altogether in reading this ten page story, he made twenty noun marker substitutions, six omissions and two insertions. He corrected four of his substitutions and one omission. Similar miscues involved other function words (auxiliary verbs and prepositions, for example). These miscues appear to have little effect on the meaning of what he is reading. In spite of their frequency, their elimination would not substantially improve the child's reading. Insistence on more precise identification of each word might cause this reader to stop seeking grammatical information and use only graphic information.

The substitution of 'hoped' for 'open' could again be regarded as careless or imprecise identification of letters. But, if we dig beyond this common sense explanation, we find 1 both are verbs and 2 the words have 'key' graphic similarities. Further, there may be evidence of the reader's bilingual French-Canadian background here, as there is in subsequent miscues ('harms' for 'arms,' 'shuckled' for 'chuckled,' 'shoose' for 'choose,' 'shair' for 'chair'). The correction of this miscue may involve an immediate rejection of the tentative choice made on the basis of a review of the graphic stimulus, or it may result from recognizing that it cannot lead to the rest of the sentence. 'I hoped a dictionary...' does not make sense. (It isn't decodable.) In any case, the reader has demonstrated the process by which he constantly tests his guesses, or tentative choices, if you prefer.

'Sounds' is substituted for sounded, but the two differ in ending only. Common sense might lead to the conclusion that the child does not pay attention to word endings, slurs the ends or is otherwise careless. But, there is no consistent similar occurrence in other word endings. Actually, the child has substituted one inflectional ending for another. In doing so he has revealed 1 his ability to separate base and inflectional suffix, and 2 his use of inflectional endings as grammatical signals or markers. Again, he has not corrected a miscue that is both grammatically and semantically acceptable.

'He' for 'I' is a pronoun for pronoun substitution that results in a meaning change, though the antecedent is a bit vague, and the inconsistency of meaning is not easily apparent.

When we examine what the reader did with the sentence 'Might as well study word meaning first,' we see how poorly the model of precise sequential identification fits the reading process. Essentially this reader has decoded graphic input for meaning and then encoded meaning in oral output with transformed grammar and changed vocabulary, but with the basic meaning retained. Perhaps as he encoded his output, he was already working at the list word that followed, but the tentative choice was good enough and was not corrected.

There are two examples, in this sample, of the reader working at unknown words. He reveals a fair picture of his strategies and abilities in these miscues, though in neither is he successful. In his several attempts at 'philosophical,' his first attempt comes closest. Incidentally, he reveals here that he can use a phonic letter-sound strategy when he wants to. In subsequent attempts he moves away from this sounding out, trying other possibilities, as if trying to find something which at least will sound familiar. Interestingly, here he has a definition of sorts, but no context to work with. 'Philosophical' occurs as a list word a number of times in the story. In subsequent attempts, the child tried 'physica,' 'physicacol,' 'physical,' 'philosovigul,' 'phizzlesovigul,' 'phizzo sorigul,' 'philazophgul.' He appears to move in concentric circles around the phonic information he has, trying deviations and variations. His three unsuccessful attempts at 'fortune' illustrate this same process. Both words are apparently unknown to the reader. He can never really identify a word he has not heard. In such cases, unless the context or contexts sufficiently delimit the word's meaning, the reader is not able to get meaning from the words. In some instances, of course, the reader may form a fairly accurate definition of the word, even if he never recognizes it (that is matches it with a known oral equivalent) or pronounces it correctly. This reader achieved that with the word 'typical' which occurred many times in the story. Throughout his reading he said 'topical.' When he finished reading, a check of his comprehension indicated that he knew quite well the meaning of the word. This phenomenon is familiar to any adult reader. Each of us has many well-defined words in our reading vocabulary which we either mispronounce or do not use orally.

I've used the example of this youngster's oral reading not because what he's done is typical of all readers or even of readers his age, but because his miscues suggest how he carries out the psycholinguistic guessing game in reading. The miscues of other readers show similarities and differences, but all point to a selective, tentative, anticipatory process quite unlike the process of precise, sequential identification commonly assumed.

Let's take a closer look now at the components the reader manipulates in this psycholinguistic guessing game.

At any point in time, of course, the reader has available to him and brings to his reading the sum total of his experience and his language and thought development. This self-evident fact needs to be stated because what appears to be intuitive in any guessing is actually the result of knowledge so well learned that the process of its application requires little conscious effort. Most language use has reached this automatic, intuitive level. Most of us are quite unable to describe the use we make of grammar in encoding and decoding speech, yet all language users demonstrate a high degree of skill and mastery over the syntax of language even in our humblest and most informal uses of speech.

Chomsky (1965) has suggested this model of sentence production by speakers of the language:

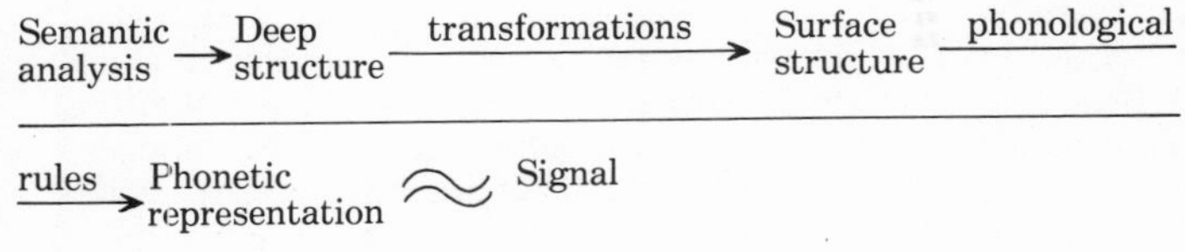

Figure 3.2

A model structure of the listener's sentence interpretation, according to Chomsky, is:

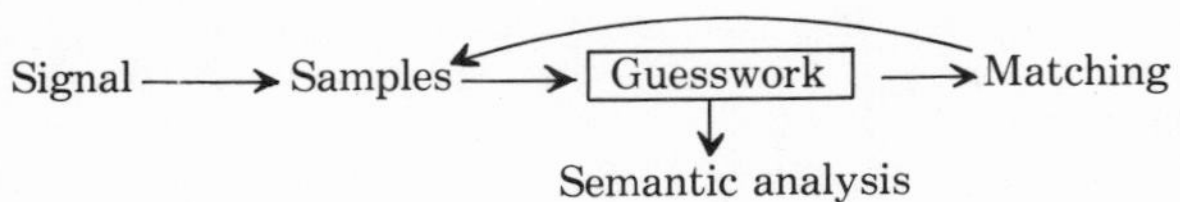

Figure 3.3

Thus, in Chomsky's view encoding of speech reaches a more or less precise level and the signal that results is fully formed. But in decoding, a sampling process aims at approximating the message and any matching or coded signal that results is a kind of by-product.

In oral reading, the reader must perform two tasks at the same time. He must produce an oral language equivalent of the graphic input which is the 'signal' in reading, and he must also reconstruct the meaning of what he is reading. The matching in Chomsky's interpretation model is largely what I prefer to call a recoding operation. The reader recodes the coded graphic input as phonological or oral output. Meaning is not normally involved to any extent. This recoding can even be learned by someone who doesn't speak the language at all, for example, the bar-mitzvah boy may learn to recode Hebrew script as chanted oral Hebrew with no ability to understand what he is chanting; but when the reader engages in semantic analysis to reconstruct the meaning of the writer, only then is he decoding.

In oral reading there are three logical possible arrangements of these two operations. The reader may recode graphic input as oral language and then decode it. He may recode and decode simultaneously. Or, he may decode first and then encode the meaning as oral output.

On the basis of my research to date, it appears that readers who have achieved some degree of proficiency decode directly from the graphic stimulus in a process similar to Chomsky's sampling model and then encode from the deep structure, as illustrated in Chomsky's model of sentence production. Their oral output is not directly related to the graphic stimulus and may involve transformation in vocabulary and syntax, even if meaning is retained. If their comprehension is inaccurate, they will encode this changed or incomplete meaning as oral output.

The common misconception is that graphic input is precisely and sequentially recoded as phonological input and then decoded bit by bit. Meaning is cumulative, built up a piece at a time in this view. This view appears to be supported by studies of visual perception which indicate that only a very narrow span of print on either side of the point of fixation is in sharp focus at any time. We might dub this the 'end of the nose' view, since it assumes that input in reading is that which lies in sharp focus in a straight line from the end of the nose. Speed and efficiency are assumed to come from widening the span taken in on either side of the nose, moving the nose more rapidly or avoiding backward movements of the eyes and nose, which, of course, must cut down on efficiency.

This view cannot possibly explain the speed with which the average adult reads, or a myriad of other constantly occurring phenomena in reading. How can it explain, for example, a highly proficient adult reader reading and rereading a paper he's written and always missing the same misprints. Or how can it explain our fourth grader seeing, 'Study word meanings first,' and saying, 'Study what it means'?

No, the 'end of the nose' view of reading will not work. The reader is not confined to information he receives from a half inch of print in clear focus. Studies, in fact, indicate that children with severe visual handicaps are able to learn to read as well as normal children. Readers utilize not one, but three kinds of information simultaneously. Certainly without graphic input there would be no reading. But, the reader uses syntactic and semantic information as well. He predicts and anticipates on the basis of this information, sampling from the print just enough to confirm his guess of what's coming, to cue more semantic and syntactic information. Redundancy and sequential constraints in language, which the reader reacts to, make this prediction possible. Even the blurred and shadowy images he picks up in the peripheral area of his visual field may help to trigger or confirm guesses.

Skill in reading involves not greater precision, but more accurate first guesses based on better sampling techniques, greater control over language structure, broadened experiences and increased conceptual development. As the child develops reading skill and speed, he uses increasingly fewer graphic cues. Silent reading can then become a more rapid and efficient process than oral reading, for two reasons: 1 the reader's attention is not divided between decoding and recoding or encoding as oral output, and 2 his speed is not restricted to the speed of speech production. Reading becomes a more efficient and rapid process than listening, in fact, since listening is normally limited to the speed of the speaker.

Recent studies with speeded up electronic recordings where distortion of pitch is avoided have demonstrated that listening can be made more rapid without impairing comprehension too.

Though the beginning reader obviously needs more graphic information in decoding and, therefore, needs to be more precise than skilled readers, evidence from a study of first graders by Goodman (1967) indicates that they begin to sample and draw on syntactic and semantic information almost from the beginning, if they are reading material which is fully formed language.

In Figure 3.4 are excerpts from two primer stories (Betts, 1963 and Betts and Welch, 1963) as they were read by a first grade child at the same session. Ostensibly (and by the intent of the authors) the first, from a second preprimer, should be much easier than the second, from a third preprimer. Yet she encountered problems to the point of total confusion with the first and was able to handle exactly the same elements in the second.

Note, for example, the confusion of 'come' and 'here' in Ride In. This represents a habitual association in evidence in early reading of this child. Both 'come' and 'here' as graphic shapes are likely to be identified as 'come' or 'here.' In Stop and Go, the difficulty does not occur when the words are sequential. She also substitutes 'can' for 'and' in the first story, but encounters no problem with either later. 'Stop' stops her completely in Ride In, a difficulty that she doesn't seem to know she has when she reads Stop and Go a few minutes later. Similarly, she calls (ride) 'run' in the first story, but gets it right in the latter one.

Though there are miscues in the second story, there is a very important difference. In the first story she seems to be playing a game of name the word. She is recoding graphic shapes as phonological ones. Each word is apparently a separate problem.

But in Stop and Go what she says, including her miscues, in almost all instances makes sense and is grammatically acceptable. Notice that as 'Sue' becomes better known she becomes 'Suzie' to our now confident reader.

RIDE IN

Run
~~Ride~~ in, Sue.

Run
~~Ride~~ in here.

Come here
~~Here~~ I ~~come~~, Jimmy.

Can Come
~~And here~~ I (stop.)

STOP AND GO

Jimmy said, 'Come here, Sue,

too
Look at my ~~toy~~ (train.)

See it go.

toy
Look at my lit/tle ~~train~~ go.'

toy
Sue said, 'Stop the ~~train~~.

Come
Stop it ~~here~~, Jimmy.'

toy
Jimmy said, 'I can stop the ~~train~~.

toy
See the ~~train~~ stop.'

too
Sue said, 'Look at my ~~toy~~.

toy
It is in the ~~train~~.

too
See my little red ~~toy~~, Jimmy.

toy
It can ride in the ~~train~~.'

toy
Jimmy said, 'See the ~~train~~ go.

Look at it go.'

Suzie too
~~Sue~~ said, 'Look at my little red ~~toy~~.

toy
See it go for a ~~train~~ ride.'

Suzie too
~~Sue~~ said, 'My little red ~~toy~~!

said too
Jimmy, my ~~toy~~ is not here.
©

toy
It is not in the ~~train~~.

toy
Stop the ~~train~~, Jimmy.

too
Stop it and look for my ~~toy~~.'

Figure 3.4

A semantic association exists between 'train' and 'toy.' Though the child makes the same substitution many times, nothing causes her to reject her guess. It works well each time. Having called (train) 'toy,' she calls (toy) 'too' (actually it's an airplane in the pictures), not once, but consistently throughout the story. That doesn't seem to make sense. That's what the researcher thought too, until the child spoke of a 'little red "too"' later in retelling the story. 'What's a "little red too,"' asked the researcher. 'An airplane,' she replied calmly. So a train is 'toy' and a plane is a 'too.' Why not? But, notice that when 'toy' occurred preceding 'train,' she could attempt nothing for 'train.' There appears to be a problem for many first graders when nouns are used as adjectives.

Common sense says go back and drill her on 'come,' 'here,' 'can,' 'stop,' 'ride,' 'and'; don't let her go to the next book which she is obviously not ready to read.

But the more advanced story, with its stronger syntax, more fully formed language and increased load of meaning makes it possible for the child to use her graphic cues more effectively and supplement them with semantic and syntactic information. Teaching for more precise perception with lists and phonics charts may actually impede this child's reading development. Please notice, before we leave the passage, the effect of immediate experience on anticipation. Every one of the paragraphs in the sample starts with 'Jimmy said' or 'Sue said.' When the reader comes to a line starting 'Jimmy,' she assumes that it will be followed by 'said' and it is not until her expectation is contradicted by subsequent input that she regresses and corrects her miscue.

Since they must learn to play the psycholinguistic guessing game as they develop reading ability, effective methods and materials used by teachers who understand the rules of the game, must help them to select the most productive cues, to use their knowledge of language structure, to draw on their experiences and concepts. They must be helped to discriminate between more and less useful available information. Fortunately, this parallels the processes they have used in developing the ability to comprehend spoken language. George Miller (1965) has suggested '...psycholinguists should try to formulate performance models that will incorporate ... hypothetical information storage and information processing components that can simulate the actual behavior of language users.'

I'd like to present now my model of this psycholinguistic guessing game we call reading English. Please understand that the steps do not necessarily take place in the sequential or stretched-out form they are shown here.

1 The reader scans along a line of print from left to right and down the page, line by line.
2 He fixes at a point to permit eye focus. Some print will be central and in focus, some will be peripheral; perhaps his

perceptual field is a flattened circle.
3 Now begins the selection process. He picks up graphic cues, guided by constraints set up through prior choices, his language knowledge, his cognitive styles, and strategies he has learned.
4 He forms a perceptual image using these cues and his anticipated cues. This image then is partly what he sees and partly what he expected to see.
5 Now he searches his memory for related syntactic, semantic, and phonological cues. This may lead to selection of more graphic cues and to reforming the perceptual image.
6 At this point, he makes a guess or tentative choice consistent with graphic cues. Semantic analysis leads to partial decoding as far as possible. This meaning is stored in short-term memory as he proceeds.
7 If no guess is possible, he checks the recalled perceptual input and tries again. If a guess is still not possible, he takes another look at the text to gather more graphic cues.
8 If he can make a decodable choice, he tests it for semantic and grammatical acceptability in the context developed by prior choices and decoding.
9 If the tentative choice is not acceptable semantically or syntactically, then he regresses, scanning from right to left along the line and up the page to locate a point of semantic or syntactic inconsistency. When such a point is found, he starts over at that point. If no inconsistency can be identified, he reads on seeking some cue which will make it possible to reconcile the anomalous situation.
10 If the choice is acceptable, decoding is extended, meaning is assimilated with prior meaning, and prior meaning is accommodated, if necessary. Expectations are formed about input and meaning that lie ahead.
11 Then the cycle continues.

Throughout the process there is constant use of long- and short-term memory.

I offer no apologies for the complexity of this model. Its faults lie, not in its complexity, but in the fact that it is not yet complex enough to fully account for the complex phenomena in the actual behavior of readers. But such is man's destiny in his quest for knowledge. Simplistic folklore must give way to complexity as we come to know.

REFERENCES

Betts, Emmett A. (1963), Ride In, 'Time to Play,' Second Preprimer, Betts Basic Readers, 3rd ed., Language Arts Series, American Book, New York.

Betts, Emmett A., and Carolyn M. Welch (1963), Stop and Go, 'All in a Day,' Third Preprimer, Betts Basic Readers,

American Book, New York.
Chomsky, Noam (1965), Lecture at Project Literacy, Cornell University, June 18.
Goodman, Yetta M. (1967), unpublished dissertation, A Psycholinguistic Description of Observed Oral Reading Phenomena in Selected Beginning Readers, Wayne State University.
Hayes, William D. (1963), My Brother Is a Genius, 'Adventures Now and Then' Book 6, Betts Basic Readers, 3rd ed., Emmett A. Betts and Carolyn M. Welch, American Book, New York, p.246.
McCracken, Glenn, and Charles C. Walcutt (1963), 'Basic Reading,' teacher's ed. for the preprimer and primer. B. Lippincott, Philadelphia, p.vii.
Miller, George A. (1965), Some Preliminaries to Psycholinguistics, 'American Psychologist,' vol.20, no.18.
Spache, George (1964), Reading in the Elementary School, Allyn & Bacon, Boston, p.12.

In 1964, when Goodman published this paper, linguistics had 'literally burst on the reading horizon.' Yet few educators knew much about linguistics. Goodman was motivated in this article by a concern that a very narrow application of linguistics to reading, a kind of phonemic phonics, was already being labeled by publishers 'the linguistic method of teaching reading.'

The central premise of this chapter is a fundamental preoccupation of Goodman's work: reading must have an interdisciplinary base, but 'it is primarily the educator who must accomplish this assimilation of linguistic knowledge to the end of producing better teaching of reading.'

The article, drawing on structural linguistics, seeks to provide a broad scientific base for the intuitive use by teachers of sound linguistic principles. In the context of this broad linguistic base the article warns that early advice of linguists to the reading profession overlooks the most significant contributions linguistics has to make to reading theory and instruction.

4 THE LINGUISTICS OF READING

To many who have labored long in the field of reading it must certainly appear that linguistics has literally burst on the reading horizon. Sessions are devoted to the subject at meetings of the International Reading Association and the National Council of Teachers of English. Books are appearing. Journal articles are multiplying. And publishers seem to be tripping over one another in a race to be the first out with a reading series that carries a linguistic label.

Linguists as well as educationists are showing grave signs of missing the essential significance that linguistics has for the teaching of reading. Reading materials, reading curriculum theory, and reading teaching have suffered from a lack of accurate knowledge of the language. This lack is not the fault of the workers in these fields. The lack is not confirmation of what the linguist suspects is poor scholarship in the field of education. Accurate, scientifically based knowledge about the English language simply has not been available. Linguists can provide this knowledge. Reading is language, and the teaching of reading must be based on the best available knowledge of language.

Educators need not come to the linguists hat in hand, but neither can educators justify ignoring the knowledge of language that the linguists are so rapidly producing. The knowledge that has been amassed in the field of reading is not bad knowledge. Psychological, sociological, physiological, and pedagogical generalizations about reading are not inaccurate. But old knowledge must be accommodated to new. And it is primarily the educator who must accomplish this assimilation of linguistic knowledge to the end of producing better teaching of reading.

The linguist is carrying on his proper function when he advances linguistic generalizations that he believes apply to the teaching of reading. He is also performing a fitting and useful function when he criticizes the teaching of reading from his linguistic vantage point. But he is not on firm ground when he produces reading programs that are based solely on linguistic criteria.

Educators who are self-conscious about their lack of linguistic knowledge would do well to consider linguistics as they have come to view psychology. Psychology has furnished many principles that are incorporated in reading programs. But a reading program cannot be built on a single psychological principle. Nor can we guarantee that a reading program that is psychologically valid will be a good reading program. Further, there are many schools of psychology as, indeed, there are of linguistics. Completely contrasting programs can have psychological or linguistic validity.

TEACHERS' LINGUISTIC SENSE

Good teachers, those with some sensitivity to what is happening to the children they teach, teachers who care whether their young charges are learning, have always instinctively used certain linguistic principles. Every time a teacher says to a child, 'Read that the way you would say it to a friend on the playground,' she is demonstrating that she senses the significance of natural intonation and its effect on comprehension. Teachers who encourage oral language expression, who build experience charts based on the child's own use of the language, who type stories dictated by children for use as reading material, may be totally ignorant of linguistic research, but these teachers have discovered for themselves some basic principles of linguistics as they have watched children striving to become literate.

Linguists, or others who have come lately to an interest in reading, should not overlook a number of important facts about reading: Most - almost all - children learn to read; in the elementary-school curriculum reading gets more time than any other subject (Austin and Morrison, 1963); most teachers make use of the best knowledge and materials available to them; more research has been done on the teaching of reading than perhaps on any other area of the curriculum (Gray, 1960).

PHONEMICS, PHONETICS, AND PHONICS

The concept of the phoneme is one important contribution that linguists have made to the understanding of language and how it communicates thoughts. Almost any variation of sound that a human being is able to produce can be significant in language. The number of these variations is almost infinite. But in any given language only a relatively few variations really do make a difference. These units of sound that make a difference are phonemes (Gleason, 1961).

The way to differentiate 'ramp' and 'lamp' in English is by the initial phonemes. But in certain oriental languages these initial sounds are not separate phonemes. The mature native speaker of Japanese has trouble producing these sounds because he has great difficulty hearing the difference between them in speech. In his native language the difference has no significance.

A branch of linguistics called phonemics has developed. It is the most highly developed branch and the one in which there is the most agreement among linguists. Two other major branches are morphemics and syntax. If phonemes are the atoms of language, then morphemes are the molecules. A morpheme is the smallest unit of language that can bear meaning. It may be a word or a combining form (as 'ed' added to a base morpheme to signal past tense). Syntax is the study of the structures in which morphemes fit together to produce language.

It is not surprising that linguists' first attempts at criticizing the teaching of reading were aimed at phonics and phonetics. Indeed, linguists found that these terms were used interchangeably and that the knowledge which supported 'phonics' programs was highly unscientific and often without basis (Fries, 1963, pp.140-6). The linguists reacted as the early scientific astronomers must have reacted to astrology. The linguists fell into the trap of concluding that phonics programs did not work because they were unscientific; that is, they were not phonemic programs.

Bloomfield (Bloomfield and Barnhart, 1962), and others who followed, advanced programs that were based on the same essential principle as phonics programs. According to this principle the child is introduced systematically to the written symbols that represent specific phonemes. In Bloomfield's approach learning is simplified because each phoneme is always represented by the same letter or digraph.

Some reading series that are now being rushed on the market are based on this essential principle, except that sound-symbol representations are always introduced in words. Fries's 'linguistically sound approach' is another slight variant (Fries, 1963, pp.186-215). He stresses contrastive patterns of letters in words that function in consistent ways. Thus, he would teach children to contrast groups of words such as 'man, Dan, ban' with 'mane, Dane, bane' and 'mean, dean, bean.'

These programs, which would more properly be labeled phonemic rather than linguistic, have been viewed by some educators as 'just another kind of phonics.' In a sense that is exactly what they are. They are based on phonemic insights - the best available knowledge of the sounds of the language - but they are not complete reading programs from either an educator's or a linguist's view.

Educators should be concerned, for example, that all these programs present groups of very similar words. Psychologists have long known that it is much harder for children to learn to differentiate things that are very similar than it is to learn to differentiate things that are quite different. Indeed, this is one basis on which intelligence tests are constructed.

Linguists should object to the isolation of words or parts of words from 'living' language. Indeed, Fries instructs teachers never to say or have the child say anything in the program that is less than a word. But he then tells the teacher to pronounce each word '*in normal talking fashion*' (Fries, 1963, p.203; italics his). His University of Michigan colleague Pike could hardly find this directive acceptable (Pike, 1945). Words pronounced out of language context cannot be pronounced in 'normal talking fashion' because the speaker has no way of knowing what intonation (stress and pitch) to use.

One danger of phonemic reading programs is that their scientific base will give them great respectability and they will gain wide use before they have been sufficiently tried. There are two other dangers. One is that fuller application of linguistics to reading will be delayed. The other is that educators will reject linguistics while rejecting phonemic reading programs.

PRIMER-ESE

Advocates of so-called new approaches to reading frequently exploit the public amusement with 'those silly primers.' 'Oh, Oh, Look, Look' is always worth a laugh. The implication is that the alternate approach to teaching reading will not produce such silly stuff.

This is an irrelevant and unfair argument when used by any person who advocates any approach to reading teaching that involves using materials that are simplified according to any criteria. Whether the criterion for simplification is word count, sound-symbol representation, or sentence structure, what results (particularly in the beginning materials) is artificial language. Witness this sentence from Fries: 'Pat a fat cat' (Fries, 1963, p.203). Stratemeyer and Smith offer this gem: 'Jump, Pud. Jump, Zip. Jump, Jump' (Stratemeyer and Smith, 1963).

Pseudopsychology was the inevitable companion of psychology. Pseudolinguistics inevitably has accompanied the development of linguistics. We can expect that reading programs that have not the vaguest linguistic justification will be described as linguistically based. The word 'linguistics' is already appearing in the promotional material of publishers of basal readers. Educators as well as linguists need to be on guard.

CONTRIBUTIONS TO EDUCATION

If we assume that linguistics has a great deal to offer education but that educators must make the application, it is important to consider carefully how linguistic knowledge can be applied in education. The following contributions deserve consideration:

1 Linguistics can provide education with an accurate description of the language.

2 Linguistics can provide techniques for language and reading research. Availability of new tools and concepts will necessitate the careful review of past research in reading. Much past research could be redone. For example, excellent research in eye movements in reading had a predominantly physiological base. But what do we know about the influence

of syntactical structure on eye movements?
3 Linguistics can provide new criteria for judging readability of reading material.
4 Linguistics and psycholinguistics can provide new insights into child language and describe more accurately how children learn languages.
5 Linguistics, together with psycholinguistics and communications theory, can give us clues on how language conveys meaning.
6 Linguistics can describe and explain the development of regional and social dialects of English.
7 Linguistics can provide sensitizing concepts that educationists and teachers can use. In this respect it is apparent that a field of applied linguistics must emerge in education - educational linguistics. The postwar developments in the teaching of foreign language in this country are the result of the use of linguistic-sensitizing concepts to improve language-teaching.

Educators will have to resist the linguists' excessive enthusiasm for their science, an enthusiasm that leads them to hope that one day every little first-grader will be an analytical linguist. There is an inconsistency here. Linguists and educationists have demonstrated that by the time a relatively normal child comes to school he has an excellent subconscious command of the syntax of the language as he hears it spoken, not to mention an immense vocabulary (Strickland, 1962). Still, some linguists somehow see the need for teaching children about the language they already use with the facility of an expert. Teachers have learned, however, that improved use of language does not depend on the child's ability to describe the language in technical terms.

GENERALIZATIONS FROM LINGUISTICS

I am not a linguist but an educationist. From linguistic resources I have gleaned a set of generalizations, the sensitizing concepts I referred to earlier, that I feel must be considered by those interested in the teaching of reading. Some of these concepts conflict with concepts currently in use in reading. Some conflict with other linguistic generalizations. But they must all be tried. They must be 'plugged in' to current reading theory and practice to produce a new and higher synthesis in reading instruction (Goodman, 1963). The generalizations follow:
1 The child comes to school with great control over his language. He derives meaning from a rapid stream of speech by responding to certain built-in cue systems such as pattern, inflectional changes, key function words, and intonations.
2 Virtually every child's language is adequate for his present needs in communication. All language is equally good.

3 Reading is an active aspect of communication. Just as the person who hears but does not comprehend is not listening, so the reader who calls words but does not comprehend is not reading.
4 The need to communicate plays a vital role in the child's language learning. His need to express his thoughts or desires and to understand the expression of others is the stimulus that causes him to develop language.
5 Language in and of itself has no meaning. It is a code, a system by which those who know the code may communicate meaning. Yet language has no existence except in association with meaning.
6 Reading materials must always say something to the child that is worth saying, in a language he can understand, involving concepts within the scope of his reach and interests.
7 If the child is to make the greatest use of built-in cue systems in language for deriving meaning, he cannot be made dependent on other systems and extraneous cues. This means that the role of pictures in early reading materials must be re-evaluated.
8 The basic units of speech are phonemes, but they have no existence outside of morphemes, the molecules of the language. Morphemes are the minimum units of language that can carry meaning, but they have no existence outside of syntactical structures. Syntactical structures, such as sentences, have reality only in the stream of language.
9 Words taken out of language context cannot be defined, pronounced, or categorized. (Can you define 'contract'? Can you pronounce 'contract'? Can you classify 'contract' as a noun or a verb? And if you could do any of these things, could you decide the proper stress and pitch to use when you said the word?) The common practice of using word lists in teaching reading must be reconsidered.
10 The tasks of teaching children to read and teaching them to speak a preferred dialect are separate and may be conflicting. This fact is well illustrated by the following incident.

> A group of second-graders were reading in round-robin fashion. It was Jim's turn. 'There was a lot of goats,' he read. 'There was black goats and white goats.'
>
> His teacher smiled encouragingly. 'Would you repeat that, please, Jim,' she said.
>
> Somewhat puzzled, Jim reread: 'There was a lot of goats. There was black goats and white goats.'
>
> Still smiling, his teacher stepped to the board. In excellent manuscript she wrote two words. 'Do you see a difference in these words,' she said.
>
> 'Yes, they have different endings,' said Jim.
>
> 'Can you read these words?' the teacher asked.
>
> '"Was," "were",' Jim read. 'Good,' said his teacher. 'This is "was," and this is "were." Now read again what you just read from the book.'

'There was a lot of...' Jim began.
'No, no!' his teacher said with some annoyance. 'It's "were."' 'There were a lot of goats.' 'Now, please reread.'
'There "were" a lot of goats. There was black goats and ...'

The parable of the goats illustrates a common dilemma in reading teaching. The teacher, using an approach that emphasizes word recognition, assumes that Jim is confusing the words 'was' and 'were.' Jim, on the other hand, is demonstrating a high level of attainment in reading. He is reading his own speech off the page, subconsciously making corrections where the book is wrong in terms of his knowledge of the language.

Reading instruction has much to learn from linguistics. Important new knowledge about language, how it functions, and how it is learned has been produced. This knowledge must be assimilated into the reading curriculum. The process must be presided over by educators primarily, perhaps under the banner of educational linguistics. In any case, the raw material for building the linguistics of reading is now available.

REFERENCES

Austin, Mary C., and Coleman Morrison (1963), 'The First R: The Harvard Report on Reading in Elementary Schools,' Macmillan, New York.

Bloomfield, Leonard, and Clarence Barnhart (1962), 'Let's Read,' Wayne State University Press, Detroit.

Fries, Charles C. (1963), 'Linguistics and Reading,' Holt, Rinehart & Winston, New York.

Gleason, H.A. (1961), 'An Introduction to Descriptive Linguistics,' Holt, Rinehart & Winston, New York.

Goodman, Kenneth S. (1963), A Communicative Theory of the Reading Curriculum, 'Elementary English,' March, pp.290-8.

Gray, William S. (1960), Reading, 'Encyclopedia of Educational Research,' ed. by Chester W. Harris, Macmillan, New York, 3rd ed., p.1087.

Pike, Kenneth L. (1945), 'The Intonation of American English,' University of Michigan Press, Ann Arbor.

Stratemeyer, Clara, and Harvey Lee Smith (1963), The Linguistic Science Readers, 'Frog Fun,' (first preprimer), Harper & Row, New York, 1963, p.8.

Strickland, Ruth G. (1962), 'The Language of Elementary School Children: Its Relationship to the Language of Reading Textbooks and the Quality of Reading of Selected Children.' Bulletin of the School of Education, Indiana University, vol.XXXVIII, no.4, Bloomington, Indiana: Bureau of Educational Studies and Testing, School of Education, Indiana University.

'Anything short of meaning, anything, that doesn't, in fact, go from code to meaning is not decoding.' That's the statement of this article's essential message. In her widely quoted book, 'Reading: The Great Debate,' Jeanne Chall had popularized the term 'decoding,' which was being used in some linguistic discussions of reading. It gained instant acceptance as a more scientific sounding alternative to phonics.

Goodman argues that *both* oral and written language are codes for meaning and that shifts from print to sound with no meaning resulting are 'recoding,' a transforming of code to code.

That enables him to reject Jeanne Chall's juxtaposing of 'code-emphasis' and 'meaning-emphasis' programs.

'There should never be an argument between whether to start with code or with meaning because the code only operates in relationship to meaning.'

5 DECODING: From Code to What?

The concept that underlies the use of the term 'decoding' has become so distorted that we need to re-examine it carefully. It has crept very rapidly into our literature and into our terminology, and has been substituted for some earlier terms that fell into disrepute, such as 'sounding-out.'

Both oral language and written language are codes. There is nothing less of a code about the noises a speaker makes and a listener reacts to than there is about those ink blotches on the page or chalk marks on a board. Both are code forms of language. Language has the capability, in the hands of people who know how to use it, of communicating meaning. Like any code it has no intrinsic meaning of its own. For literate people there are two code forms that complement each other, a written code and an oral code.

But if you look carefully at the term 'decode,' that term implies that one is going from code to something other than code. If, in decoding, we go from code to something else, what else is that something else? An immediate answer is that if the reader moves from code to code, no decoding has taken place. If he moves from written language to oral language in some form, however distorted or complete, he has not decoded anything. In a similar manner the army signal corps operator receives a coded message that comes to him as a dot-dash signal over a radio. He then transcribes that into letter sequences. But he can't take that piece of paper with the letter sequences and say 'Here, I've decoded the message.' In fact, he has to get a code book out and somehow reconstruct the message which has been carefully obscured through several different encodings in order to keep other people from getting the message.

It isn't until he gets the message that any decoding has taken place. Anything short of meaning, anything that doesn't, in fact, go from code to meaning is not decoding.

There are some non-decoding kinds of things that happen in reading. These are short circuits that can develop and that unfortunately are apparently taught, and which kids unfortunately then learn. Kids have a nasty habit of learning what they are taught. Then teachers become very unhappy about the fact that they did, not realizing what brought the learning about. These short-circuits will be discussed more fully later.

Decoding must move the language user from language to meaning. But there isn't any intrinsic meaning in language. If we ask any physicist to describe from a physical point of view what, in fact, is going on when language is spoken, he would not find any property of that sound that had any intrinsic meaning. Even the quaint notion that maybe people started to learn to talk by imitating the sounds around them and using them as symbols is a pretty thin theory to explain language development. Obviously, very few noises any speaker makes have anything to do with the meaning he's trying to produce. As users of language we've gotten so used to thinking of ourselves as dealing directly with meaning we very often lose sight of the fact that the speaker cannot be projecting meaning into his listener's brain. He's broadcasting, taking his message and encoding it, and what the listener is doing, on the basis of what he's learned about language, is taking that sound signal, the noises that the speaker has made, and decoding for meaning. The listener reconstructs the message or attempts to reconstruct the message that the speaker was broadcasting. There's no direct pipeline from mind to mind. There's no way of the speaker insuring, short of doing the best job he can of encoding, that decoding is going to be successful.

The speaker can try to think about what the listener brings to the task. That is, he can be 'audience minded,' as any speaker or writer tries to be. But all he can do is broadcast. From that point on it's the listener's job. The meaning is always in the speaker and the listener or in the writer and the reader.

Literate users of language, as listeners, can reconstruct the meaning from spoken language. As readers they can take written language and reconstruct the meaning. There are obviously some differences in the way the forms are used. Listeners can usually see speakers. They make motions with their hands. They make facial gestures and body movements. They may point to things. If speakers are conversing, they might show each other something or hold something or exchange something. There's a situational context that operates. Written language is always more removed from that which it refers to. It's most frequently out of any situational context. But an exit sign over the door is in a context. It has meaning partly because of its location. Even if you didn't know what it said, if it were in a foreign language, you'd be able to know what it must mean because of the context in which you find it.

At international airports, besides the words for men and women there are also picture clues to help get the meaning across.

To understand how language is decoded for meaning, psycholinguistic theory is needed. This theory has not grown out of a desire to promote a particular theory of language and a particular grammar, but rather from research on what people do when they read and when they listen.

The listener must cope with a stream of sounds which he has learned to organize according to certain perceptual categories that he has, the kinds of things that certain linguists call phonemes. In terms of certain contrastive features of the sounds, he's learned two very important things as he learned the language: what to pay attention to and what not to pay attention to. If he didn't know what not to pay attention to, it wouldn't do him much good to know what to pay attention to. He'd be constantly distracted.

But what's more important, the listener has to be able to take what's coming at him and from it induce its underlying structure. He has to be able to plot it into structural units and be able to handle the interrelationships of those units. If the speaker produces a statement which is a series of clauses, joined and interrelated and embedded in each other, the listener has to sort out those interrelationships, organize the clauses and assign meaning once he has the underlying, or deep, structure. That's the way the message is recreated. Listeners can't go directly from the signal, that stream of sounds, to meaning. There is no way of explaining how one could unless he has dealt with its structure. Everybody has the experience both in listening and in reading of finding that he's assumed the wrong underlying structure, one that doesn't make sense. So the listener has to reorganize, reprocess, and try a different underlying structure and then get the meaning.

Whether one starts with speech or with print, the task is to determine what the underlying grammatical structure is and then assign meaning. This sequence is virtually simultaneous. The language user is immediately getting some meaning sense. If language is anything, it is a meaning-seeking process. And it's only when the user of language is actively seeking meaning that, in fact, it operates as language.

If teachers doctor up language, if they select it in such a way that it turns out not to be language which is meaningful, or acts like language, then both the attempt to reconstruct the underlying language structure and the attempt to get at the meaning are frustrated and it becomes an experience in nonsense. Psychologists should have recognized in their own research, year after year after year, that whenever they used a language-learning task which was meaningful it was easier to learn than something that was nonsense. Whenever they tried something that had the grammatical sequence of natural language, even if it wasn't meaningful, that was easier to handle than unstructured nonsense. That's because a language user engages in the process of seeking meaning through the grammatical structures. He uses the surface structure, the sequences of sounds or the letters, only as signals or means of getting at, or inducing or recreating, the deep structure.

Because of the way language works, language users in decoding have to go from a surface structure to an underlying structure and then to meaning.

Now let's contrast speaking and writing with how listening and reading work. The contrast is between the encoding part of language and the decoding part of language. By this time the reader should understand that decoding is not being used here in any sense as a letter-to-sound shift. Decoding here means going from language to meaning and contrasts with encoding: from meaning to language. It doesn't even quite matter whether the person is successful. What's most important is that the activity he's engaged in is one in which he is seeking meaning or moving from meaning.

Encoding starts with meaning. The language uses a message to communicate a need, a feeling, an idea, a reaction to the world. When you turn to somebody and say something and he's standing on your foot, you hope he'll get off your foot. If he doesn't understand, he may continue to stand on it for a while. So, you start out with a message; then you assign a deep structure. As a language user you're not quite aware of the process because it's become so well learned, but you could not call this an unconscious process because you obviously control it.

One of the evidences that the process is controlled is that it sometimes comes out not quite the way we intended it to. It's not a totally unconscious process but language users are so agile that they're not quite aware of how it works. Users assign a deep structure, then they use a set of rules that they learned as youngsters. While learning the language, language users induced the set of rules for generating it and got to the point where they could use them almost automatically. In the meantime as they learned to use them they produced some funny sounding kinds of things like 'I taked it' instead of 'I took it.' They tried to overgeneralize the rule and had to learn its exceptions. As they learned to use the rules they produced language, not on the basis of imitating what they heard, but on the basis of this set of rules that move language toward a surface representation.

It would appear at first that reading and listening are mirror images of speaking and writing. However, we have to be aware of the way the human mind works and what is possible in the language situation. The human mind finds it possible to make receptive language a different process, not a mirror image.

Receptive language use is not the directly opposite sequence of language encoding. The receptive language user does have to get to the deep structure in order to get to the meaning, but he doesn't have to use all the surface structure; that is, he doesn't have to use every feature of every sound and every relationship of every sound. He doesn't have to perceive it all. He doesn't have to hear it all accurately. He can hear partially, in fact, and still handle the situation just as he can read a text that has smudged print. The reason for that is that in getting at that deep structure he can make giant leaps, can interpret a few key clues or cues (either one applies here) and on that basis make a quick guess, a quick prediction, of what the structure is. Once he has predicted the structure, then all he has to do is sample from the subsequent signal, sounds or letters, in order to confirm what he has already predicted. He makes a giant leap. What's very important in the effectiveness of his guessing or predicting are the tactics or strategies that he's developed for knowing, before he sees them, which are the most important cues to look for. A reader, like a listener, develops strategies for picking out the most productive cues before he encounters them. It's been known for years that all the letters in a word are not equally important; the initial consonant is quite important. From an information theory point of view, the initial consonant carries more information; therefore, the reader learns to zero in on it, search for it, even before he sees it.

What a reader thinks he sees, just as what a listener thinks he hears is only partly what he actually processed, and mostly what he expected. The language user knows what to expect so that there's a process of guessing, of using minimal cues, of selecting the cues that carry the most information. Beginning cues in reading are graphic, obviously. Language users may attach, because they're listeners before they're readers, some generalizations about the relationship between the writing system and the speech system and use some phonological cues then. But there has been an exaggeration of the importance of these cues. They are misused when taught out of language context, because they are of value only in language contexts. The reader, like the listener, brings to the task his knowledge of the way the language works. His knowledge of the grammatical system makes it possible for him to predict from key graphic symbols what, in fact, the structure could be. Of course, the more complex it is the more processing he has to do, and the more interrelationships there are. A series of short simple sentences is easier to process than one sentence that contains several clauses embedded and conjoined. But the reader has to get the underlying structure. That's what he moves toward. As he brings his knowledge of grammar into play, he may be much more interested in the grammatical functioning of 'the' than in its graphic qualities. Equally important, though, since this is a meaning-seeking process, the reader has anticipated, and is setting up, an expectation semantically. He builds a semantic context in which he tries things out, and he keeps saying to himself as he processes and guesses, 'Does it make sense?' In language, meaning always is both input and output. One can't read and understand something that one doesn't have the conceptual development to handle. If, when he's done, a reader doesn't know if something makes sense, he doesn't know whether he's been successful or not. And if he doesn't know whether he's been successful he can't judge whether the strategies he used are ones that he should keep on using or ineffective ones that he should drop.

This need to confirm the guess on the basis of one's knowledge of the language and of the meaning that one brings to it is perhaps the strongest argument for why kids from the very beginning have to encounter meaningful natural language in their reading materials. It's an old cliché in education: 'First you learn to read and then you read to learn.' Essentially that's true but we have to put it into context of saying that the meanings that the reader gets from early reading experiences have to be broadly within his experience already, and broadly within his conceptual grasp. If there are new ideas that he's not yet able to handle, then the task is self-defeating right from the beginning.

The relationships between oral and written English have to be understood in a couple of contexts. Everybody knows we have an alphabetic system. An alphabetic system means that at least in origin there's an attempt to represent not simply the meanings graphically as idiographic writing systems do, but to actually represent the oral language so that there is in fact a set of relationships between oral and alphabetically written languages. Language changes over time. The fit between the oral and written language tends to change, not just for English but for all languages. Some languages have less complex relationships than English, but there is no such thing (and can never be any such thing) as a written system that is a perfect representation on a one-to-one basis of the oral languages. Language changes; dialects drift apart, the sound systems of all dialects are not the same. Scottish speakers, for instance, have a closer correspondence in those 'night,' 'light' words than we do. The 'gh' was taught to me as silent letters, because they don't relate to anything in my sound system. To Scottish speakers they do relate to something in their sound system, and a spelling shift to accommodate my sound system would be a shift away from theirs. The correspondences in alphabetic writing systems turn out not to be between letters and sounds but between patterns of letters and patterns of sounds. And those are necessarily complex. Sounds shift in relationships to the sounds around them as affixes are combined with bases to achieve certain meaning sequences, certain grammatical interrelationships. In the word 'situation,' for instance, neither 't' represents the phoneme that is most frequently associated with the letter 't.'

Because the child is a listener before he's a reader, the complexity illustrated by 'situation' turns out never to be a reading problem. Systems of teaching reading that have treated it as a problem have created more difficulties than they've solved. A child normally would have no tendency to read 'situation' as 'sit u a ti on,' unless someone had taught him an inappropriate rule, one that didn't fit with the phonological rules he had already learned. As soon as he tries to say a word sequence, the rules that he's applying in producing that language take over, and it comes out a certain way. In fact, it's very difficult for him to say it any other way.

Having dealt to some extent with the relationship of reading and listening and the relationship of writing to speech in English, let's consider just what breaks down in the reading process that might cause concern as we look at the ways reading has been taught and the kinds of problems that result. The listener has already learned a very efficient language process. He has become competent with the oral language to the point where he can go from that oral signal to the underlying structure, to meaning, efficiently and rapidly. He knows which cues to select and knows how to plug in to the grammatical system to pick up grammatical cues and get at the underlying structures. He can plug in the meaning from his experiences and from concepts that he has developed. All that is working already. Now if the difference between reading and listening is a matter of going from a written signal rather than an oral signal what, in fact, he has to learn is not how to match letters to sounds but how to get from that written signal to the underlying structure in much the way that he has learned to get from the oral signal to the underlying structure.

The task in reading is not to hear the word or recognize the word or name it. The task is to get the underlying structure, to get at the meaning, and constantly to keep the meaning in mind. And that means that even when teachers set out to teach the relationships between oral and written language they turn them into a set of abstractions unless they keep these relationships within the context of language as it functions. The task in reading is to get at that underlying structure; teaching reading often turns into an unrelated task, one that can now be labeled 'recoding,' going from the graphic code to an oral code. At that, the oral code is fragmentary, because in order to do a real job of encoding orally I have to already have the meaning.

Readers, as we said earlier, can be taught to have short circuits. Instead of going from print to meaning, they wind up with something that isn't meaning at all.

Grunting sounds in response to print is one kind of short circuit. Among early readers in some instructional programs there's a strong tendency to go through an unfamiliar text and name the words they know and then sit back complacently. Or they'll point to a word and they'll say, 'We haven't had that word yet.' The task for them is to produce an oral name for the word and the notion that this is supposed to be a language process and a meaning-seeking one hasn't come through to them. Kids who have learned the whole galaxy of word attacks can come up with very close correspondence in oral reading. As a matter of fact, if you listen superficially to their reading you would think they must understand because they're so accurate. And then you discover that all that they were doing was efficiently attacking words; that is, they have achieved a complex kind of recoding that functions extremely well but short-circuits the meaning-seeking process.

In our research there are subjects that recode so effectively that they even handle the syntactic structures. They go from the print to a kind of non-semantic underlying structure and then right back to oral language, still without understanding. Many in-school activities teach them to do that, by the way. Pupils are given a chapter in a book on Brazil, for example. Then they are asked the question, 'What are the principal products of Brazil?' The readers go back through and find a line that starts out 'The principal products of Brazil are ...' and copy it, knowing that the end of that sentence is the answer. What they have done is a complex kind of recoding, but still really recoding, in the sense that the child has not sought meaning. In fact, some readers may have come to the conclusion that for them reading doesn't really yield sense.

SUMMARY

Simply speaking, reading is a meaning-seeking process. Listeners have learned to handle listening as a meaning-seeking process. What a reader has to do is to get from print to that same underlying structure, from which he can get to meaning. And he always has to keep in mind that language has as its purpose to get the meaning. It's not an end in itself but always a means to an end.

To summarize in one short statement: there should never be an argument between whether to start with code or with meaning because the code only operates in relationship to meaning.

In 1969, Goodman was invited to speak on reading at the Congress for Applied Linguistics in Cambridge, England. He took the occasion to extend his view of the reading process in English to a view of reading as a single, universal process in all languages.

This paper takes issue with a common view among linguists: that written language is a secondary representation of oral language and that readers must go through oral language to get to meaning. Goodman argues that alphabetic writing is a convenience and not an essential to literacy and that, in any case, both language forms, oral and written, directly represent meaning. Subsequent studies of the reading process in other languages, using miscue analysis, have largely supported Goodman's assertions in this chapter.

6 PSYCHOLINGUISTIC UNIVERSALS IN THE READING PROCESS

Reading is a psycholinguistic process by which the reader, a language user, reconstructs, as best he can, a message which has been encoded by a writer as a graphic display.

Through research on children reading English who are native speakers of some dialect of American English, I have evolved a basic theoretical view of the reading process. I hope it will be understood that some of what I will be saying is an extension of and projection of my theoretical view into dimensions that go beyond the research on which it is based. In this sense what I will say is hypothetical and I invite other scholars to test and challenge the hypotheses in terms of languages and orthographies other than English.

GENERATIVE AND RECEPTIVE ASPECTS OF LANGUAGE

It is ironic that although most researchers agree that receptive control of aspects of language precedes generative control, more attention has been given to the process of language production than to the process by which language is understood. Many linguists have assumed that listening and reading are simply the mirror images of speaking and writing. They have assumed that since generative processes begin with meaning and result in a fully formed phonological or graphic display that receptive processes begin with the encoded display and reverse the process, step by step, to get back to meaning.

In this too simple view not enough consideration has been given to the variant nature of the productive and receptive tasks that are involved in language use. In producing language, the language user has thoughts which he wishes to express. In a transformational view, he creates a deep language structure which represents his meaning, applies a set of compulsory and optional transformational rules and generates a surface structure. If the language user is literate this surface structure may utilize a phonological signal and require the application of a set of phonological rules or it may utilize a graphic signal and require use of a set of orthographic rules.

The choice will be dictated, of course, by the language user's purpose. The receptive process does start with the phonological or graphic display as input, and it does end with meaning as output, but the efficient language user takes the most direct route and touches the fewest bases necessary to get to his goal.

He accomplishes this by 'sampling,' relying on the redundancy of language, and his knowledge of linguistic constraints. He predicts structures, tests them against the semantic context which he builds up from the situation and the ongoing discourse and then confirms or disconfirms as he processes further language.

Receptive language processes are cycles of sampling, predicting, testing and confirming. The language user relies on strategies which yield the most reliable prediction with the minimum use of the information available.

Neither listening nor reading is a precise process, and in fact even what the language user perceives is only partly what he sees or hears and partly what he expects to see or hear. This is necessarily so not only because of the prediction in which the language user engages but also because he has learned to organize his perceptions according to what is and is not significant in the language. The language user must not simply know what to pay attention to but what not to pay attention to.

The producer of language will be most successful if the signal he produces is complete and well-formed. With such a signal, the receiver of language is free to utilize his sampling strategies.

The necessary concern for oral language which had been neglected for so long caused many scholars to dismiss written language without adequate consideration as a secondary representation of oral language. But written language in a literate culture is not simply a way of preserving and recording oral language. It designates streets, places, and directions, it labels and classifies. It makes communication possible over time and space.

A key difference between oral and written language is that speech is most commonly encountered within the situations in which it is most relevant. Speakers may rely on the situational context to make referents explicit. Listeners may infer from the situational context and from the movements, actions, and gestures of speakers a great deal of semantic information to augment and constrain what they derive from the language.

Written language tends to be out of situational context. The writer must make referents and antecedents explicit, he must create contexts through the language to replace those which are not present. He must furthermore address himself to an unseen and frequently unknown audience. He gets no immediate linguistic or visual feedback to cue him as to whether his communicative efforts are successful.

Written language is perfectible in that the writer may edit it to be sure he has said exactly what he wished to say. It is not perishable in the sense that oral language is.

These differences should not obscure the basic similarities between the alternate language forms for literate language users, but they should make clear that reading and listening will employ variant psycholinguistic strategies to cope with the variant characteristics of the two forms. Reading employs a strategy of regression to reread, for example, whereas listening cannot employ a comparable strategy. The listener must ask the speaker to repeat and that is not always feasible.

One misconception which has caused considerable confusion in dealing with the reading process is the notion that meaning may only be derived from oral language. It is assumed by some that readers engage in a process of recoding graphic input as aural input and then decoding. While this may in fact take place in beginning stages of the acquisition of literacy among some learners, it is not necessary or characteristic of proficient reading. An analogy can be found in the early stages of learning a second language. The learner may be going through a process of continuous translation into his first language before he decodes. But eventually he must be able to derive meaning directly from the second language with no recourse to the first. Just so the proficient reader becomes as skillful at deriving meaning from written language as he is from the aural form with no need to translate one to the other.

It must be remembered that oral language is no less an arbitrary code than written language. Neither has any direct relationship to meaning and the real world other than that which its users assign it.

Alphabetic writing systems have a number of virtues among which is that there is a built-in correspondence to the units and sequences of the oral language form. But this is not an unmitigated blessing. A writing system which is directly related to ideas and concepts has the virtue that it can be used for communication by speakers of different languages. The system of mathematical notation has that advantage. 6 + 9 = 15 is a mathematical statement that will be immediately understood by speakers of a wide range of languages, whereas six and nine equal fifteen can only be understood if the reader knows English.

The Chinese writing system may indeed have its faults but it has the virtue of being understood by speakers of oral languages which are not mutually comprehensible. And of course the Chinese writing system once it is mastered, does function quite well for its users. Alphabetic writing systems are not in fact necessary for literacy.

THE READING PROCESS

The readers of English I have studied utilize three cue systems simultaneously. The starting point is graphic in reading and we may call one cue system 'graphophonic.' The reader responds to graphic sequences and may utilize the correspondences between the graphic and phonological systems of his English dialect. I should point out that these are not phoneme-grapheme correspondences but in fact operate on morpho-phonemic levels (that is, spelling patterns relate to sound sequences). In

English as in other languages the spelling system is fixed and standardized. This means that correspondences will vary from dialect to dialect and that, over time, changing phonology will loosen the fit of even the tightest alphabetic system.

The second cue system the reader uses is syntactic. The reader, using pattern markers such as function words and inflectional suffixes as cues, recognizes and predicts structures. Since the underlying or deep structures of written and oral language are the same, the reader seeks to infer the deep structure as he reads so that he may arrive at meaning.

The third cue system is semantic. In order to derive meaning from language the language user must be able to provide semantic input. This is not simply a question of meaning for words but the much larger question of the reader having sufficient experience and conceptual background to feed into the reading process so that he can make sense out of what he is reading. All readers are illiterate in some senses, since no one can read everything written in his native language.

These cue systems are used simultaneously and interdependently. What constitutes useful graphic information depends on how much syntactic and semantic information is available. Within high contextual constraints an initial consonant may be all that is needed to identify an element and make possible the prediction of an ensuing sequence or the confirmation of prior predictions.

Proficient readers make generally successful predictions but they are also able to recover when they produce miscues which change the meaning *in unacceptable ways.*

No readers read material they have not read before without errors. It must be understood that in the reading process accurate use of all cues available would not only be slow and inefficient but would actually lead the reader away from his primary goal which is comprehension. In fact in my research I have encountered many youngsters who are so busy matching letters to sounds and naming word shapes that they have no sense of the meaning of what they are reading. Reading requires not so much skills as strategies that make it possible to select the most productive cues.

These strategies will vary with the nature of the reading tasks. For example literature has different characteristics than discursive language. The writer will use unusual terms and phrases rather than the more trite but also more predictable ones which would be used to express the same meaning in everyday conversation. The reader needs strategies that adjust to the very different constraints in literary materials.

Because reading involves visual input, characteristics of the visual system do affect the reading process. The material must be scanned from left to right as English is printed and the eye must focus at specific points since it cannot provide input while it is in motion. At each fixation a very small circle of print is in clear sharp focus. Some have argued that only print in sharp focus can be used in reading. But there is a large area of print in the peripheral field at each point of fixation which is not seen clearly but is sufficiently seen to be usable in the sampling, predicting and confirming aspects of reading. The reader can in fact work with partial, blurred, even mutilated graphic input to a considerable degree.

That, too briefly, is what my research has told me about the process of reading English among native American speakers. I have no reason to believe that this process would vary except in minor degrees in the reading of any language. Whether the graphic sequence is from left to right, right to left, or top to bottom would be of little consequence to the basic reading process. The reader needs to scan appropriately but he will still sample and predict in much the same way.

With alphabetical orthographies the regularity of correspondence rules for letter-sound relationships is not nearly as important as many people have believed. Readers are able to use syntactic and semantic cues to such a considerable extent that they need only minimal graphic cues in many cases. They can tolerate a great deal of irregularity, ambiguity, and variability in orthographies without the reading process suffering. There is in fact a wide range in which an alphabetic orthography may exist and still be viable. Only minor adjustments in the reading process are required to deal with any unusual correspondence features.

An example in reading English is the variability of vowel representation. This is particularly confused since the unstressed vowel schwa, may be spelled by any vowel letter. Readers learn to rely more heavily on consonants, particularly initial ones for their minimum cues and to use vowel letters only when other information is inadequate.

I confess to knowing nothing about problems of reading non-alphabetic writing systems but I strongly believe that readers of languages which employ them will still be sampling using minimal graphic cues to predict grammatical structures.

Grammatical patterns and rules operate differently in each language but readers will need to use their grammatical competence in much the same way. Some special reading strategies may result from particular characteristics of the grammatical system. Inflections are relatively unimportant in English grammar but positions in patterns are quite important. In a highly inflected language the reader would find it profitable to make strong use of inflectional cues. In English such cues are not terribly useful.

Semantic aspects of the reading process cannot vary to any extent from one language to another since the key question is how much background the reader brings to the specific reading.

To sum up it would seem that the reading process will be much the same for all languages with minor variations to accommodate the specific characteristics of the orthography used and the grammatical structure of the language.

LEARNING TO READ ONE'S NATIVE LANGUAGE

In the personal history of each individual in a literate society he learns first to control the spoken language and several years later to control the written language. He masters speech with no organized instruction. Normally he learns to read and write in school. It is puzzling that far less success is achieved in learning to read than in learning to speak.

Obviously there is not time to explore this vexing problem. But several key points need to be made:

1 Children who learn oral language should be able to learn to read.
2 Children who know oral language should be able to use this knowledge in learning to comprehend written language.
3 Reading instruction should center on comprehension strategies.
4 The reading process cannot be fractionated into sub-skills to be taught or subdivided into code-breaking and comprehension without qualitatively changing it.
5 Reading instruction should use natural meaningful language within the conceptual grasp of the learners. (This implies of course that the content should always be relevant as well.)
6 Where it is at all feasible the child should achieve initial literacy within his own language (in fact within his own home dialect!).

READING A SECOND LANGUAGE

Here are some implications I see from my study of the reading process for learning to read a second language:

(a) Learning to read a second language should be easier for someone already literate in another language, regardless of how similar or dissimilar it is.
(b) Reading will be difficult as long as the student does not have some degree of control over the grammatical system.
(c) Strong semantic input will help the acquisition of the reading competence where syntactic control is weak. This suggests that the subject of reading materials should be of high interest and relate to the background of the learners.
(d) Reading materials in early language instruction should probably avoid special language uses such as literature and focus on mundane, situationally related language such as signs, directions, descriptions, transcribed conversations, etc. This would depend of course on the background of the learner. Scientists should do very well with materials dealing with their own interests.
(e) It will always be easier for a student to learn to read a language he already speaks. For young learners this clearly

suggests a sequence of early focus on oral language and later introduction of reading, even in situations where the second language will be the medium of later education. But the motivation and needs of older highly literate students may suggest that oral and written language receive equal attention even at early stages.

(f) As in learning to read a first language reading instruction should always involve natural, meaningful language and instruction should avoid the trivial and keep the focus on comprehension strategies.

The following article, prepared for a Japanese audience, extends Goodman's view on the universality of the reading process across languages and across orthographies.

'I ask this question:' ... says Goodman, 'if alphabetic writing made learning to read much easier, wouldn't Japan have shifted totally to an alphabetic system, instead of the mixed system which prevails and seems to serve well, judging by the extent of literacy in Japan?'

7 WHAT IS UNIVERSAL ABOUT THE READING PROCESS

All human societies are linguistic. They have one or more languages that they use to communicate needs, wishes, concepts, emotions, experiences to each other. Humans use language, not only to communicate, but as a medium of thought and learning.

When human societies reach a point in their culture where communication is necessary over time and over space, then written language develops. Oral language is used in immediate face-to-face communication, but to preserve ideas for future generations, or to communicate over a wide distance, written language is needed.

Just as listening is a receptive oral language process, so reading is a receptive written language process. In productive language, speaking and writing, the language user begins with meaning and encodes it in language. In receptive language, the user starts with language and constructs meaning from it. The principal difference is that oral language use usually involves a speaker and listener interacting within each other's hearing while in written language interaction, writer and reader may not even know each other. The writer may be far away, or even dead.

Reading is then the process of getting meaning from print.

MISCUE RESEARCH

In my research, I've sought to use the scientific insights of linguistics and psycholinguistics to understand how the readers are able to process print, language in written form, to obtain meaning.

The basic research procedure has been to have a subject read aloud a complete story or other text he or she has not seen before. A text is chosen that will be somewhat difficult for the reader. The reader is informed that no help will be given during the reading and that he or she will be asked to retell what has been read upon completion.

The analysis focusses on the miscues of the reader. A miscue is an oral response to the text that does not match the expected response. All readers produce these unexpected responses, though some readers produce many more than others do.

In miscue analysis, miscues are examined by comparing the expected responses and the observed responses. I have been concerned with the similarities and differences in appearance, sound, grammar, and meaning, as well as with changes that result from miscues on the acceptability of the meaning and grammar of the resulting text. I have looked at spontaneous self-corrections of miscues by readers. I am particularly concerned with which miscues lead to self-correction.

In the analysis, I have assumed that nothing is accidental, that miscues represent the same process as expected responses except that the cues have somehow been used in an unexpected manner.

I have used the concepts of linguistics to describe the miscues and have also drawn on psycholinguistics, the study of the relationships between thought and language.

Let's suppose that a reader reads the following sentence:

> large It
> Japan is a country with a small land area, which has
> a large population.

A possible miscue could be the insertion of the word 'large' before country. Insertions are often words that make sense and that appear elsewhere in the printed text. Another possible miscue is ending the sentence after 'area' and at the same time substituting 'it' for 'which.' The result of the miscue is a transformed text that has acceptable syntax and meaning.

In the following example, the reader finds the miscue disrupts meaning and makes a self-correction, regressing to the point where meaning has been lost:

> C was
> Japan is a country with a small land area, which has
> a large population.

In this case, the reader substitutes 'was' for 'has.' Both are verb forms of similar appearance. 'Was' is very common, so it is something the reader might be expecting. When the reader realizes that meaning is lost, he knows something is wrong and self-corrects.

Miscues like these are like windows on the reading process since we can infer what the reader is thinking as the miscues occur.

My research has convinced me that there is only one reading process for English, and that reading is very much a matter of using language to create meaning.

The differences that are found between proficient and poor readers is their relative ability to integrate efficiently the cycles and strategies so that they are able to effectively get meaning. Poor readers seem to get lost in the detail, they are less able to keep their focus throughout reading on meaning.

It has been traditional in teaching children to read English to build from part to whole, from letter-sound relationships to words, to meaningful wholes. I think this is quite wrong, that it violates both the evidence for how language is most naturally learned and that it turns written language from a meaningful whole to a set of abstract bits and pieces, which are hard for young children to learn and which lose their relationship to meaning.

If the language children are using to learn to read is natural, meaningful and relevant to them, then they will be strongly motivated to learn. They will be able to use their knowledge of oral language, and they will be able to judge their own success by asking themselves whether what they have read makes sense to them.

READING OTHER LANGUAGES

So far I have been discussing reading and learning to read English. There is evidence from studies of children reading Spanish, Polish, German, and Yiddish that the same process is at work in these languages.

Lopez has found that children reading Spanish can read many words in a story that they were unable to recognize in a list. That result matches the result of my own research in English. Barrera found children reading in Spanish producing miscues which preserved meaningful syntactically acceptable language. She found that readers would sometimes change verb, noun, and adjective endings, so that they would be consistent, acceptable and meaningful.

The reader is dealing appropriately with the Spanish syntax and thus producing miscues which the same bilingual readers would not produce reading English, yet in both cases there is clear evidence of the reader predicting syntactic structures to get to meaning.

Romatowski found pupils bilingual in Polish and English, also effectively dealing with the difference in syntax, adapting the reading process to the linguistic and orthographic differences, but doing much the same things to get to meaning.

Hodes studied pupils bilingual in Yiddish and English. They were able to adapt to two different orthographies. Yiddish uses the Hebrew alphabet and is written from right to left, but the essential process of reading proved to be the same for both languages.

Hofer reports similar results in studying monolingual German children learning to read their native language.

I am unaware of any studies of children's miscues in reading non-alphabetic writing systems to date.[1] I would predict, however, that the basic process of reading would be the same as it is in alphabetic systems with necessary modifications for the differences in the writing systems. In alphabetic writing, there is a direct relationship of written and oral language. But they also are related through the meaning and syntax common to both. In non-alphabetic writing there is no direct relationship between print and speech, but both still are related through the meaning they represent and the syntax they use.

I would expect to find readers sampling from the graphic display, predicting syntactic structures and meaning, producing miscues, and correcting miscues when they produce unacceptable syntax and meaning.

In learning to read, I would expect pupils to be able to use syntactic and semantic context to assign meaning to new graphic symbols, so that there would not be any strong need for symbols to be formally taught as a prerequisite to successful reading. There seems to be no reason why any writing system should be learned any differently than any other for the purpose of reading with comprehension.

It is the search for meaning that motivates and unifies the reading process. Learning to read any system will be most successful when it is kept within the context of this search for meaning.

I believe the movement in reading through optical, perceptual, syntactic, and semantic cycles is universal in reading all languages regardless of the orthographies they employ. The use of sampling, predicting, confirming and correction strategies is also universal in all forms of reading.

Once learned, it is very unlikely that it is harder to read any language or any writing system than any other. Whether it is harder to learn to read any language or any writing system, alphabetic or non-alphabetic, is a harder question to answer. On the basis of the view of the reading process I have evolved, I believe that there are probably no important differences in the difficulty for people learning to read as long as the focus is kept on the relationships of written language to meaning during instruction. Learning to write in different orthographies is probably a different matter. The number and complexity of symbols and their forms in the writing systems may make it harder to write legibly and efficiently in some systems than in others. The invention and use of alphabetic writing systems with limited numbers of characters may be more useful to writers than readers. In fact, it may be that minimizing complexity may be a greater benefit to writers than the relationships between the symbols of speech and print alphabets establish. I ask this question in this regard: if alphabetic writing made learning to read much easier, wouldn't Japan have shifted totally to an alphabetic system, instead of the mixed system which prevails and seems to serve well, judging by the extent of literacy in Japan?

NEEDED RESEARCH

Clearly when I have gone beyond the discussion of how reading English works, I have argued on the basis of theory and implications of research and I have cited little direct research. The aspects, I believe to be universals of reading across languages and orthographies, must be verified, modified or rejected by direct research.

I believe that the methodology of miscue analysis is appropriate for research in reading any language. I think that analysis of the miscues of readers at varying levels of proficiency, reading, in each language, can help to explore the validity of my model of the reading process or any model for that language.

Such research can also illuminate how this process is varied or adapted by the readers to the particular characteristics of the language or writing system it uses. Research is also needed on the relative ease of reading the same language written in different orthographies; again miscue analysis is a useful tool for such research.

The research I am suggesting is not simply for the sake of knowledge. Too many decisions about reading, writing and literacy are being made in the world today, without sufficient exploration of the realities of written language. Good research should provide the sound basis for more effective literacy instruction in the world's schools.

NOTE

1 Since this was written, Tien, Su-O L., at Michigan State University, has produced an unpublished study analyzing miscues of Taiwanese pupils reading Chinese. The miscue patterns were consistent with the Goodman model.

> There is no justifiable gap between theory and practice in reading. Sound practice can only be built on sound theory. Theory which is impractical is bad theory, and much of current practice is bad because it is not based on an examined, coherent, defensible theory of reading.

This chapter, originally published in a depth presentation of the findings of miscue research, argues the need for a comprehensive theory of reading to underlie not only practice, the teaching of reading, but research as well. Without such a theory, we are like the proverbial blind men of Hindustan who sought to know about elephants. 'Too much has been done in reading by blind men who have quickly decided that the elephant is a tree trunk and run home to create a method and materials for training elephants.'

As a theoretically based approach to research, miscue analysis is contrasted with other research views. Of particular importance, the concept of 'comprehending' is developed in this chapter. 'Comprehending' is the degree of concern for meaning the reader's miscue patterns display.

8 WHAT WE KNOW ABOUT READING

The parable of the blind men and the elephants offers an apt analogy to the ways in which reading has been viewed in the past. Just as each blind man limited his definition of an elephant to his own superficial experience with its overt characteristics, so reading has been defined by narrow, superficial, observable aspects. The blind man who approached the leg called it a tree; the one who touched its side called it a wall; the one who grasped its tail thought it a rope. In reading, some look and see only words, hence for them reading is a matter of attacking words; some see letters and the sounds they represent, so reading is phonics; some see patterns of letters, so reading is spelling. Some stand at the end of reading and proclaim that reading is thinking. Even had the blind men combined their impressions into an eclectic view of the elephant it would remain superficial. An elephant is certainly not two walls supported by four tree trunks with a hose at one end and a rope at the other.

One must develop a theory of the elephant which makes it possible to interpret superficial observations and get at its essential nature, its elephantness. It's not that the blind men are wrong in their observations; it's their unwillingness to infer from their data the essential unity which underlies it that is the problem. Our research has above all else had as its goal to seek out the unity in reading, to infer from observation of reading behavior the process that underlies the behavior.

From every vantage point we could find, we have looked at the miscues readers produce. We have created a taxonomy to clarify the interrelationships between the parallel observations. We have constructed a model and theory of the reading process to predict and explain what we have observed, and then we remodeled the theory and reconstructed the model on the basis of further observations. Though we can not see into the heads of readers and observe their minds at work, we are not blind.

Certain basic premises provide a foundation for the understanding of reading which we've built. One of these is that *reading is language*. It's one of two receptive language processes. Speaking and writing are the generative, productive language processes. The other receptive language process is listening. Reading and listening, at least for the literate, are parallel processes.

Readers are users of language: that's another key premise.

They use language to obtain meaning. Through seeking to comprehend the writer's meaning, they in fact construct the meaning, through a process which is strongly dependent on their own experience and conceptual development. In reading, meaning is thus both input and output, and the persistent search for and preoccupation with meaning is more important than the particular meaning the reader arrives at. *What* message the reader gets is less important than the fact that the reader is trying to get a message. What message the reader produces is partly dependent on what the writer intended, but also very much dependent on what the reader brings to the particular text.

It's a constructive process, this search for meaning. As users of language, children learning to read their native language are already possessed of a language competence and an ability to learn language which are powerful resources, provided that literacy is treated by schools as an extension of their natural language learning.

Simply speaking, reading researchers in the past have treated reading as if it were something new and foreign, and in the process they have lost the opportunity to capitalize on the immense language competence that children have before we ever see them in school.

Here's another premise: *language is the means by which communication among people is brought about*. It's always, therefore, in close relationship to meaning. When it's divorced from meaning it is no longer language. It becomes then an intriguing, manipulable, abstract system. You can play games with language apart from meaning, but it is no longer language. If that intriguing system is fragmented into sounds or letters or patterned pieces, it quickly loses its power even to intrigue and becomes a collection of abstractions.

The significance of regarding language as the means and meaning as the end in language use is that it explains why language is learned easily, why young children are able to treat language as if it were part of the concrete world, why meaningful language is easier to learn, to remember, to manipulate. It also explains why instructional reading programs that begin with bits and pieces abstracted from language, like words or letters, on the theory that they're making learning simpler in fact make learning to read much harder. The very sequencing that we thought we were doing to make the learning simpler turns language into something that isn't language anymore. The kids treat it, then, not as concrete learning, but as abstraction.

I'm digressing from my central concern for the reading process to point this out because I want to emphasize my conviction that there is no justifiable gap between theory and practice in reading. Sound practice can only be built on sound theory. Theory which is impractical is bad theory, and much of current practice is bad because it is not based on an examined, coherent, defensible theory of reading. Too much has been done in reading by blind men who have quickly decided that the elephant is a tree trunk and run home to create a method and materials for training elephants.

We've learned that certain atheoretical commonsense notions are totally inappropriate to understanding the reading process. One such commonsense notion is that accuracy in and of itself is important in reading. That seems so logical. A second related to the first is that being careful to perceive, recognize, and process each letter or each word is necessary to successful reading. I don't know how many times I've had teachers say to me: 'After all, how can you read a sentence if you don't know all the words in it?' Those are commonsense views and like most commonsense views they come from superficial observation of reality, not totally invented, of course, but the kind of superficial observation that the blind men were engaging in.

Our theory tells us that these commonsense notions are wrong, and our research confirms our theory. Effective and efficient readers are those who get to meaning by using the least amount of perceptual input necessary. Readers' language competence enables them to create a grammatical and semantic prediction in which they need only sample from the print to reach meaning. They already have the language competence to do that. Psycholinguists helped us to understand this by demonstrating that readers can not possibly be reading language a letter or a word at a time, since the time it takes to do that far exceeds the time the reader actually devotes to the given sequence. Through their miscues children helped us to understand this by demonstrating their driving concern for structure and meaning, even in the first grade, even from the very beginning, as soon as they catch on to the fact that reading is language and that it is supposed to yield meaning.

Some kids get distracted from this understanding; some kids have a little trouble finding their way back to it; but we keep noticing it even in the least proficient readers: this compulsion to try and find some meaning somewhere. They can leap to meaning while only touching base in print.

In reading, as in listening, the language user must continuously predict underlying grammatical patterns because it is from these that meaning may be decoded. Essentially meaning relates to grammar through clauses and their interrelationship.

> It must have been around midnight when I drove home, and as I approached the gates of the bungalow I switched off the headlamps of the car so the beam wouldn't swing in through the window of the side bedroom and wake Harry Pope.

The paragraph above is the beginning of a story that we have used extensively with tenth graders in our reading research; it's from a short story, 'Poison,' by Roald Dahl. This first paragraph is composed of a single sentence in which the author has done a very interesting job of creating a setting for his story. There's a lot of information here that isn't of vital importance and yet it creates a background against which things are going to happen. How did he get all this into a single sentence? The first sequence, 'It must have been around midnight,' is a clause. Now we come to another clause, 'when I drove home.' Two basic statements are combined in such a way that we get the idea of time and we get the idea of what's taking place at the time because he uses 'when' to join them.

But now the author is going to join the main clause, which is 'It must have been around midnight' with another main clause. How does he do that? That's what the 'and' is there for. However, before he gets to the next main clause we have another dependent clause introduced by 'as.' So we have a main clause, a dependent clause, a conjunction, then another dependent clause and than another main clause: 'It must have been around midnight/when I drove home/and/as I approached the gates of the bungalow/ [and here comes the next main clause] I switched off the headlamps of the car.' If one omits the 'and' there, as some of our readers have done, there isn't any particular problem, in fact 'and' is a kind of optional element. One might ask, since it isn't necessary, why the author chooses to put it there in the first place. Had he written this in a high school English class or a freshman composition class his teacher probably would have written 'run-on sentence' and crossed out 'and.' Somehow the author feels the necessity to keep you propelled forward, to give you the feeling that this is all a kind of unity.

But now read the same sentence keeping the 'and' but leaving the 'as' out. What happens now? 'It must have been around midnight when I drove home and I approached the gates of the bungalow.' One can either put an 'and' in, [we've had kids who've done that] or one can go back and figure out what went wrong. The point is that in order to get meaning from this sentence one must work through the grammatical structure and one must somehow get at the clauses and their interrelationship. That's really what's significant about the concept that readers have to get to deep structure here; they have to go beyond the surface; they have to see those underlying relationships that are not even sentence relationships.

It is our conclusion that the sentence isn't nearly as important a unit in language as linguists have been saying. The trouble is that instead of looking at language, they've been looking at sets of sentences that they made up. In the task of looking at kids reading real stories, we've had to deal with paragraphs like this and we've become aware that what really is important is the clauses and their relationships, whether within or across sentences. Every teacher is familiar with the kid who shifts clauses when reading a sentence that starts with a left-branching clause. For instance, suppose that a sentence started: 'As I approached the gates of the bungalow I switched off the headlamps of the car so the beam wouldn't...'

Now if the subject reads: 'It must have been around midnight when I drove home as I approached the gates of the bungalow ...,' he is treating the 'as' not as dependent on the clause that follows it but on the clause that precedes it, which means a subtle kind of change.

Teachers have tended superficially to think that these shifts occur because the kids don't see the punctuation. But the problem in reading is that the punctuation comes at the end and one already must have made a prediction about what is being dealt with before one gets to the punctuation. Instead of indicating when to end the sentence, the punctuation, at best, simply confirms whether the reader was right or wrong in the initial decision of what kind of structure is being dealt with. The sentence above is a complex sentence from a short story that wasn't written for reading instruction. We found it in a twelfth-grade literature anthology but it wasn't written for twelfth-grade literature anthologies either.

Here's a sentence that was written for reading instruction: 'See Spot run.' It could come from any of a number of basal readers. It illustrates how the same process is operating with this short sentence.

How does a child get to the meaning of this sentence? People who developed reading programs and who were obviously trying to get the best knowledge they could into their programs thought that the psychologist had given them proper advice when he said the main problem is exposure to words, that you control the number of words you introduce, and once you introduce a word you use it as often as you can. The problem is that psychological theory treats language as a bag of words. The notion was that once a word is introduced it is learned through repetition. Basal readers avoided inflected forms in primers because they're new words (so they didn't use 'sees,' they used 'see').

But since this type of sentence first appeared first-grade teachers have been aware of an interesting phenomenon. A kid could read these words from flash cards and have difficulty reading the three-word sentence. Let's analyze that as we did the more complicated structure. What's the subject of this three-word sentence: 'See Spot run'? My second-grade teacher said it was 'you understood.' I don't know if she understood what that meant. A transformational grammarian now has translated that. What he would say is that there is, in the deep structure, a subject, and the subject is 'you.' Well, not really, because 'you,' after all, is a pronoun that represents some noun which has already been identified. When do you use 'you'? When one person is addressing another and the subject is identified because of the situation of the discourse. In the book, however, there might be a preceding word like 'father.' 'Father! See Spot run.' What does 'you' represent then here? Father. Which just happens to be the word which precedes 'see.'

The child must dredge up from the deep structure the missing subject. How does he know he's supposed to do that? He will know if he recognizes this as a grammatical pattern in which the subject 'you' is deletable. How does he recognize that? Sentences that start with verbs are often imperative. He has the language competence to know that. If his mother says, 'Take out the garbage,' he understands because he recognizes that command form, and he knows that the deleted subject is 'you' and that in this case 'you' is himself. But notice that what we're saying is that in order to get the subject of the sentence, he must recognize this as an imperative grammatical pattern. He must predict the pattern from the start.

Now that we know the subject is 'you,' what verb goes with that subject? This is a rather odd sentence: verb-noun-verb. So the reader has to do what we were doing up above in that longer sequence; he has to identify what amounts to two clauses and their interrelationship. The first clause is (you) see (something). The whole second clause, not just 'Spot,' is the object of that verb 'see.' You see (something), and the something is: 'Spot run.'

We've got another problem. Why do we have a verb that doesn't have an 's' on it following a noun that's third person singular and which is clearly the subject of the verb in that clause? Again the reader must go to deep structure and say that the underlying clause is really 'Spot runs.' How do we get from 'Spot runs' to 'Spot run'? We do it by two transformations; first we make an infinitive out of the verb, and instead of 'Spot runs' it's 'Spot to run;' and then we apply another deletion as we did with the 'you,' and we get from 'see' (Spot runs) to 'See Spot to run' and then 'See Spot run.' 'Run' is really an infinitive with the 'to' deleted. The funny thing about this is not how complicated it is, but how many kids don't have trouble reading it, even though this is a complex pattern with very little meat on the bones. In contrast to the earlier sentence, if you miss anything here you're really out of luck. But, still, many kids learned to grasp this pattern in listening. If a kid can understand his mother when she says, 'Take out the garbage,' he can understand 'See Spot run.'

The problem with that three-word sentence, then, is not so much that kids can not understand it but that it throws a number of complicated curves at them, one being the invisible subject. It is just at this early point that textbooks should be, instead, maximizing children's ability to predict by presenting more common and more natural sentence patterns. As a matter of fact, the text probably should not have used 'see' (which was chosen here because it had already been introduced as a word). It should have said something like 'watch' or 'look at,' which would then have sounded more natural and been more predictable.

What do kids do with that sentence when they have to read it? One possibility is to read it as a series of three words.

Teachers may teach kids to do so by emphasizing accuracy. When the kid says 'See' and then there is a long pause, the teacher may say 'Spot.' The kid may not have been wondering what the word was, he may have been trying to figure out what it was doing there. Inadvertently what the teacher teaches him is to say the word even if it doesn't make sense to him.

If the focus were on meaning rather than identification of words, there wouldn't be as many reading problems. There's no way to get to the meaning except through the clause relationship. But don't misunderstand the significance of this. What we have to understand is that the search for meaning is itself what makes it possible for the reader to predict the grammatical structures. None of us, even at our current stage of education and linguistic sophistication, can go very far getting into these complicated descriptions while we're trying to understand what somebody's saying; in fact, it works the other way around.

A little girl who was learning to read said it well. She read something that her mother didn't believe she could read and her mother asked, 'How did you know that?' The little girl said, 'It just popped into my mouth.' That's what happens with language. With the focus on meaning, the control over the grammatical system is so well developed that the meaning actually pops into one's mind, and the words, then, into one's mouth. The reader doesn't need to say, 'Oh, I see. That is a clause embedded into another clause which is functioning as the object of the verb "see" with the deleted subject "you".' She doesn't have to consciously say that and yet she's automatically processing that information. She thinks she's attending only to the meaning and yet obviously she can't get to the meaning without processing the language.

The meaning makes possible the prediction of the structure *if* the reader is concerned for meaning. One can then try on grammatical structures for fit, that is to see if they do in fact yield something that makes sense, and then accept and decode them or reject and correct them to an alternate pattern. Decode here means get to meaning.

Somehow the idea became current in reading circles that written language was a code but oral language wasn't. Somehow oral language by virtue of its primacy was something other than code. If you didn't speak English, would you get any meaning from what is issuing from a speaker's mouth? There's no meaning being exchanged in speech. The speaker is simply producing sound and the listener is processing that sound and creating for himself a meaning; but what exchanges between them is a code. No intrinsic meaning is in any of the noises the speaker makes, any more than in the scratches or print on this page. Code to code is recoding; in order to go from code to something else you have to be going to meaning.

We're going to need to understand that concept if we're going to get away once and for all from the misconception that somehow one can divide reading into a physical, mechanical act of translating print to speech and a cognitive act of going to meaning.

Research has demonstrated that readers, proficient or otherwise, can not really be going from print to oral language and then to meaning. Very early readers learn to do in parallel fashion with reading what they have learned to do with listening; to go from code, this time in a graphic form, to meaning. Most literate adults can do that much faster than they can produce speech.

In our research we're trying to get beyond reading performance to a competence which can not be directly observed. We can't see the reading process happening; we can not tune in on it directly; we must infer it from some kind of external behavior.

But how can comprehension, which is the end product, be inferred? All along I've been emphasizing meaning as input, meaning as output, and meaning as what makes the whole thing go. When we try to find out, after the person has read, what he understood, we're dealing with one or another kind of measure of his performance. It is a great mistake to equate that performance with the competence itself.

That's what is so objectionable about the current interest in reading tests that's been brought about by accountability programs and by behavioral objectives programs. Such programs assume that getting a kid to perform in certain ways in fact makes that child a reader. If teachers were asked, they would make clear that kids perform without competence and have competence without performance. For example, someone says to you, 'The marlup was poving his kump,' and asks you comprehension questions such as: 'What was the marlup poving?' 'What was the marlup doing to his kump?' Has your comprehension been measured because you answered the two questions correctly? Did you understand that nonsense sentence? What happens to kump when it gets poved, particularly by a marlup? The point of course is that that's precisely what a lot of comprehension questions are like. What we're getting is the child's underlying linguistic competence. She can manipulate grammatical structures. But we aren't in fact getting any insight into what she learned as a result of her reading, which is what we think we're getting at.

This problem is not one our group feels we've solved, but we think we have a grasp of it which we want to share with you. This represents research recently completed.

Figure 8.1 shows five groups of readers in eighth and tenth grades. All of them read Story 61. Four of the same groups read a second story, Story 60. The figure indicates the percentage of the miscues those readers made which we were able to code as syntactically and semantically acceptable or syntactically acceptable but not semantically acceptable. Story 61 is one that even our high group found somewhat difficult.

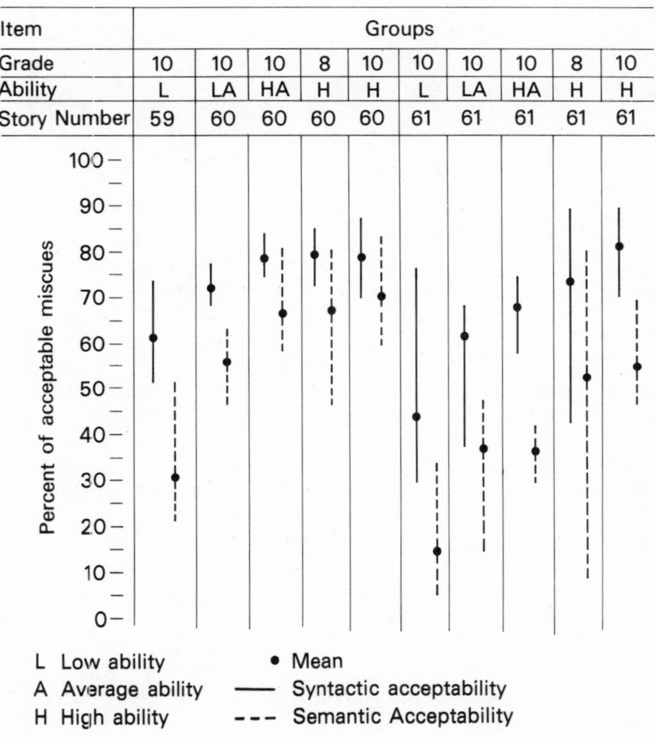

Figure 8.1 Percent of syntactic and semantic acceptability of miscues by student readers (range and mean by groups)

The left column in each pair represents the syntactic acceptability of their miscues. The right column represents the semantic acceptability. Things can be syntactically acceptable and not make sense, but they can't be semantically acceptable unless they're syntactically acceptable. So it's not a surprise that the former is lower than the latter.

Notice the stepladder effect (on Story 61) when you look at our high tenth-grade group, our high average tenth-grade group, our low average tenth-grade group, our low tenth-grade group, and our high eighth-grade group. The high eighth graders look quite a bit like the high average tenth graders; in fact, they come up a little higher in the syntactic acceptability. But each tenth-grade group is successively lower.

Story 60 is the Roald Dahl story referred to earlier. Notice how much more similar the groups are. In this story where the conceptual load isn't as great, where there isn't as much to keep track of as in the harder story, semantic acceptability and syntactic acceptability are much more similar and the high eighth-grade group comes up to just about where the high tenth-grade group is. This figure does not show a measure of performance 'after' reading, it shows reading as it takes place. It's still performance, but we're asking ourselves: 'When the kid produced the miscue, did it make sense?' That gives us an indication then of how much attention to and concern for meaning each reader is showing and how successfully that reader is able to stay with meaning.

In the less complex story, the groups are more alike, but the harder material with heavier conceptual load takes its toll. You also notice that, though there is more gradation between the lowest and the highest group in the semantic acceptability on Story 61, there still are some pretty difficult sentence structures in the complex story and without the ability to handle meaning that syntax gets too hard to manage.

When we put two things together we come up with something that we've labeled 'comprehending;' not comprehension but comprehending. It looks as if comprehending, the concern for meaning while reading, can be measured by taking the percentage of miscues that are originally acceptable semantically and adding to that the percentage that aren't semantically acceptable but which are corrected. Those that are fully semantically acceptable plus those that are corrected to make them acceptable give us a percentage of miscues which we call the comprehending percentage.

Figure 8.2 shows the range for five groups; the 10L group read only Story 61, the harder story. They didn't read Story 60. Instead they read another story which is from an eighth-grade book. The range on Story 60 ('Poison') for our 10H group in comprehending is from about 67 percent up to about 94 percent with a mean of 77 percent. All the students in the group were doing a lot of comprehending, either because the text makes sense with their miscues or they corrected. Percentage of correction doesn't necessarily have to be high to achieve that, if in fact their miscues are successful in the first place in retaining meaning. The 10H group with the more difficult story still has some pretty high comprehending activity going on, but the range has slipped to 55-95 percent with a mean of 70 percent. The group has a much greater spread than on the other task.

The 10HA group has a high range and mean for Story 60 (74-92 percent, M = 81 percent), but on Story 61 the whole range falls to 42-55 percent, with a mean of 51 percent. The 10HA group is not comprehending as well; they're not as able to get to the meaning or to do something about it when they lose the meaning.

The range for the low average group overlaps the higher tenth grade in comprehending: For Story 60, it is 63-88 percent with a mean of 75 percent, but on Story 61 comprehending range drops to 21-64 percent, with a mean of 43 percent. The difference in reading competence shows on the harder story.

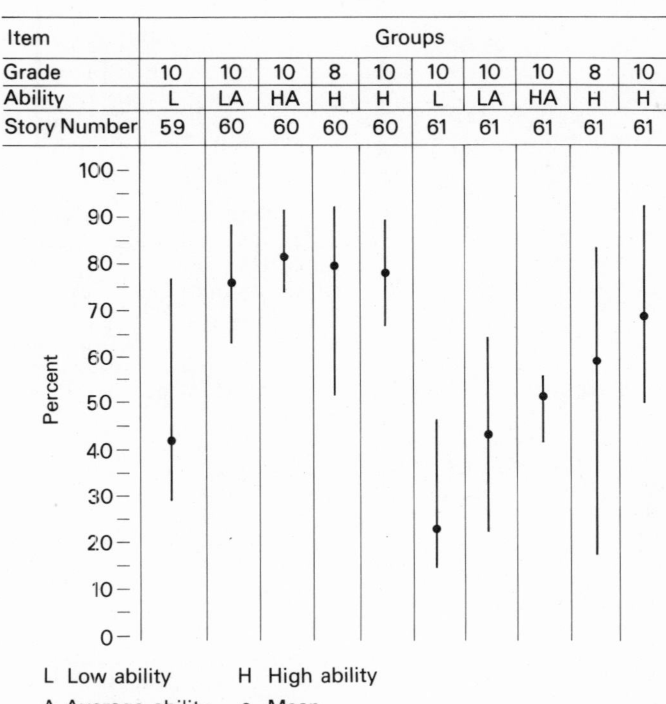

Figure 8.2 Comprehending scores of eighth and tenth graders (range and mean by groups). Comprehending score = percent of semantically acceptable miscues added to percent of semantically unacceptable miscues that are successfully corrected.

There were kids in the low average group who did better in comprehending than kids in the high average group, or in the high group. This finding has considerable significance, because what we used for grouping these kids originally was their percentile ranking on a standardized reading test. What you see is that some kids who are not particularly high achievers on standardized reading tests do as well in this measure of retaining meaning or correcting to get meaning as the high achievers. Even the low group with the difficult story still overlaps the low average group.

The 8H group comes up as high as the 10H group but has a wider range on Story 60. Their mean, 78 percent, is almost the same. On the harder story the range of the 8H group becomes very wide, 18-82 percent, and mean drops to 57 percent.

The point this data emphasizes is that we can, by looking at reading in process, by judging the miscues that kids produce in terms of their effect, get some powerful insights into how each reader is operating: we can get at his or her basic competence.

To summarize, what we know of how readers operate is something like this: First of all, more proficient readers make better miscues; they're better miscues not in the sense that we like them but in terms of their effect. They're less likely to produce unacceptable grammar. Furthermore, more proficient readers have an ability to recognize when their miscues need correction. When a reader is correcting a lot of miscues that don't change the meaning and *not* correcting a lot that *do* change the meaning, there is a pretty powerful insight that he's operating on a wrong model, that in effect he's not very efficient because he's wasting a lot of time trying to achieve accuracy that's unnecessary, while not being able to handle the situation where he loses the meaning.

The difference between more and less proficient readers is not a difference in the reading process but in how well they are able to use it. Our research has made it possible to infer from their miscues the control that readers are exercising over the reading process. It should also provide a basis for instructional procedures designed to improve that control.

Part Two
MISCUE ANALYSIS

The organization of Part Two of this volume follows the general pattern of the first part. It begins with a pair of complementary articles (Chapters 9 and 10) that present a comprehensive coverage of miscues and miscue analysis. Chapter 11 presents the very beginnings of miscue analysis research and this historical perspective is continued in Chapter 12. The following article (Chapter 13) is a technical report on the influences of the peripheral field when reading, and Part Two is suitably concluded by Chapter 14, a recent attempt to show the importance and relevance of miscue studies as a means of studying language and thought in process.

> Because we worked with real kids reading real books in real schools, the practical applications of the lessons we have learned and even the research procedures we used are more evident.

This chapter, a general introduction to miscue analysis, demonstrates the value of studying reading, both for researchers and teachers, in the context of reality. That makes it possible to adapt miscue analysis, originally developed as a research device for the diagnostic needs of teachers and clinicians.

9 MISCUES: Windows on the Reading Process

Reading miscue research was undertaken for the express purpose of providing knowledge of the reading process and how it is used and acquired. In turn, this knowledge can form the basis for more effective reading instruction toward the achievement of the goal of universal literacy.

Some scholars see research as a quest for knowledge for the sake of knowledge. They see a sharp separation between research and the application of knowledge to the solution of real problems. This is a point of view which the authors of this work do not share.

We do not grudge the pure researcher his disinterest in the practical. In the course of our research we have frequently found uses for concepts that such pure research has produced. In interactions with linguists, psychologists, psycholinguists, and other academicians we have found it possible to raise issues and ask questions which stimulated them to conduct research and thereby provide further useful knowledge.

Now we are at a point in our research where we feel we know enough about how reading works that we can share with teachers and other practitioners some of our insights and their implications for reading instruction. Had our research not been reality oriented and rooted in our concern for the practical, this task of translating research into application might have been more difficult. Because we worked with real kids reading real books in real schools, the practical applications of the lessons we have learned and even the research procedures we used are more evident. Everything we know we have learned from kids. Our purpose here is to show our fellow teachers how they also may learn from kids.

Miscue analysis, which will be explained below in some detail, must be viewed as part of a pervasive re-ordering and restructuring of our understanding of reading. It is a tool which in research has contributed to development of a comprehensive theory and model of reading; in the classroom or clinic it can be used to reveal the strengths and weaknesses of pupils and the extent to which they are efficient and effective readers. But it is only useful to the extent that the user comes to view reading as the psycholinguistic process it is. Miscue analysis involves its user in examining the observed behavior of oral readers as an interaction between language and thought, as a process of constructing meaning from a graphic display. The reader's use of graphic, phonological, syntactic, and semantic information is considered.

Fortunately, one of the most powerful uses of miscue analysis is in teacher education. In the process of analyzing the miscues of a reader, the teacher or potential teacher must ask questions and consider issues he may never have thought about. Was the meaning acceptable after the miscue? Did the reader correct the miscue if it was not? If a word was substituted for another word, was it the same part of speech? How close was it to the sound and shape of the text word? Was the reader's dialect involved? Through these questions, instead of the teacher's counting errors, the quality of the miscues and their effect on meaning are the central concerns. Miscue analysis then is rooted in a psycholinguistic view of reading (one that sees thought and language interacting), but it is also a way of redirecting the focus of teachers so that they may see reading in this new perspective.

When we try to understand how reading works, we must look beyond the superficial behavior of readers. We must try to see what is happening that is causing that behavior. When we teach reading we are trying to build the competence which underlies the superficial behavior, we are not trying simply to change the behavior.

A miscue, which we define as an actual observed response in oral reading which does not match the expected response, is like a window on the reading process. Nothing the reader does in reading is accidental. Both his expected responses and his miscues are produced as he attempts to process the print and get to meaning. If we can understand how his miscues relate to the expected responses we can also begin to understand how he is using the reading process.

Here is a sentence from one story used in our research, and the miscues one pupil produced in reading it:

> But I remember the cameras moving close to the crib and Mr Barnaby bending over and saying soothing things to Andrew — but not too loudly.
>
> (Handwritten miscue markings: Ⓒ; "that" inserted after "remember"; "s" of "cameras" circled; "Barny" over "Barnaby"; "and" circled; "some" over "soothing"; Ⓒ "words" over "things"; "ly" of "loudly" circled.)

The reader omits a word and some word parts, inserts a word, substitutes other words, goes back at times to correct himself, and comes out with a meaningful sentence. We must be concerned with more than his superficial behavior. We must infer from it the process he has used and his competence with that process. He inserted 'that' but corrected when he realized the pattern he had created was not acceptable syntax. He omitted 'and' but did not correct because it was not a necessary element.

We start in miscue analysis with observed behavior, but we do not stop there. We are able, through analysis of the miscues, to see the process at work.

MISCUE ANALYSIS

Miscue analysis as a research tool began in 1963. I started with the goal of describing the reading process. The most basic task in doing this seemed to be to have subjects read, orally, a story they had never seen before, one which was somewhat difficult for them.

Even in the very earliest research attempts two things became clear. First, it was obvious that oral reading is not the accurate rendition of the text that it has been assumed to be. Readers, even good ones, make errors. Second, it was clear that linguistic insights, scientific views of language, were very much appropriate to describing reading behavior. The things the readers did were linguistic things - they were not random.

When a beginning reader substitutes 'a' for 'the' in a sentence like:

A
The little monkey had it.

the reader is substituting one noun marker for another. When a more advanced reader sees:

There were glaring spotlights.

and says:

There was a glaring spotlight.

that reader is processing language, he is not just saying the names of words.

In these early studies I naively looked for easily identified cause-effect relationships. For each miscue I looked for some 'one' cue. In this I was operating as others had done in research on error analysis. The difference was that I was using scientific linguistics to categorize the phenomena. So when I found myself saying a miscue had a graphic cause, I found myself aware that there also were grammatical relationships involved; 'lad' and 'lady' look quite a bit alike but they are also both nouns and they have related meanings. Both are kinds of people. So if a reader substitutes 'lady' for 'lad' which of these factors is the cause?

I was led then to development of an analytic taxonomy which considers the relationships between the expected response (ER) and the observed response (OR) from all possible angles. Each miscue is considered on all variables that are pertinent, and no attempt is made to establish a single cause-effect relationship. Reaching this point in understanding was dependent on coming to see that one had to look at the whole process and that the various kinds of information a reader used always interacted with each other.

This taxonomy was used then in studies of reader's miscues and modified continuously to deal with the phenomena we found in the actual reading of kids. The more we understood the more we were able to modify the miscue analysis so that in turn it could deal more completely with the miscues. A recent version of the taxonomy appeared in the 'Reading Research Quarterly' (Goodman, 1969).

Miscue studies have now been completed on readers ranging from near beginners to proficient high school students. Miscue research studies have included black and white readers, urban and suburban, non-native speakers of English, pupils labeled perceptually handicapped and many others. Studies have been done of miscues in languages other than English. Studies have involved subjects reading basal texts, science, social studies, mathematics, fiction, and nonfiction. One series of studies followed a small group of readers over several years of reading development (Goodman, 1971).

In examining miscues some variables have emerged as being more significant than others or more indicative of proficiency than others. It is possible then to get powerful insights into a child's reading or into the reading process in general using a less complete miscue analysis than the taxonomy.

In working with teachers we have used a variety of less formal versions of miscue analysis. The 'Reading Miscue Inventory' is a published program for use of miscue analysis in classroom and clinical settings (Goodman and Burke, 1972). It concentrates on nine key variables and the patterns of miscues pupils produce. Many teachers are also applying miscue analysis to the use of traditional informal reading inventories for selecting stories from their current instructional materials to use in miscue analysis.

In all miscue analyses, procedures are relatively uniform:

1 *An appropriate selection for the pupil is made.* This is a story or other reading selection which is somewhat difficult for the pupil. He reads the entire story, so it must not be longer than he can handle at a single sitting. It must be long enough to generate 25 or more miscues (50 or more in the case of research studies). More than one selection may need to be tried to find one that is appropriate. The selection should have the continuity of meaning that unified stories or articles provide.

2 *The material is prepared for taping.* The pupil reads directly from the book. The teacher or researcher needs to have a worksheet on which the story is retyped, preserving the lines of the story exactly as they are in the book. Each line on the worksheet is numbered with page and line of the story, so that miscues may be identified as to where they occur.

3 *The reader is audiotaped and the code sheet is marked.* The reader is asked to read the story. Before he begins,

light conversation puts him at ease. He is told that he will not be graded for his reading and that he will be asked to retell the story after he has read.

He is also told that no help will be given while he is reading. He is encouraged to do the best he can to handle any problems. He can use any strategies he knows, he can guess or skip a word and go on.

As he reads, the teacher or researcher follows, marking the miscues on the typescript. Too much happens for everything to be noted as it occurs, so the entire reading, including retelling, is tape-recorded. Later the tape is replayed to complete the marking of the miscues on the worksheet. The worksheet becomes a permanent record of the session. It becomes the basis for the miscue analysis.

4 *The subject retells the story*. After he has read, the subject is asked to retell the story without interruption. Following the unaided retelling, the reader is asked open-ended questions to probe areas he omitted in his retelling. These questions do not use any specific information which the reader has not himself reported. The teacher or researcher does not steer the reader to conclusions. The reader's mispronunciations are retained in the questioning. A comprehension rating is based on an analysis of the retelling.

5 *The miscues are coded according to the analytic procedure used* (Taxonomy, Reading Miscue Inventory, or other).

6 *The patterns of miscues are studied.* Because miscue analysis gets at the process and goes beyond the superficial, it produces information that can become the basis of specific instruction. If the reader shows insufficient concern for meaning, the teacher can devote attention to building this concern. If a specific problem occurs, such as confusion of 'wh' and 'th' words (what, that; when, then; where, there), strategy lessons can be designed to help the reader cope with the problem.

In noting such a problem the teacher can carefully find its limits. The reader does not interchange other words starting with 'w' or 't'. He does not mix words like 'whistle' and 'thistle.' Only these function words are confused. In this way the teacher can design a lesson which will help the reader use meaning and grammatical structure to detect when he has made a miscue of this type. The instruction will help the reader correct when he makes the miscue, and in the process such miscues will begin to disappear as the reader makes better predictions.

The ability to use the information gained from miscue analysis in working with learners is, as was said earlier, dependent on the teacher's moving to a view of reading and reading instruction consistent with views of reading as a meaning-getting, language process.

WHAT WE KNOW ABOUT READING

Reading instruction in the last four decades has been word oriented. Basal readers have been built on this word centered view. Controlled vocabulary, a system of carefully introducing new words starting with those in very frequent use, has been the central organizing strand in reading instruction.

Phonics vs whole word arguments are concerned with the best way to teach words. Miscue research has led us away from a word focus to a comprehension focus. As we have looked at reading from a psycholinguistic perspective, we have come to see that the word is not the most significant unit in reading. Word bound reading instruction must be reconsidered in light of what is now known about the reading process.

Three kinds of information are available to the reader. One kind, the graphic information, reaches the reader visually. The other two, syntactic and semantic information, are supplied by the reader as he begins to process the visual input. Since the reader's goal is meaning, he uses as much or as little of each of these kinds of information as is necessary to get to the meaning. He makes predictions of the grammatical structure, using the control over language structure he learned when he learned oral language. He supplies semantic concepts to get the meaning from the structure. In turn his sense of syntactic structure and meaning make it possible to predict the graphic input so he is highly selective, sampling the print to confirm his prediction. In reading, what the reader thinks he sees is partly what he sees, but largely what he expects to see. As readers become more efficient, they use less and less graphic input.

Readers test the predictions they make by asking themselves if what they are reading makes sense and sounds like language. They also check themselves when the graphic input they predict is not there. In all this it is meaning which makes the system go. As long as readers are trying to get sense from what they read, they use their language competence to get to meaning. The extent to which a reader can get meaning from written language depends on how much related meaning he brings to it. That is why it is easier to read something for which the reader has a strong conceptual background.

Readers develop sampling strategies to pick only the most useful and necessary graphic cues. They develop prediction strategies to get to the underlying grammatical structure and to anticipate what they are likely to find in the print. They develop confirmation strategies to check on the validity of their predictions. And they have correction strategies to use when their predictions do not work out and they need to reprocess the graphic, syntactic, and semantic cues to get to the meaning.

When a reader's miscues are analyzed, the most important single indication of the reader's proficiency is the semantic acceptability of his miscues before correction. The reader's preoccupation with meaning will show in his miscues, because they will tend to result in language which still makes sense.

Even when readers produce nonwords they tend to retain the grammatical endings and intonation of the real word which is replaced. If they cannot quite get the meaning, they preserve the grammatical structure.

Effective readers also tend to correct miscues which result in a loss of meaning. They do this selectively. They will often not even be aware they have made miscues if meaning is not changed.

The reader, when he experiences difficulty, first asks himself what would make sense, what would fit the grammatical structure, and only after that what would match the graphic cues that would fit into the twin contexts of meaning and syntax. This keeps the value of graphic information in proper perspective and does not cause the reader to use any more information than is necessary.

Readers who are inefficient may be too much concerned with word-for-word accuracy. This may show in their miscues in a variety of ways, such as:

1 High degree of graphic correspondence between expected and observed responses in word substitution even when meaning is lost.
2 Frequent correction of miscues that do not affect the meaning.
3 Multiple attempts at getting a word's pronunciation even when it makes little difference to the comprehension of the story (proper names or foreign words, for example).

When the conceptual load in a particular selection gets too heavy for the reader he may begin to treat it as grammatical nonsense, manipulating the grammatical structure without getting to meaning. This may be reflected by a relatively high percentage of grammatical acceptability of miscues and relatively low percentage of meaning acceptability. If the reader is getting to the meaning both should be relatively high.

In judging how proficiently a reader is using the reading process, a teacher might use a procedure something like this:

1 Count the reader's miscues.
2 Subtract all those which are shifts to the reader's own dialect; these are not really miscues since they are what we should expect the reader to say in response to the print.
3 Count all the miscues which result in acceptable meaning (even if changed) before correction.
4 Count all miscues which result in unacceptable meaning but which are successfully corrected.
5 Add the miscues in steps 3 and 4. The result is the total number of miscues semantically acceptable or corrected.

This last score, expressed as a percentage of all miscues, is what we have come to call the 'comprehending' score. It is a measure of the reader's ability to keep his focus successfully on meaning. It is a measure of the *quality* of the reader's miscues. What is important is not how many miscues a reader makes but what their effect on meaning is.

EMERGENCE OF NEW METHODOLOGY FOR READING INSTRUCTION

With the new, revolutionary way of viewing reading and learning to read, a new methodology is gradually emerging. This is not a psycholinguistic method of teaching reading. Psycholinguistics is the foundation on which sound methodology must be built, but psycholinguistic knowledge does not automatically translate into a method of teaching reading.

Nor is miscue analysis a method of teaching reading. It is a technique for examining and evaluating the development of control of the reading process in learners. It can, in the hands of a knowledgeable teacher, provide the basis for useful instruction. But it does not lead to a total method.

Rather, as we come to understand better the process we are trying to teach when we teach reading, we can examine current practices and methodology - keeping some, rejecting some, reshaping some, and adding some totally new elements.

What changes most is the perspective. But that is a pervasive change because it leads to a new set of criteria for judging what is of value in reading instruction.

This new perspective is process-centered, language-centered, meaning-centered. It requires a new respect for language, a new respect for the learner, and a new respect for the reading teacher.

Language is seen, in this developing methodology, as much more than the bag of words we used to think it was. It is a structured, systematic code which can be used to represent meaning.

The *learner* of reading has a highly developed language competence which is his greatest resource in learning to read. In fact, the key to successful reading instruction is as it has always been, in the learner. With a new respect for the learner, we can make learning to read and write an extension of the natural language learning the child has already accomplished without professional assistance.

The *teachers* in this new methodology have a new and very important role to play. The teachers must come to understand the reading process so well that they can guide the progress of the learners. The teachers must know the signs of progress and be able to provide appropriate materials and instruction to aid the child's growth in proficiency.

Miscue analysis can be of great use to the teachers in this role because of the specific and general insights it provides about the learner's strengths and weaknesses. His miscues reflect his control and use of the reading process.

In many diagnostic procedures the teacher is frequently advised to administer a dose of phonics regardless of the pattern the child has shown. Miscue analysis shows the process at work and will reveal changes in how this process is used.

One problem that plagues teachers is judging how much progress pupils are making toward reading proficiency. When we judge the progress of infants in learning oral language, we do it very simply. If they can make themselves understood, they are learning to talk; and if they can respond to what is said to them, they are making progress in listening. We judge, in other words, by the learners' success with the process as they use it. Reading also should be judged by the extent to which learners can understand an increasing range of written materials.

We let ourselves confuse published reading tests with the competence in reading they are trying to assess. The subskill tests, skill check lists, and word lists do not test the ability to understand written language. They test, in large part, ability to perform with the abstract bits and pieces of language.

Miscue analysis can bring us back to reality.

REFERENCES

Goodman, K. (1969), Analysis of Oral Reading Miscues: Applied Psycholinguistics, 'Reading Research Quarterly,' vol.5, pp.9-30.

Goodman, Y. (1971), Longitudinal Study of Children's Oral Reading Behavior (USOE Final Report, Project 9-E-062), US Dept of Health, Education and Welfare.

Goodman, Y., and C.L. Burke (1972), 'Reading Miscue Inventory,' Macmillan, New York.

This chapter develops the concepts of miscue analysis and illustrates it with the actual miscues of readers. It shows how readers' miscues continuously illustrate their use of the reading process. The article concludes with a sequence of new answers for old questions and new questions in need of answers.

10 MISCUE ANALYSIS: Theory and Reality in Reading

More than ten years ago this researcher set himself a simple task: he wished to examine, from the perspective of modern linguistics, what happened when people read. It seemed logical to ask subjects to read material they had not seen before, so that what they did could be analyzed.

This examination of oral reading is not new. Analysis of reading errors in oral reading has been going on for several decades. What is new is the linguistic perspective that is applied. Error analysis had largely followed two assumptions. First, it was assumed that oral reading should be accurate and therefore that errors represented undesirable events in reading. Second it was assumed that errors grew from weaknesses or deficiencies in the reader. The number of errors was counted but little attention was given to qualitative difference among miscues or their effect.

In miscue analysis, from the very beginning reading has been treated as a language process, the receptive aspect of written language and therefore the parallel process to listening. The reader is regarded as a user of language, one who constructs meaning from written language.

Everything the reader does is assumed to be caused in this linguistic process. Unexpected events in oral reading thus reveal the way the reader is using the reading process itself. The term error is a misnomer, then, since it implies an undesirable occurrence. The term 'miscue' has emerged instead. A miscue is any observed oral response (OR) to print that does not match the expected response (ER). Miscue analysis reveals the reader's strengths and weaknesses and provides a continuous window on the reading process.

In this last sense miscue analysis is a uniquely powerful tool in linguistic and psycholinguistic research, since it makes it possible to monitor a language process continuously as it proceeds.

Shifting the focus in this analysis from errors as undesirable phenomena to be eliminated, to miscues as the by-product of the reading process, has made possible a revolution in viewpoint in which both the reader and the reading process may be regarded positively. The reader, particularly of a native language, may be regarded as a competent user of language whose language competence is reflected in miscues produced as a proficient reader and at all stages of acquisition of reading proficiency.

By moving away from a simplistic view that reading must be

accurate we are able to see, through miscues, how the efficient and effective reader operates. We can further define effectiveness in reading as the ability to construct a message (comprehend) and efficiency as the ability to use the least amount of available cues necessary to get to the meaning. Miscues are produced in efficient reading but they are likely either to leave meaning unaffected or be corrected by the reader. As efficiency increases, frequency of miscues tends to decrease but this is the result and not the cause of efficiency.

AN EMERGING MISCUE TAXONOMY

In early miscue research we sought for simple cause-effect relationships. We began to recognize that there were graphic cues from the perception of the print itself, phonic cues that relate print to speech, syntactic cues that derive from the structure of the language and semantic cues from the meaning. But we looked for a one-to-one cause-effect relationship. We tried to classify some miscues as graphophonic (combining the first two since the cues are the same), some as syntactic, some as semantic. We soon became aware that we could not fragment the process of reading, that every event involved the use of all three systems. Consider this example:

Text: Wait a *moment*.
Reader: Wait a *minute*.

The reader substitutes 'minute' for 'moment.' The observed response (OR) looks like and sounds like the expected response to some extent. But 'minute' and 'moment' also have the same grammatical function and mean the same thing. All of the three sorts of cues and their interaction contribute to the miscue. Furthermore the reader who is American is more likely to use 'minute' than 'moment' which the British writer has used. So the reader has shown that the influence of dialect is also at work.

A taxonomy for the analysis of oral reading miscues has emerged over a period of years in a series of studies. Each miscue is examined by asking a number of questions about the relationship of expected to observed response. All relevant questions are answered independently. What emerges then is the pattern of how the cuing systems are used in ongoing reading.

Here are the questions that are asked:

1 Is the miscue self-corrected by the reader?
2 Is the reader's dialect involved in the miscue?
3 How much graphic similarity is there between ER and OR?
4 How much phonemic similarity is there?
5 Is the OR an allolog of the ER? 'Typing' and 'typewriting' are allologs of the same word. Contractions are also allologs.

6 Does the miscue produce a syntactically acceptable text?
7 Does the miscue produce a semantically acceptable text?
8 Does a grammatical retransformation result from the miscue?
9 If the miscue is syntactically acceptable, how much is syntax changed?
10 If the miscue is semantically acceptable, how much is meaning changed?
11 Is intonation involved in the miscue? In English changed intonation may reflect change in syntax, meaning or both.
12 Does the miscue involve the submorphemic language level?
13 Does the miscue involve the bound morpheme level?
14 Does the miscue involve the word or free morpheme level?
15 Does the miscue involve the phrase level?
16 Does the miscue involve the clause level?
17 What is the grammatical category of the OR?
18 What is the grammatical category of the ER?
19 What is the relationship between function of ER and OR?
20 What influence has the surrounding text (peripheral visual field) had on miscues?
21 What is the semantic relationship between ER and OR word substitutions?

Miscue analysis using this taxonomy is suitable for depth research on small numbers of subjects. Typically our research has involved 3-6 subjects selected because they have common characteristics. These subjects are asked to read one or more full selections. In our most recent research our subjects have been asked to read two stories. Comparing profiles on both stories adds to the depth of our insights into the process.

A simpler form of miscue analysis dealing with only the more significant questions has been developed by Yetta M. Goodman and Carolyn Burke. This form has been used in some research studies, but it is designed for use by teachers and clinicians as a diagnostic tool. It also has found wide use in teacher education as a means of helping pre-service and in-service teachers to understand the reading process.

PSYCHOLINGUISTICS AS A BASE FOR STUDY OF READING

Reading and listening are receptive language processes. Speaking and writing are generative, productive, language processes. The reader or the listener is actively involved in the reconstruction of a message. He must comprehend meaning in order to be considered successful.

Meaning is not a property of the graphic display. The writer has moved from thought to language, encoding his meaning as a graphic display just as the speaker moves from thought to language encoding his meanings as a phonological sequence. The reader decodes the graphic display and reconstructs meaning.

Whether one wishes to understand reading as a process to teach initial literacy or to help readers become more effective, one must start from a base of psycholinguistics, the study of the interrelationships of thought and language. All the central questions involved in reading are psycholinguistic ones, because reading is a process in which language interacts with thought. Psycholinguistics is foundational to all understanding of the reading process.

In research and instruction learning to read has been commonly equated with learning to match an alphabetic orthography with its oral language counterpart. Reading instruction has frequently either been minimal, considered to be complete once the orthography is mastered, or endlessly repetitious and barren for those learners who persist in not acquiring correspondences between oral and written language. Skills have been taught on the basis of tradition with no insight into their relationship to the basic function of reading, reconstructing the message. The result is the most common, persistent and disabling reading problem in all cultures: people who have learned to respond orally to print but who can not or do not comprehend what they are reading. Reading becomes a print-to-speech short circuit. Those who can not get meaning from written language are just as functionally illiterate as those who never received instruction.

A PSYCHOLINGUISTIC THEORY OF READING ENGLISH

A theory and model of the reading process has grown out of research with young American readers of English. The theory has evolved as a means of interpreting the differences between OR and ER in order to understand the process of reading.

Behavior, whether linguistic or any other, is the end product of a process. The external behavior is observable and serves as an indicator of the underlying competence. Behavior can be observed but it can not be understood without some theory of how it is produced. Seemingly identical behaviors may result from very different processing. Very different behaviors may prove closely related if they are seen within a theoretical framework.

Comparison of OR and ER in miscues is a powerful means of inferring the process readers are using in dealing with specific reading tasks. When reading is as expected the process is not discernible but when it has produced miscues then the information used by readers and the ways in which they use it may be seen.

The following is the beginning of a short story as read by five relatively proficient readers aged 13-15. It will serve to illustrate the miscue phenomena and to introduce the theory of the reading process.

Subject 1

It must have been around midnight when I drove home, and as I approached the gates of the bungalow I
© lights
switched off the head lamps of the car
on
so the beam wouldn't swing in through
the window of the side bedroom and
wake Harry Pope.

Subject 2

It must have been around mid-
©
night when I drove home and (as) I approached the gates of the bungalow I
© lights
switched off the head lamps of the car
so the beam wouldn't swing in through
the window of the side bedroom and
wake Harry Pope.

Subject 3

It must have been around mid-
As
night when I drove home; (and) as I approached the gates of the bungalow I
© lights
switched off the head lamps of the car
so the beam wouldn't swing (in) through
©
the window of the side bedroom (and)
where was -
wake Harry Pope.

Subject 4

It must have been around midnight when I drove home, and as I ap-
© 1. bung- 2. bung-
proached the gates of the bungalow I
(I)
switched off the head lamps of the car
(I) (I)
so the beam wouldn't swing (in) through
the window of the side bedroom and
wake Harry Pope.

Subject 5

It must have been around midnight when I drove home, and (as) I ap-
bagalog and
proached the gates of (the) bungalow I
lights
switched off the head lamps of the car
©
so the beam wouldn't swing (in) through
at of the
the window of the side bedroom and
Henry
wake Harry Pope.

Figure 10.1 Miscues of five readers

The first phenomenon that can be seen here is a common tendency among these readers to substitute 'lights' for 'lamps' in line 4. The two words start with the same sound and letter but the relationship between the words is clearly semantic. Unless one assumes some kind of pervasive habitual association between these two words, one must conclude (a) that the readers are anticipating what they will in fact see, and (b) that they are more likely to expect 'lights' than 'lamps.' Notice, in fact, that subject 2 says 'lamps,' rejects that in favor of 'lights,' and then goes back to 'lamps.' This is a good example of the reading process at work. This British writer has used the term 'head lamps.' Our American subjects prefer the term 'head lights' and have already predicted it. Subsequent graphic input, however, contradicts the prediction. Some of the readers reprocess, however they have already gotten the meaning from the initial processing and must have done so before they said 'lights' if it is meaning that influenced their choices.

The words that are omitted by these five readers offer more insights into the process. 'As' in line 2 is omitted by two readers, one of whom corrects. 'In' in line 5 is omitted by three readers, one of whom corrects. Subject 1 substitutes 'on' for 'in.'

If we examine these for both cause and effect these insights emerge:

'As' may produce miscues (unexpected responses), because it follows 'and' and introduces a dependent clause that precedes the independent clause it relates to. That requires that the 'as' clause be processed, stored, and held until the following clause is processed before the meaning is fully clear. Omission of 'as' changes the structure so that the hitherto dependent clause is independent conjoined by 'and' to the preceding independent clause. A problem is then created since now there is no signal left as to the relationship between the new independent clause and the clause starting with 'I' at the end of line three. The omission of 'as' creates a sequence with an unacceptable grammatical structure. The reader who corrected seemed aware of this problem before he was aware of the precise omission because he repeated 'and I' three times before a successful correction. The reader who did not correct inserts a conjunction 'and' before 'I' in line 3, producing parallel independent clauses.

Subject 3 omits 'and' before 'as' on line 2. This conjunction turns out to be optional since the prior clause is independent.

The omission of 'in' before 'through' on line 5 results in little loss of semantic or syntactic information. The readers appeared to omit an element perhaps redundant in their American dialects. One substitutes 'on' for 'in' which may be more likely in her dialect in this context.

Subject 5 replaces 'of the side bedroom' with 'at the side of the bedroom.' In doing so he makes a minor change in the meaning but produces a new structure which is both meaningful and grammatical.

Subject 3 moves even farther away from the text at the end of the paragraph. He substitutes 'where Harry Pope was' for 'and wake Harry Pope.' Apparently he expected it to conclude with 'sleeping.' He realizes his expectation is not borne out and regresses, reprocesses and corrects.

The miscues of these readers can not be explained by viewing reading as a process of sequential letter or word identification. If it were so, then miscues would be more evenly distributed and be confined to words or word parts.

Even with the one word in this paragraph that did cause some recognition problems, 'bungalow,' the problems can not be seen simply as letter-sound (phonics) or word recognition based. It may be that the problem comes from a mismatch between the reader's definition and concept of a bungalow and the writer's. Americans commonly use bungalow to refer to a very modest house or vacation home. Furthermore we can't be sure that those readers who exhibited no difficulty with 'bungalow' understood its use by this author in this context.

Several key concepts about the reading process are required to begin to explain the miscues of these readers.

1 Anticipation or prediction is an important part of the reading process.
2 Readers process syntactic or grammatical information as they read and this plays an important role in their ability to predict what they have not yet seen or processed.
3 Meaning is the end product of the reading process and effective readers are meaning-seekers.
4 Meaning is also input in the reading process. The success of the reader in comprehending is largely a function of the conceptual and experiential background he brings to the task and which his processing of the writer's language evokes in him.
5 Graphic information (letters, letter constituents, and patterns of letters) is by no means the sole input in the reading process. Nor is the matching of such information to phonological information a necessarily significant part of the reading process.
6 Accuracy in oral reading is not a prerequisite to effective reading. Comprehension is the basic goal and a focus on accuracy may be counter-productive.

The reader must begin with this graphic display and somehow decode it in such a way that he reconstructs the author's message.

Any passage may be analyzed for letters, words or meaning. The last focus is a much more efficient one in that the amount of information needed to get to the meaning is far less than if words or letters must be first analyzed. Thus to be both *effective* and *efficient* reading must be focussed on meaning.

An effective, efficient reader uses the least amount of information necessary to reconstruct the writer's message. This is only possible if he is able to sample from available cues those that are most productive, that is those that carry the most information. To do so he must utilize strategies that he develops that make it possible to predict and guess at the other available information without actually processing it. The reader's knowledge of the grammatical system of the language and the constraints within the system, as well as the semantic constraints within the concepts dealt with, constitute the parameters within which the reader's strategies are operating.

To get from print to meaning, the reader must treat the graphic display as a surface representation of an underlying structure. He must not only process the graphic display as a grammatically structured language sequence but he must assign an underlying or deep structure in order to process the interrelationships between clauses.

Consider, for example, the paragraph cited above as read by these subjects. This paragraph is a single sentence composed of clauses combined in complex ways so that the meaning of the whole is more than that of any one clause. Rewritten as a string of one-clause sentences that express about the same meaning, it might read like this:

> It must have been around midnight. I drove home at midnight. I approached the gates of the bungalow. [At the same time] I switched off the head lamps of the car. [In order that] the beam wouldn't swing in through the window of the bedroom. The bedroom was at the side. [In order that] the beam wouldn't wake Harry Pope.

The reader must deal with an underlying structure by interpreting signals in the surface structure because meaning relates not to the surface structure but to underlying structure.

The writer has produced the graphic display starting with meaning, assigning a deep grammatical structure, then transforming this deep structure by use of transforming rules and subsequently applying a set of orthographic rules to produce a surface representation in the form of a graphic display.

This process is much the same as speaking except that the final rules are orthographic rather than phonological. In use, the graphic display and oral language are alternate surface representations of the deep structure. Writing is *not* a secondary representation of speech. This is obvious in non-alphabetic writing systems. It is no less true in alphabetic systems even though there are direct relationships between the two surface representations.

The alphabetic systems are economical in that they are able to use a small number of symbols in patterned combinations to express an unlimited number of meanings just as oral language does. And using the oral language symbols as a base for the written symbols is both convenient and logical. But if readers found it necessary to identify letters and match them with sounds or even identify word shapes and match them with oral names then efficient reading would be slower than speech. But efficient readers use distinctive features of letters to move from print to deep structure and meaning. Their ability to identify letters or words they have read *follows* rather than *precedes* their assignment of deep structure and meaning. Once they know what they have read they also know the words they have read and their spellings. In this manner they *appear* to identify graphic elements much more rapidly than they could actually do so.

Essentially the same deep language structure underlies both speech and writing. There are, of course, different circumstances in which oral and written language are used. The former is much more likely to be in a situational context that may be indicated by gesture or which needs no explanation. Written language on the other hand, is most often abstracted from the situations it deals with. It must create its own setting and be a much more complete representation of the message to achieve effective communication. But these differences are more those of use than of process.

The reader samples the three systems of cues in order to be aware of and predict surface structure and induce deep structure and meaning.

The reader responds to what he sees or what he thinks he sees. His experience with and knowledge of the graphic symbols (letters), spelling patterns, sequencing rules and redundancies sets up expectations. He is able to use distinctive features to form perceptual images that are partly the result of what he expects to see.

Subject 5 thought the name was 'Henry' rather than 'Harry.' The two names differ graphically in very minor ways. She had no reason to reject that having produced it since it fits both meaning and grammar constraints.

A minimum amount of syntactic information, that 'as' is a marker of a clause for example, makes it possible to predict a surface structure and almost simultaneously begin to induce an underlying structure. Punctuation, part of the graphic cue system, comes mostly at the end of sequences in English and therefore is of little use except as a check on prediction. One must predict the pattern in order to process subsequent elements.

For a proficient reader to get directly to meaning he must draw on his knowledge of the patterns, rules, constraints and redundancies of the grammatical system.

Even beginning readers in our research substitute 'a' for 'the,' an indication that they use grammatical as well as graphic cues. As the surface structure is predicted, the rules by which that structure is linked to the underlying deep structure are evoked and serve as additional cues.

Because of the limited number of patterns, the constraints within these patterns (only certain elements may follow certain others), and the redundancy of language (every cue does not carry a new bit of information) a reader is able to sample those cues that carry the most information and predict whole patterns on that basis.

Sampling, selecting and predicting are basic aspects of reading. They require development by the reader of 'comprehension strategies' which control the choice and use of cues and keep the reader oriented to the 'goal' of reading, which is meaning.

When miscues affect meaning the reader must be aware that they do and correct. He uses a set of confirmation strategies as he proceeds. He asks himself: (a) whether he can predict a grammatical sequence on the basis of information processed (b) whether he can assign a decodable deep structure (c) whether what he has decoded as meaning in fact makes sense.

As he continues to process information he is constantly alert to information that contradicts his prediction. As long as subsequent information confirms he proceeds. If any contradictory information is encountered he must reprocess to reconcile the conflicting information. This may require a new hypothesis about what is coming. The problems with 'as' that our subjects had and their subsequent response illustrates this process at work.

Reading then becomes a sample, predict, test, confirm, and correct-when-necessary process.

The constant concern for meaning as output makes meaning input as well. The deep structure must be decodable, the reader must know whether what he has decoded makes sense. Furthermore, experience and concepts must be evoked to create a semantic context and a set of semantic constraints which correspond to the syntactic constraints.

Memory functions as a kind of highly cross-referenced lexicon feeding the most appropriate referential meaning into the processing to complete the set of semantic cues.

No person, however literate, is ever able to read all that is written in his native language. The ability to read any selection is a function of the semantic background one brings to it. Without substantial meaning input, effective reading is not possible. Literacy is by no means a constant for any individual for all reading tasks.

NEW VIEWS OF OLD QUESTIONS

Miscue analysis and the psycholinguistic view of reading suggest the need for reconsidering old issues. Here, a few of these can only be listed. In each case the traditional view seems to be at odds with this new view.

1 Where should reading instruction begin? Not with letters or sounds but with whole real relevant natural language, we think.

2 What is the hierarchy of skills that should be taught in reading instruction? We think there is none. In fact in learning to read as in learning to talk one must use all skills at the same time.

3 Why do some people fail to learn to read? Not because of

their weaknesses but because we've failed to build on their strengths as competent language users.
4 What should we do for deficient readers? Build their confidence in their ability to predict meaning and language.
5 Can anyone learn to read? Yes, we say. Anyone who can learn oral language can learn to read and write.

SOME NEW QUESTIONS

There is still a lot to be learned about reading. Many new questions emerge as reading is seen from a new vantage point. For example:

1 How does the difference in grammatical structure of different languages influence the reading process?
2 How does the reading process differ in non-alphabetic writing systems as compared to alphabetic systems?
3 How do variations among readers in conceptual development influence their reading and their comprehension?
4 Can methods be devised for teaching people to read languages they don't speak? This question is of particular importance in countries where college texts are in languages other than the national language.

Perhaps the most basic question we need to ask is how can we put these new scientific insights to use in achieving the goal of universal literacy.

This brief research report, originally presented at AERA in 1964, was the first public statement of miscue analysis research. In this exploration, Goodman had first-, second-, and third-graders read stories at appropriate levels of difficulty. For this study he had them read lists of words taken from the stories prior to reading the stories. He wanted to see the ability of children to read words in and out of context. The results were dramatic: even first-graders could read two-thirds of the words in context that they could not read in lists. That was a satisfying but not surprising result: it supported the intuitive feeling of many teachers that children's reading of words out of context was very different from their reading of connected text; it was consistent with a large body of research that showed that whole meaningful language was easier to read, to learn, to remember than were isolated sentences, lists of words, or nonsense syllables.

Though the study was replicated numerous times in English and Spanish (Huddleson-Lopez) the conclusions were challenged by Samuels and Singer because they seemed to contradict Samuels's focal attention hypothesis: that things are easiest to learn when all distracting stimuli are removed - hence words are easiest to learn in isolation.

The study, however, does not deal with learning words - which Samuels and Singer equate with learning to read - it deals with reading words in and out of context.

11 A LINGUISTIC STUDY OF CUES AND MISCUES IN READING

This is a report of the conclusions to date of a descriptive study of the oral reading of first-, second-, and third-grade children. It is a study in applied linguistics, since linguistic knowledge and insights into language and language learning were used.

ASSUMPTIONS

In this study, reading has been defined as the active reconstruction of a message from written language. Reading must involve some level of comprehension. Nothing short of this comprehension is reading. I have assumed that all reading behavior is caused. It is cued or miscued during the child's interaction with written language. Research on reading must begin at this point of interaction. Reading is a psycholinguistic process. Linguistic science has identified the cue systems within language. The child learning to read his native language has already internalized these cue systems to the point where he is responding to them without being consciously aware of the process. To understand how children learn to read, we must learn how the individual experiences and abilities of children affect their ability to use language cues. We must also become aware of the differences and similarities between understanding oral language which uses sounds as symbol-units and written language which depends on graphic symbols.

CUE SYSTEMS IN READING

Here is a partial list of the systems operating to cue and miscue the reader as he interacts with written material. Within words there are:

Letter-sound relationships
Shape (or word configuration)
Known 'little words' in bigger words
Whole known words
Recurrent spelling patterns.

In the flow of language there are:

Patterns of words (or function order)
Inflection and inflectional agreement (examples: The boy runs. The boys run.)
Function words such as noun markers (the, a, that, one, etc.)
Intonation (which is poorly represented in writing by punctuation)
The referential meaning of prior and subsequent language elements and whole utterances.

Cues external to language and the reader include:

Pictures
Prompting by teacher or peers
Concrete objects
Skill charts.

Cues within the reader include:

His language facility with the dialect of his sub-culture
His idiolect (his own personal version of the language)
His experiential background (the reader responds to cues in terms of his own real or vicarious experiences)
His conceptual background and ability (a reader can't read what he can't understand)
Those reading attack skills and learning strategies he has acquired or been taught.

PROCEDURES

The subjects of this study were 100 children in grades 1, 2, and 3 who attend the same school in an industrial suburb of Detroit. Every second child on an alphabetic list of all children in these grades was included. There were an equal number of boys and girls from each room.

For reading materials, a sequence of stories was selected from a reading series not used in the school. With the publisher's permission the stories were dittoed on worksheets. A word list from each story was also duplicated.

An assistant called each subject individually out of the classroom. The subject was given a word list for a story at about his grade level. If the child missed many words, he was given a list for an earlier story. If he missed few or none he was given a more advanced story. Each child eventually had a word list of comparable difficulty. The number of words that each child missed on the lists, then, was a controlled variable.

Next the child was asked to read orally from the book the

story on which his word list was based. The assistant noted all the child's oral reading behavior on the worksheets as the child read. The assistant refrained from any behavior that might cue the reader. Finally, each subject was to close his book and retell the story as best he could. He was not given advance notice that he would be asked to do this. The reading and retelling of the story was taped. Comparison between the structure of the language in the book and in the retold stories is underway utilizing the system of the Loban and Strickland studies.[1] It is not complete and will not be reported here.

WORDS IN LISTS AND IN STORIES

One concern of the research was the relative ability of children to recognize words in the lists and read the words in the stories. The expectation was that children would read many words in stories which they could not recognize in lists. I reasoned that, in lists, children had only cues *within* printed words while in stories they had the additional cues in the flow of language. I was not disappointed.

Table 11.1 Average words missed in list and in story

	List average	*Also missed in story*		*Ratio*
		Average	*Percent*	
Grade 1	9.5	3.4	38%	2.8:1
Grade 2	20.1	5.1	25%	3.9:1
Grade 3	18.8	3.4	18%	5.5:1

Table 11.2 Ability to read words in context which were missed on list

	Less than ½	*More than ½*	*More than 2/3*	*More than ¾*	*More than 4/5*	*N*
Grade 1	11%	89%*	69%	49%	26%	35
Grade 2	3%	97%	81%	66%	50%	32
Grade 3	6%	94%	91%	76%	67%	33

* Cumulative percents of subjects

As shown in Table 11.1, the children in this study were able to read many words in context which they couldn't read from lists. Average first-graders could read almost two out of three words in the story which they missed on the list. The average second-grader missed only one-fourth of the words in the story which he failed to recognize on the list. Third-graders were able to get, in the stories, all but 18 per cent of the words which they did not know in the list.

As Table 11.2 shows, except for a small group of first-graders and a very few second- and third-graders, all the children in this study could read correctly in the story at least half of the words that they could not recognize on the lists. Sixty-nine percent of first-grade children could 'get' two-thirds or more of their list errors right in reading the story. Sixty-six percent of the second-graders could read three-fourths or more of their errors in the story. The comparable group of third-graders could get better than four out of five. The children in successive grades in this study were increasingly efficient in using cue systems outside of words.

Table 11.3 Total errors and substitution errors on lists

	List errors average	*Included substitutions Average*	*Percent*	*Ratio*
Grade 1	9.5	4.9	52%	1.9:1
Grade 2	20.1	11.5	57%	1.7:1
Grade 3	18.1	14.3	79%	1.3:1

At the same time, as Table 11.3 shows, children in successive grades were making greater attempts to use word attack skills, here defined as responses to *cue systems within words.* About half of the listed errors of first-graders were omissions. The children did not attempt to figure the words out by using any available cues. Second-grade children showed an increased tendency to try to 'get' the word. This is shown by the somewhat higher percent of substitutions among the list errors of second-grade children. Third-graders showed a pronounced increase in the percent of substitutions among their list errors. Children in successive grades used word attack skills with increased frequency though not necessarily with increased efficiency.

Table 11.4 One-time substitutions for known words in stories

	Average substitutions	*Average lines read*	*Substitutions per line read*
Grade 1	3.7	50.2	.074
Grade 2	14.9	126.2	.118
Grade 3	16.9	118.7	.142

There is no instance of a child getting a word right on the list but missing it consistently in the story. But often children made an incorrect substitution in the reading of the story in individual occurrences of known words. As Table 11.4 indicates, second- and third-graders made more than twice as many one-time substitutions per line read as first-graders. Third-graders made more substitutions per line than second-graders. Three possible causes of these one-time substitutions may be 1 overuse of cues within words to the exclusion of other cues, 2 miscuing by book language which differs from the language as the child knows it, and 3 ineffective use of language cues.

REGRESSIONS IN READING

This study also was concerned with regressions in reading, that is repeating one or more words. No statistics are needed to support one observation: virtually every regression that the children in this study made was for the purpose of correcting previous reading.

When a child missed a word on a list, unless he corrected it immediately he seldom ever went back. In reading the story, however, children frequently repeated words or groups of words, almost always to make a correction. Regressions themselves, then, were not errors but attempts (usually but not always successful) to correct prior errors.

Table 11.5 Regressions in reading

	First grade		*Second grade*		*Third grade*	
	Per child	*Per line read*	*Per child*	*Per line read*	*Per child*	*Per line read*
Word Only						
To correct word	2.40	.048	10.11	.090	10.30	.087
To correct intonation on word	.09	.002	.49	.004	1.42	.012
Total	2.49	.050	10.60	.094	11.72	.099
*Phrase**						
To correct word by repeating phrase	1.54	.031	5.77	.052	7.54	.061
To rephrase	.29	.006	1.97	.018	1.03	.009
To change intonation	.52	.011	2.83	.026	2.76	.023
Total	2.35	.048	10.57	.096	11.33	.093

* For these purposes a phrase is considered *any* two or more consecutive words

If regressions are divided into two groups, word regressions - those which involve one word immediately repeated - and phrase regressions - those which include repeating two or more words - the two types each represent almost exactly half the regressions at each of the grade levels (see Table 11.5).

Regressions seem to function in children's reading about like this: if the child makes an error in reading which he realizes is inconsistent with prior cues, he reevaluates the cues and corrects his error before continuing. Otherwise, he reads on encountering more cues which are inconsistent with his errors. Eventually he becomes aware that the cues cannot be reconciled and retraces his footsteps to find the source of the inconsistency. Thus, regressions in reading are due to redundant cues in language. They are self-corrections that play a vital role in children's learning to read. In two cases errors go uncorrected: 1 if the error makes no difference to the meaning of the passage, and 2 if the reader is relying so heavily on analytical techniques using only cues within words that he has lost the meaning altogether.

A PRELIMINARY LINGUISTIC TAXONOMY

In a third phase of the study I categorized all errors of the subjects according to linguistic terminology. This analysis produced the 'Preliminary Linguistic Taxonomy of Cues and Miscues in Reading.'

It should be noted that the 100 subjects of this study, though all attend the same school and have learned to read with a fairly consistent methodology, exhibited virtually every kind of reading difficulty and deviation which I could predict linguistically.

IMPLICATIONS OF THIS STUDY

There are several implications to be drawn from the description of the oral reading of these children. Some practices in the teaching of reading are made suspect.

1 Introducing new words out of context before new stories are introduced to children does not appear to be necessary or desirable.
2 Prompting children or correcting them when they read orally also appears to be unnecessary and undesirable in view of the self-correction which language cues in children.
3 Our fixation on eye fixations and our mania for devices which eliminate regressions in reading seem to be due to a lamentable failure to recognize what was obvious in this study: that regressions are the means by which the child corrects himself and learns.
4 Shotgun teaching of so-called phonic skills to whole classes or groups at the same time seems highly questionable in view of the extreme diversity of the difficulties children displayed in this study. No single difficulty seemed general enough to warrant this approach. In fact, it is most likely that at least as many children are suffering from difficulties caused by overusing particular learning strategies in reading as are suffering from a lack of such strategies.
5 The children in this study found it harder to recognize words than to read them in stories. Eventually I believe we must abandon our concentration on words in teaching reading and develop a theory of reading and a methodology that puts the focus where it belongs: on language.

NOTE

1 Walter Loban, 'The Language of Elementary School Children,' National Council of Teachers of English, Champaign, 1963; and Ruth Strickland, 'The Language of Elementary School Children,' Bulletin of The School of Education, Indiana University, vol.38, July, 1962.

This chapter presents to a research audience the rationale and basic concepts of miscue analysis as a research methodology. It puts miscue analysis into a historical perspective of studies of reading errors. It introduces the research taxonomy which, because of its bulk, will be found in the Appendix.

12 ANALYSIS OF ORAL READING MISCUES: Applied Psycholinguistics

Though it is only recently that attention has been given in reading research to linguistic and psycholinguistic insights, reading research has always dealt with linguistic questions if only by ignoring them. Every study of reading materials, reading instruction, the reading process, and reading errors has involved decisions about language units, language sequences, and the explanation and categorization of linguistic behavior.

The reader, whether proficient or beginner, is a user of language. During the reading process this user of language responds to a graphic display, physically no more than patterned ink blotches, and works at reconstructing a message encoded in the graphic display by the writer. No matter how this process is fractionated or atomized, linguistic and psycholinguistic questions are always involved. Understanding of the process must depend on understanding how language works and understanding how language is used, that is how language and thought are interrelated. Psycholinguistics is the study of these relationships. Until now, researchers in reading have been but dimly aware of the fact that research in reading is applied psycholinguistics. It is the contention of this paper that, just as the solution of problems in space exploration would be impossible without applied physics, so research in reading is impossible without scientifically based psycholinguistics.

This article presents a psycholinguistically based analysis for use in the study of oral reading. The research in which this analysis has been used is basically descriptive, the goal being to describe what happens when a reader, at any stage of proficiency, reads orally.

Researchers and classroom teachers have known that the errors readers make provide insights into reading development. Although for decades oral reading errors have been subjected to scrutiny, this scrutiny has been atheoretical. Without a theoretical framework in which to deal with errors and other oral reading phenomena, many insights into the reading process have been lost.

Spache (1964) summarized a number of studies (Barbe, et al., Daw, Duffy and Durrell, Fields, Gilmore, Payne, Swanson, Wells) and a number of analytical systems in a discussion of informal reading inventories. It is clear from his summary that analysis of oral reading errors has been characterized by establishment of arbitrary, often nonparallel, and overlapping, categories such as fluency, word attack, and posture, posture being hardly a reading error.

Spache (1964, pp.104-5) attempted to compare the findings of ten studies of reading errors in terms of frequency rank of error types, but since all investigators did not use the same categories in the same way with the same definitions, the results were really not comparable. For example, what one classified as substitution, another called mispronunciation.

Weber (1968, pp.96-119) summarized the classification systems used in studies of reading errors and the deficiencies in these systems. She found that most systems focussed on words or letters or some combination of both. The variability among definitions of categories from researcher to researcher, however, made comparison very difficult. Furthermore, many classification systems included overlapping categories. Also confusions over the function of oral reading introduced a bias that caused the researcher to be distracted by extraneous phenomena (poor enunciation, hesitation, inadequate phrasing, posture), and a number of studies viewed reading errors as simple misperceptions of words and letters. Another recurrent shortcoming, Weber found, was the lack of concern for the linguistic function of the errors. Often errors were lumped together that were by no means of equal significance. Lastly, legitimate language differences due to the dialect of the reader were treated frequently as mispronunciations.

The analytical system presented here begins with the premise that all responses to the graphic display are caused and are not accidental or capricious. In every act of reading, the reader draws on the sum total of prior experience and learning. Every response results from the interaction of the reader with the graphic display. Responses that correspond to expected responses mask the process by which they are produced. But observed responses (ORs) which do not correspond to expected responses (ERs) are generated through the same process as expected ones. By comparing the ways these miscues differ from the expected responses we can get direct insights into how the reading process is functioning in a particular reader at a particular point in time. Such insights reveal not only weaknesses, but strengths as well, because the miscues are not simply errors, but the results of the reading process having miscarried in some minor or major ways. The phenomena to be dealt with will be called miscues, rather than errors, in order to avoid the negative connotation of errors (all miscues are not bad) and to avoid the implication that good reading does not include miscues. After a series of studies, the present author is convinced that only in rare special circumstances is oral reading free of miscues and that silent reading never is miscue-free. In fact, it appears likely that a reader who requires perfection in his reading will be a rather inefficient reader.

A few other researchers have also recently moved away from prior error studies. Weber (1967) studied errors of first-grade readers in Ithaca, New York. Clay (1966) in studies in Auckland, New Zealand, also looked at reading errors of beginners using linguistic criteria. Y. Goodman (1967) used the taxonomy presented here to look at first-grade reading development whereas Kolers (1969) analyzed the errors of adult readers.

During several years of research on miscues, an analytical system and a theoretical base has evolved in order to accommodate the actual observed reading responses of subjects. A theory must explain and predict and a taxonomy must provide for all phenomena without loose ends and with a minimum of arbitrary decisions. Both the theory and the taxonomy begin with psycholinguistic theory and are modified and explicated in terms of reality. In such a way the research does not stop with the description of superficial behavior, but goes beneath it to the competence which it involves. It is not enough to say that readers sometimes substitute 'a' for 'the.' It must be seen that such behavior can only result from the linguistic competence of the reader which makes it possible for him to produce a determiner, where one is needed. It must also be seen that something more than word recognition or letter perception is involved.

APPLICATIONS OF LINGUISTICS TO READING

Early applications of linguistics to reading have been narrow. Bloomfield (1963) concentrated almost exclusively on phonemics. He went only as far as seeking phoneme-grapheme regularity in materials. He did not study the process of reading nor make a full application of linguistics to it. Fries (1964) looked at reading theoretically, but he also focussed on a narrowly defined method of reading based upon spelling patterns and the descriptive linguistic principle of minimal contrast. Lefevre (1964), in a theoretical work, partially developed a sentence approach to reading instruction which included attention to syntax and intonation. Educationists, with a few rare exceptions, have either completely accepted or completely rejected one or another of these methodological points of view.

Strickland's (1962) research was an exception because she studied the structure of children's language and compared it with the language in basal readers. Loban (1963) used similar analysis in his longitudinal studies of children's language development. Bormuth (1966) conducted studies of the relationship of linguistics to readability, using a transformational count. Bormuth also carried out psycholinguistically based research on reading comprehension. Hunt (1965) studied grammatical structures in children's composition and identified differences in complexity at successive ages, as indicated by increasing use of transforms. Hunt dealt with written expression, an encoding process. Reading is basically decoding, but oral reading also involves at least some encoding, since the reader must produce an oral version of what he reads.

The narrowness of early applications of linguistics to reading has led to the development of two unfortunate misconceptions: 1 that a linguistic method of teaching reading exists, and 2 that linguistics can be applied to reading only to explain phoneme-grapheme correspondences. The first is patently untrue. There can be no linguistic 'method' of reading instruction any more than there can be a 'psychological' method. The second misconception is even more unfortunate because some linguists have written 'linguistic' reading texts building on this unexamined assumption rather than doing the research necessary to determine the full scope of linguistic and psycholinguistic implications for reading.

The theoretical base

'The major deterrent to research on the reading process is the inefficiency of techniques for investigating the problems,' says Helen M. Robinson (1968, p.400). She suggests that 'a wealth of information about processes could be secured from carefully planned...examination of children's reading behavior' (Robinson, 1968, p.401).

With no theory underlying the detailed descriptions Robinson has called for, much could be added to the existing collection of data without making any contribution to coherent understanding of the reading process. Although researchers such as those associated with Project Literacy (Project Literacy Reports, 1964-6) have taken a broad view of reading, they have been content to look at one portion of the reading process at a time, applying insights from psychology, linguistics, and psycholinguistics. Useful knowledge has been produced, but it has not contributed to a theory that could generate hypotheses and predict and explain reading behavior.

One of the best known theories of reading, Holmes's substrata-factor theory, is not a theory at all, but rather an artifact of manipulation of statistics generated by a set of reading tests (Holmes, 1965). As Clymer (1968) points out, it is not possible to explain or predict cause and effect relationships on the basis of the Holmes's analysis, nor does it generate testable hypotheses.

Theories in reading have been thinly built on partial views of the process of reading. Notably missing has been any awareness of the nature of language and language use. Research programs designed to test such theories have been nonexistent, unless one includes classroom testing of materials based on theoretical assumptions. Such studies, however, have rarely been designed to yield any direct evidence about the validity of the underlying theory.

In the theory of the reading process which is evolving, reading is seen as information processing. The reader, a user of language, interacts with the graphic input as he seeks to reconstruct a message encoded by the writer. He concentrates his total prior experience and learning on the task, drawing on his experiences and the concepts he has attained as well as the language competence he has achieved.

In this process, thought and language interrelate, but they are not the same. Reading can be described as a psycholinguistic process, in which meaning is decoded from a linguistic medium of communication rather than a thinking or linguistic process. Furthermore, while reading, the reader may experience cycles of reflective thinking in response to the reading; these cycles cannot be considered part of the reading process itself any more than following directions after having read them can be considered a part of the reading process.

It is important, therefore, to draw a line between reading and the results of reading. But, such a line should not be drawn short of meaning, because the entire reading process should be geared to the reconstruction of the message. Fractionating the process into constituent bits or skills for the purpose of research or instruction qualitatively changes not only the process, which through its interrelationships is much more than the sum of its parts, but also changes the nature of the parts since they normally function as part of a complex process.

Recent attempts by Chall (1967) and others to justify the separation of 'code-breaking' from reading for meaning have been based on misunderstandings of how the linguistic code operates and is used in reading. A language is not only a set of symbols (phonemes for oral language, graphemes for written) it is also a *system* of communication in which the symbols are patterned to create sequences capable of carrying an infinite variety of messages. The system of language is grammar. In the process of acquiring his language in pre-school years, each language user acquires control over the rules by which his language is generated. These rules make it possible for him to generate original language utterances which are grammatical and understood by his listeners.

Though it is convenient to think of utterances as composed of units, which are basic symbols, these units are themselves affected by their settings. Compare these words for example: 'site,' 'situate,' 'situation.' Note that the affix creates a sequence which requires the final consonant in 'site' to shift to /č/ in 'situate' and the final consonant in 'situate' to shift to /š/ in 'situation' (Halle, 1969). Furthermore, constraints are imposed in all languages on the permissible sequences so that 'lamp' is a possible English word, but 'mpal' is not. The language user learns not only the symbols, but the rules by which they adapt to their settings and the constraints on them. He learns the small number of significant differences in sounds which differentiate the units, and he also learns to ignore differences which are not significant in his language. He must ignore these differences or those which are significant will be lost in a maze of irrelevant noise.

Two key facts have thus been overlooked by those arguing

for code-emphasis programs: 1 Phonemes do not really exist outside of the full system of constraints in which they are found. 2 Oral language is no less a code than written language.

Those who argue that one may think of reading as matching oral units with written units, have frequently labeled such an operation decoding. But, decoding is a process of going from code to message in information theory.

Going from code to code is recoding (Goodman, 1967a). One may think of a hypothetical stage in reading in which the fledgling reader recodes graphic input as speech which he then treats as aural input and decodes for meaning as he does in listening. Research has indicated that this view is not appropriate for proficient readers (Goodman and Burke, 1968) and may not fully apply even to beginners (Y. Goodman, 1967). Rather, proficient reading can be seen as direct decoding of graphic input. But even in this stretched out view, the reader must operate in response to real meaningful, grammatical language if he is to have all the information available to him in proper interrelationship, and he must be able eventually to reconstruct and comprehend a message.

Even in an alphabetic system, the interrelationships between the oral and written forms of the language are not simple phoneme-grapheme correspondences, but are relationships between patterns of sounds and spelling patterns. The concept of regularity, i.e. consistent representation of oral language by written units, should be seen in relation to constrained sequences. 'S' is a regular representation of /š/ in 'sure' and 'sugar,' just as 't' is a regular representation of /š/ in 'action.' The correspondence is consistent, though it operates in limited circumstances (Venezky, 1967). Many of these minor-pattern regularities are so firmly based in the operation of the language as the user of language has come to know it, that they cause no particular problem in reading.

The most basic reason why the reading process cannot be fragmented is that the reader does not use all the information available to him. Reading is a process in which the reader picks and chooses from the available information only enough to select and predict a language structure that is decodable. It is not in any sense a precise perceptual process. As Kolers has indicated, it is only 'incidentally visual' (Kolers, 1969). It is not a process of sequential word recognition. A proficient reader is one so efficient in sampling and predicting that he uses the least (not the most) available information necessary (Goodman, 1965).

All the information must be available for the process to operate in the reader and for the sampling strategies it requires to develop in the beginner.

Three basic kinds of information are used. They are graphophonic, syntactic and semantic.

Since the value of any bit of these three types of information must be related to the other available information, the choice of which bit to select can only be made in full context and the strategies for making those selections can only be learned in response to real language materials (not flash cards or spelling matrices or phonics charts). Also, the reader cannot judge the effectiveness of his choices unless he has subsequent input which can tell him whether his choice fits the semantic, syntactic, and graphophonic constraints.

Consider Betts' (1963, p.135) primer story paragraph as it was read by a first-grader:

Mrs Duck looked here and there.
But she did not see a thing
under the (old) apple tree.
(c) the
And on she went
for a walk.

By omitting 'old,' the child produced a sequence that was still acceptable both syntactically and semantically. Furthermore, he corrected a minor flaw in the writing. The phrase, 'the big old apple tree,' was used early in the story. Subsequently, the phrases 'the tree' or 'the apple tree' were used. In connected discourse, a rule operates that generally requires the speaker to delete descriptive adjectives from subsequent references to the same noun. Perhaps the writer or editor of the story wanted to provide one more use of 'old.' In any case, the child omitted it and did not correct or indeed appear to be aware of the miscue.

On the next line, the child substituted 'the' for 'she' and attempted to read on, but found that subsequent choices were not syntactically or semantically consistent. He then returned to the beginning of the line and reread the entire sentence, this time correctly. 'The' and 'she' are graphically similar (though phonemically, totally dissimilar). But, this reader was evidently concerned that what he reads be decodable, that is, make sense. The omission of 'old' did make sense, but the 'the' substitution resulted in an unacceptable sequence which he corrected. The process would have been totally different if he had encountered 'old' and 'she' on word lists.

POTENTIAL OF ANALYSIS OF MISCUES

It should be clear from the detail of the analysis (see the Appendix) that studies using the taxonomy are depth studies and the number of subjects in any single study must necessarily be quite small. It is a technique most suitable for seeking to understand thoroughly how a few readers use the reading process. It stands in sharp contrast to statistical studies of many subjects on a few key, isolated variables.

The studies that have utilized the taxonomy (Goodman, 1965;

Goodman and Burke, 1968; Y. Goodman, 1967; Allen, 1969), have sought to understand the reading process and perfect the theoretical model of the process. They have compared small groups of children at different levels of proficiency, have studied children over time to see how the reading process changes, have looked at some phenomena such as substitutions and transformations in considerable depth. Continuing research aims at understanding the full range of variation in the operation of the reading process and of the strategies that readers use.

Reading has been focussed on, but analysis of reading miscues offers some interesting possibilities for linguistic and psycholinguistic research in general. Such analysis, for instance, utilizes natural language rather than contrived quasi-linguistic tasks. It also provides an expectation model (the ER) with which to contrast the actual performance of the subject (the OR). It can make possible the more scientific use of reading tasks in psychological, linguistic, and psycholinguistic research. Ironically, use of the reading tasks in such research is quite common, but the influence of the task on the results has frequently been ignored. Reconsideration of the results of such research and replication of the research may throw considerable new light on the findings.

Though the current analysis is complex and time consuming, limited application of the concepts and insights involved may provide new classroom and clinical diagnostic procedures. Y. Goodman and Burke (1969) have already suggested an informal classroom procedure based on the taxonomy.

The descriptive research now being carried out hopefully will generate hypotheses about the reading process that can be empirically tested and lead to new insights into methods and materials for reading instruction.

Ultimately, the test of the value of this research, like all reading research, is in the contribution it makes to more effective learning of reading.

REFERENCES

Allen, P. (1969), A Psycholinguistic Analysis of the Substitution of Miscues of Selected Oral Readers in Grades 3, 4 and 6, and the Relationships of these Miscues to Reading Process, a Descriptive Study, unpublished doctoral dissertation, Wayne State University.

Betts, E.A., and Carolyn M. Welch (1963), 'The ABC up the Street and Down' 3rd ed., Betts Basic Readers, The Language Arts Series, American Book Company, New York.

Bloomfield, L., and C. Barnhart (1963), 'Let's Read Series,' C.L. Barnhart, Bronxville, New York.

Bormuth, J.R. (1966), Readability: a New Approach, 'Reading Research Quarterly,' vol.1, no.3, pp.79-132.

Burke, Carolyn L. (1969), A Psycholinguistic Description of Grammatical Re-structuring in the Oral Reading of a Selected Group of Middle School Children, unpublished doctoral dissertation, Wayne State University.

Chall, Jeanne (1967), 'Reading: the Great Debate,' McGraw-Hill, New York.

Clay, Marie M. (1966), Emergent Reading Behavior, unpublished doctoral dissertation, University of Auckland, New Zealand.

Clymer, T. (1968), What Is 'Reading'?: Some Current Concepts, in Helen M. Robinson (ed.), Innovation and Change in Reading Instruction, 'Yearbook of the National Society for the Study of Education,' vol.67, part II, pp.7-29.

Fries, C.C. (1964), 'Linguistics and Reading,' Holt, Rinehart, & Winston, New York.

Gephart, W. (1969), Application of the Convergence Technique to Reading, 'Occasional Paper No.4, Phi Delta Kappa,' January.

Goodman, K.S. (1965), A Linguistic Study of Cues and Miscues in Reading, 'Elementary English Journal,' vol.42, pp.39-44.

Goodman, K.S. (1967a), 'The Psycholinguistic Nature of the Reading Process,' Wayne State University Press, Detroit.

Goodman, K.S. (1967b), Reading: a Psycholinguistic Guessing Game, 'Journal of the Reading Specialist,' vol.4, pp.126-35.

Goodman, K.S., and C. Burke (1968), 'Study of Children's Behavior while Reading Orally,' (Report of Project No.5425), United States Department of Health, Education, and Welfare.

Goodman, Yetta M. (1967), A Psycholinguistic Description of Observed Oral Reading Phenomena in Selected Beginning Readers, unpublished doctoral dissertation, Wayne State University.

Goodman, Yetta M., and C. Burke (1969), Do They Read what They Speak? 'The Grade Teacher,' vol.86, pp.144-50.

Halle, M. (1969), Some Thoughts on Spelling, in K. Goodman and J. Fleming (eds), 'Psycholinguistics and the Teaching of Reading,' International Reading Association, Newark, Delaware.

Holmes, J.A. (1965), Basic Assumptions Underlying the Substrata-factor Theory, 'Reading Research Quarterly,' vol.1, no.1, pp.4-28.

Hunt, K. (1965), Grammatical Structures Written at Three Grade Levels, 'National Council of Teachers of English Research Report,' no.3.

Kolers, P.A. (1969), Reading is Only Incidentally Visual, in K. Goodman and J. Fleming (eds), 'Psycholinguistics and the Teaching of Reading,' International Reading Association, Newark, Delaware.

Lefevre, C.A. (1964), 'Linguistics and the Teaching of Reading,' McGraw-Hill, New York.

Loban, W.D. (1963), The Language of Elementary School Children, 'National Council of English Research Report,' no.1.

McCullough, Constance M. (1967), Linguistics, Psychology, and the Teaching of Reading, 'Elementary English,' vol.44, no.4, pp.353-62.

Project Literacy Reports (1964-6), Project Literacy, Cornell University, Ithaca, New York, nos.1-8.

Robinson, Helen M. (1968), The Next Decade, in Helen M. Robinson (ed.), Innovation and Change in Reading Instruction, 'Yearbook of the National Society for the Study of Education,' vol.67, part II, pp.397-430.

Spache, G.D. (1964), 'Reading in the Elementary School,' Allyn & Bacon, Boston.

Strickland, Ruth G. (1962), The Language of Elementary School Children: Its Relation to the Language of Reading of Selected Children, 'Bulletin of the School of Education,' Indiana University, vol.40, no.4.

Venezky, R. (1967), English Orthography: Its Graphic Structure and Its Relation to Sound, 'Reading Research Quarterly,' vol.2, no.3, pp.74-106.

Weber, Rose-Marie (1967), Errors in First Grade Reading, unpublished manuscript, Cornell University Library.

Weber, Rose-Marie (1968), The Study of Oral Reading Errors: a Survey of the Literature, 'Reading Research Quarterly,' vol.4, pp.96-119.

> The reader is constantly predicting what he will encounter and hypothesizing what syntactic pattern he is dealing with as he reads. He must do this in order to be able to make use of new perceptual information and get to meaning. If something, however fuzzy, in the peripheral field fits the prediction and the hypothetical syntactic pattern, the reader may use it. Perception, hypothesis, and prediction are operating together.

This is the essential explanation that Goodman offers for the phenomena of miscues involving the substitution or insertion of words in the surrounding text, that is in the visual periphery.

Most of the research done by Goodman and his colleagues has been reported only in lengthy technical reports. This chapter extracts the evidence from the research on this one phenomenon: influence of peripheral field.

13 INFLUENCES OF THE VISUAL PERIPHERAL FIELD*

Teachers and others have often noted a tendency for readers to pull words from the adjacent text into their oral reading. Such phenomena appear to indicate that the reader is influenced as he processes written language for meaning either by graphic images which are at places in his visual field other than at the point of focus or by memory of what he has already seen before the current point of focus.

When someone reads, his eyes must stop and fix at points along the printed line in order for the graphic display to be in focus. At the point of fixation there is a small area of sharp focus surrounded by a larger area which is out of focus to various degrees but still seen. It is this surrounding area which is the peripheral visual field.

If, as some people believe, reading involves the processing of print in an orderly sequence with words being processed one by one as the reader meets them on the line, then the peripheral field would have little effect on reading. Only an occasional miscue might appear from the peripheral field *if* the reader loses his place or his eyes wander in some random direction.

But reading is a sampling, selecting, predicting, comparing and confirming activity in which the reader selects a sample of useful graphic cues based on what he sees and what he expects to see. The graphic symbols are not processed one by one or in a strictly serial manner. Rather the reader samples from the print on the basis of predictions he has made as he seeks meaning. As a result it is not surprising that graphic information which is often appropriate to the reader's prediction is sometimes pulled in from the peripheral field.

Miscues, points in oral reading where observed responses do not match expected responses, result when the reader has used cues in the peripheral visual field. As we shall demonstrate with research data this is not a simple case of miscue of graphic information in the peripheral field causing the miscues. They are, like all miscues, products of the reading process. The reader makes predictions based on his search for

*This article is based on Goodman, K.S., and Burke, Carolyn, 'Theoretically Based Studies of Patterns of Miscues in Oral Reading Performance,' USOE Project No.9-0375. Points of view or opinions stated do not necessarily represent official Office of Education position or policy.

meaning and his assumptions of grammatical structures. When he uses peripheral graphic cues it often is because the information fits his expectation.

In this article the influence of the peripheral visual field on oral reading is examined. The data for the examination comes from an extensive study of oral reading miscues. In the larger research, oral reading of second-, fourth-, sixth-, eighth-, and tenth-grade pupils was tape recorded. At each grade, three or four groups at different proficiency levels were included. Each group read a story appropriately difficult for them. The miscues the subjects produced were examined in depth. Only the aspects that relate to peripheral field influences are reported here.

THE PERIPHERAL FIELD

We can imagine the peripheral visual field as a series of ovals around the point of focus. Since print is arranged horizontally the ovals are flattened at the top and bottom because the reader is less likely to be influenced by images on the vertical axis of his visual field. Figure 13.1 illustrates such a view of the peripheral field. The inner circle includes the area which is in relatively sharp focus. The next circle out, which includes a large proportion of the line above and below the point of focus, is less clearly seen. It can be called the near periphery. The second circle out includes major portions of the text, two lines above and below the focal point.

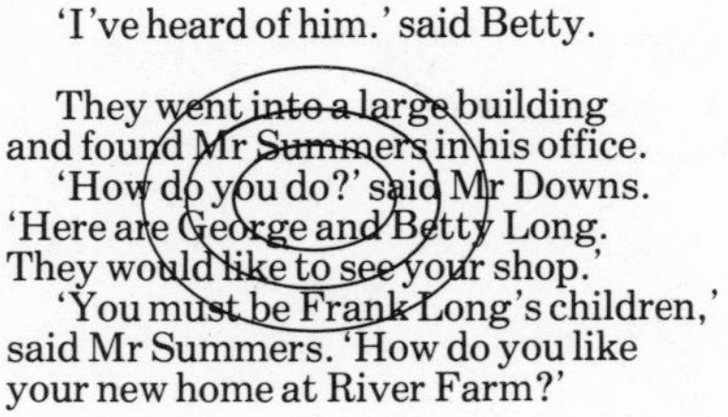

'I've heard of him.' said Betty.

They went into a large building
and found Mr Summers in his office.
'How do you do?' said Mr Downs.
'Here are George and Betty Long.
They would like to see your shop.'
'You must be Frank Long's children,'
said Mr Summers. 'How do you like
your new home at River Farm?'

Figure 13.1 Peripheral field model

In our research we search the peripheral field within these concentric circles for words which match words which are substituted or inserted by readers. The miscues which may potentially involve peripheral field influences are only a portion of the whole, however. Omissions and complex miscues which involve several words are among those not considered for peripheral visual influences. We use a computer program to search the text in the peripheral field. Because of limitations of this program we have redefined the peripheral field as the line in which a word occurs and the two lines above and below. Figure 13.2 shows the redefined categories.

The computer first searches the line on which the miscue is located. This is treated as the area of relatively sharp focus. If the computer fails to find a matching word in the sharp focus, the computer checks the line above and below, the near periphery. If no match is found here the computer checks the second line above and below, the far periphery.

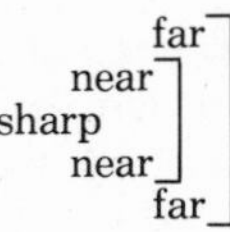

looking at the stores and buildings. — far
When they came to the workshops, — near
the busman let them off. — sharp
'Here we are,' said Mr Downs. — near
'Mr Summers runs this shop. — far

Figure 13.2 Peripheral field categories

Here are some examples of peripheral field miscues:

They
1 'What are *they*?' asked Sue, ...

We
2 ... as *we* are. They know reck-
3 ... *said* Mrs Duck.
Said
'My new hat is at the house.

In the first example 'they,' which occurs in the same line, is substituted for 'what.' Example 2 shows 'we' substituted for 'they.' In example 3 'said,' found in the line above, is substituted for 'my.'

There is some distortion in our procedure in dealing with whole lines since we cannot consider the absolute distance of the matching words.

the
4 ... standing on a rock in *the* rose garden.
'It's *the* best picture I ever saw!'
5 ... back upstairs. Pulling *the* kitchen stepladder out into
the
the hall and climbing up on it, he found *the* transom...

In examples 4 and 5 the substitution is 'the.' It is found in the text twice in both examples at varying distance but is counted as sharp periphery in both cases since the word on the same line as the miscue is found first by our procedure.

Another limitation of our procedure is that it only counts exact matches and cannot deal with partial matches such as inflections of the same word. It somewhat underestimates the total peripheral effect.

pieced
7 ...and carefully placed the pieces of glass inside.

The word 'pieces' is in the same line in example 7 but is not found because it is not an exact match.

The lines above and below the line in which the Expected Response (ER) word is found are as likely to contain a word which matches the Observed Response (OR) as is the line in which the ER occurs. Since there are two lines in this *near* area the percents tend to be double that of the single line in the sharp focus area. Table 13.1 shows these percents with the groups in the study arranged in the approximate order of ascending proficiency.

Table 13.1 Percent of miscues in each peripheral area

				Far		Near			Total
Grade	Proficiency level	Story*	Not found	Total	Per line	Total	Per line	Sharp	Total percent in periphery
2	L	22/24 (P)	73.3%	5.6%	2.8%	17.8%	8.9%	3.3%	26.7
4	L	26/28 (1)	83.9	6.1	3.1	7.7	3.9	2.3	16.1
2	LA	44 (2)	77.4	8.5	4.3	10.2	5.1	3.9	22.6
6	L	47 (3)	85.9	3.1	1.6	5.8	2.9	5.2	14.1
2	HA	47	76.4	4.6	2.3	9.7	4.9	9.3	23.6
4	A	51 (4)	82.7	5.7	2.9	6.5	3.3	5.1	17.3
2	H	51	71.9	8.4	4.2	10.7	5.4	9.0	28.1
8	L	53 (6)	77.2	4.1	2.1	11.3	5.7	7.4	22.8
4	H	53	74.6	3.9	2.0	14.1	7.1	7.3	25.4
6	A	53	75.9	5.1	2.6	11.9	6.0	7.1	24.1
10	L	59 (8)	89.4	2.3	1.2	5.2	2.6	3.1	10.6
8	A	59	74.6	6.7	3.4	9.7	4.9	9.0	25.4
6	H	59	78.2	5.8	2.9	10.8	5.4	5.3	21.8
10	LA	60**	77.0	5.2	2.6	12.6	6.3	5.2	23.0
10	HA	60	71.4	7.8	3.9	12.3	6.2	8.4	28.6
8	H	60	67.5	8.0	4.0	14.3	7.2	10.3	32.5
10	H	60	66.1	7.0	3.5	17.2	8.6	9.7	33.9
10	L	61***	90.4	2.8	1.4	4.1	2.1	2.6	9.6
10	LA	61	87.1	3.5	1.8	7.1	3.6	2.4	12.9
10	HA	61	81.0	5.6	2.8	9.1	4.6	4.3	19.0
8	H	61	81.2	3.3	1.7	12.2	6.1	3.3	18.0
10	H	61	82.1	2.5	1.3	13.0	6.5	2.5	17.9

* Numbers are assigned to each story. Figure in parentheses is the intended level of difficulty.
** Story 60 is an adult short story.
*** Story 61 is an adult essay.

The far periphery seems to exert about half as much influence as the sharp and near periphery areas. The percent for the two lines in the *far* area are about half those for *near* and about equal the single sharp focus line.

The three lowest proficiency groups (2 low, 4 low, 2 low average) show relatively more spread of influence, the sharp area percent is relatively low and in the cases of 4L and 2LA readers the far periphery is almost as influential as the near. Two reasons may exist for this apparent greater use of the whole periphery. It may in fact show the inefficiency of the readers in using the most useful graphic information in their reading. But it may also reflect the limited controlled vocabulary of these beginning basal reader materials. With a small vocabulary the chance of a particular word being in adjacent lines is comparatively high.

Readers of the third- and fourth-grade stories (stories 51 and 53) show a relatively stronger influence of the sharp focus line. It is nearly as likely to contain a match for the OR as the two near periphery lines together. Perhaps we see here a 'zeroing in' phase, a period in which the reader is concentrating his attention more deliberately on what is in sharper focus. With both stories note, however, that the younger more proficient group in each pair (2HA for story 47 and 2H for story 51) have higher percents of related miscues with peripheral field involvement than the less proficient groups (6L and 4A).

Starting with readers of the sixth-grade story (53) the groups all tend to show the pattern of the three lines in sharp and near focus exerting about equal influence. For average eighth- and tenth-grade readers (8A, 10LA, 10HA) of stories 59 and 60 the sharp focus line shows disproportionately high tendencies to contain an OR match. Perhaps again this indicates that average, as compared to the poorer and better readers, are the more 'careful.'

Our computer program does not distinguish between those near and far area OR matching words which are above and those which are below the line of the ER. We analyzed one story, the sixth-grade story 53, manually to see if there were any important differences between the upper and lower halves of the peripheral field. In the reading of this story a match for the OR word was found in the line above 131 times and in the line below 90 times. In 54 cases the match was in the second line above and 42 times in the second line below. This apparent greater tendency to be influenced by the field above than below may result from two factors:

1 Retention in memory of graphic cues which are processed later at points where they are likely to occur.

2 Greater attention to and use of the upper part of the visual field. Perhaps these work in combination. Memory pulls the reader's attention back to previously seen cues.

PERIPHERAL INFLUENCES AS PROFICIENCY INCREASES

Low proficiency groups in all grades, with the exception of the second, show a tendency for lower percentages of their miscues to involve the peripheral field than average and high groups. Low tenth graders read two stories (59 and 61) with about 10 per cent peripheral field involvement on each. Average and high groups tend to be more consistent within a narrow range around 25 per cent of miscues with peripheral involvement. An exception is the average fourth-graders who have only 17 per cent miscues with peripheral involvement.

An interesting contrast is provided by the groups that read both the adult short story (60) and the more difficult adult essay (61). In all cases the percent of miscues with peripheral cue involvement was almost double for the easier story (60). This, together with the tendency for more proficient readers of other stories (47, 51, 59) to produce higher percent of miscues involving peripheral cues, suggests that better readers are more likely to be influenced by peripheral visual cues.

Actually, however, the percentages exaggerate the picture. The frequency of miscues (our measure is MPHW- miscues per hundred words) tends to decrease as proficiency increases and to increase as difficulty increases. We calculated, therefore, the Peripheral Field Miscues Per Hundred Words (PFM-PHW) for each group.

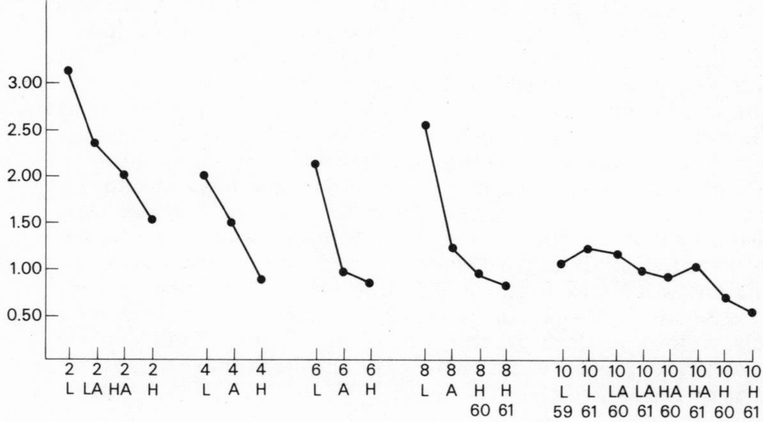

Figure 13.3 Peripheral field miscues per hundred words

Figure 13.3 shows that in fact there is a steady drop in relative frequency of peripherally involved miscues as proficiency increases. What this means is that peripheral field cues are a relatively stable factor within a decreasing tendency to produce miscues. Since other factors contributing to miscues drop off sharply as proficiency increases, the percent of miscues for more proficient readers of a particular story tends to be relatively high. The same is true with more difficult material. Readers will produce more miscues involving other factors so a smaller percentage will show peripheral involvement.

Table 13.2, using the three fourth-grade groups, illustrates these phenomena.

For the low group which has 12.45 miscues per hundred words, 16.1 per cent of these 12.45 miscues (or 2.00 MPHW) are miscues from the peripheral field. Whereas for the high group there are only 3.63 miscues per hundred words but 25.3 per cent of those (or .92) are miscues from the peripheral field. Even though the percent of peripheral field miscues increases (16.1 per cent - 25.3 per cent) the actual frequency of PF miscues decreases (2.00-.92).

Table 13.2 Peripheral field miscues and MPHW of fourth grade

Group	MPHW	PFM	PFMPHW
4L	12.45	16.1	2.00
4A	8.61	17.3	1.49
4H	3.63	25.3	.92

SUBSTITUTIONS AND INSERTIONS

So far we have looked mainly at quantitative aspects of peripheral cuing of miscues. Now we can examine the quality and effects of those miscues. Peripheral cues may be involved in substitutions of words in the peripheral field for other words or the insertion of such peripherally seen words at unexpected places.

Figure 13.4 shows the percentages of substitution and of insertion miscues where the OR matches a word in the peripheral field. For all groups except low second grade a much higher percent of matches for insertion miscues are found in the peripheral field than for substitutions.

While the percent of substitution miscues with peripheral visual cuing ranges between 15 per cent and 25 per cent for most groups the percent of insertion miscues involving peripheral cues is at or over 50 per cent for most groups.

Word insertions are not nearly as frequent for any group of readers in the study as are word substitutions. Substitutions constitute 52 per cent to 86 per cent of word level miscues for the groups in the study while insertions range from 1.5 per cent to 19 per cent. More proficient groups within each grade show higher percents of insertions and lower percents of substitutions than less proficient groups. These frequency comparisons make it remarkably clear that insertions are very likely to involve peripheral cuing.

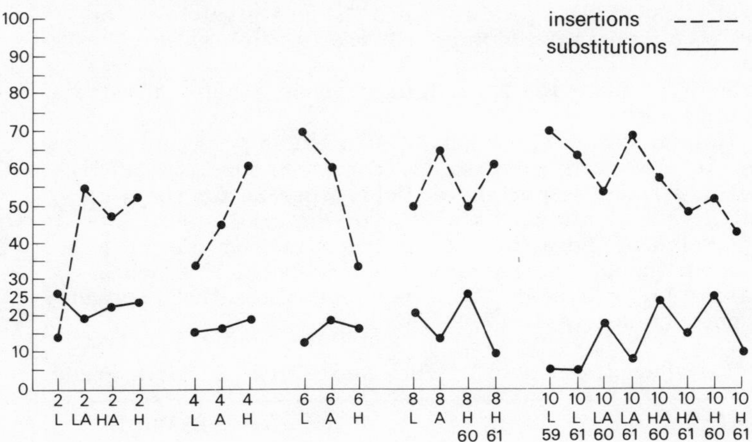

Figure 13.4 Peripheral field influence: substitutions and insertions

It is not hard to see how these insertion miscues use the peripheral cues. The reader is constantly predicting what he will encounter and hypothesizing what syntactic patterns he is dealing with as he reads. He must do this in order to be able to make use of new perceptual information and get to meaning. If something, however fuzzy, in the peripheral field fits the prediction and the hypothetical syntactic pattern, the reader may use it. Perception, hypothesis, and prediction are operating together. The apparently more accurate reading of the more proficient reader may in fact be due to more successful prediction and hypothesizing rather than more careful use of visual information.

WHAT KINDS OF WORDS ARE INVOLVED?

If the miscues that involve peripheral visual cues were simply the result of the processing of the wrong cues or cues out of sequence, any words would be as likely to be involved as any other that occurred in the text with the same frequency. We would expect nouns, verbs, adjectives, adverbs, and function words to appear about as frequently among peripheral field involved miscues as they do in the running text. If on the other hand factors such as those we have suggested influence the use of peripheral cues then a different pattern would emerge.

We can examine these propositions by looking at the involvement of function words among the miscues with peripheral cues. Such words are few in number but make up a very large proportion of the running text of written English including the stories used in our study.

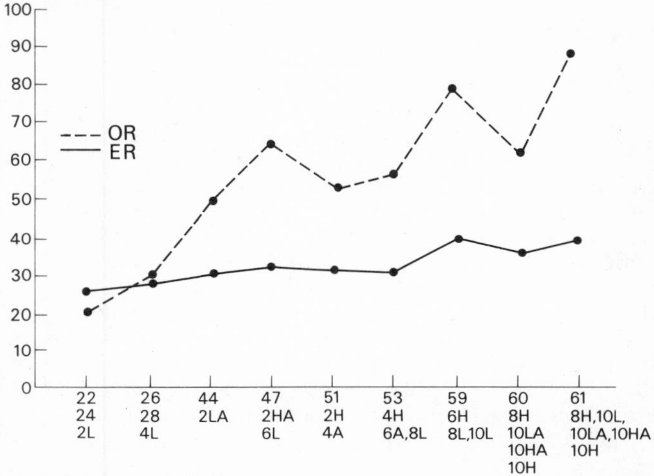

Figure 13.5 Percent of ER function words in stories and percent of OR function word miscues from peripheral field

Figure 13.5 shows the percent of all words in the stories which are function words and the percent of function word ORs among the miscues involving peripheral cues produced by all readers of each story. While the percent of text function words increases slightly in successively more advanced stories, the percent of peripheral field miscues involving function words increases dramatically. Low second-graders have somewhat lower occurrences of function words in these miscues than occur in the stories they read. Low fourth-graders produce such miscues on a par with function word frequency in the stories.

But in all groups other than these two lowest proficiency groups, function words occur far more frequently among peripheral field miscues than in the stories. Often the percent of such miscues is double their rate in the story. In story 61, the adult essay, with 39 per cent function words, 87 per cent of the miscues with peripheral field cues involve function words. Non-function words conversely are less likely to be involved in miscues with peripheral cues. They make up 61 per cent of the running text yet only 11 per cent of such miscues in the reading of story 61.

This spectacular involvement of function words among miscues with peripheral cuing is related to the strong tendency for insertions to have peripheral cues. The majority of these insertions are function words.

Often the inserted function words are optional elements the author has not used. The following examples show the insertion of a function word which is present at the deep structure level of the ER but not at the surface level.

8 At *that* moment we
that
both thought he had been bitten and...
the
9 a lucky few can climb into lifeboats and survive...

A few function words like 'the' occur so frequently in the running text that the chance of it being found in any five line sequence is quite high. It is possible then that for some of the insertions and substitutions of function words the peripheral occurrence of a matching word is coincidental, and not really involved. Another possibility however is that almost every time a reader predicts such a word he finds it someplace in the visual field and uses it.

One reader in our average eighth grade group made frequent miscues involving 'the' and 'and.' Of 52 peripheral field involved miscues he had 16 insertions of 'the' and 14 insertions of 'and.'

the
10 ...and built fires on high points...
the the
11 Herder and dog stopped...
and a
12 ...at his throat the tendon above
and
13 When it became quiet...

Notice in these examples that the inserted elements are grammatically optional and have little or no effect on meaning.

Less proficient readers produce a higher proportion of miscues with peripheral visual cues which alter or disrupt meaning and which may interfere with the reader getting the grammatical pattern. About half of the peripherally involved miscues of one low proficiency reader were substitutions with changed grammatical function. He also substituted pronouns which involved changing number or person.

Here are some examples of this low proficiency reader's miscues:

him
14 As the lady led me...
He
15 We could put it...
A
16 As little brothers go...

now
17 ...be better not to have a contest.
our
18 ...came to the house.

A low proficiency sixth-grade reader produces these miscues with peripheral cues:

to
19 Billy liked the winter, too.
his was then
20 ...he and the fawn would race together through...
e their
21 ...house was done they built one for...
the for of
22 At this season of the year all the...

Care needs to be taken in assigning cause-effect relationships however. The reading process requires the reader to use graphic cues within the context of a predicted grammatical structure and his expectations of elements. Reading is trying to make sense out of written language. One cannot, therefore, say that these less efficient and effective readers are losing meaning because they are misusing peripheral visual cues. Rather the miscues they produce are symptomatic of a more basic difficulty in controlling the process to get to the meaning with the least amount of effort and confusion. All readers are likely to be influenced by the peripheral visual field. Less proficient readers are less able to screen the peripheral cues in relation to the pattern and meaning. Admonishing such readers to be more careful may produce greater word for word accuracy but it is unlikely to improve their comprehension, because it is their difficulty in making sense out of the reading which is revealed by disruptive miscues. Care with the pieces may mean greater loss of the sense of the whole.

The individuals in our study in average and low proficiency groups who show the lowest percentage of miscues with peripheral cues are those with the highest proportion of miscues which disrupt the meaning.

SUMMARY

All readers produce observed responses which match words graphically in the visual peripheral field. Readers in higher grades and groups of higher proficiency in the same grades tend to show a higher percentage of such miscues. However, because MPHW drops with greater proficiency the actual frequency of peripheral field miscues declines at the same time that percentage increases.

This seems to show that the tendency to be influenced by

the graphic display in the visual peripheral field remains relatively constant as proficiency increases, while other factors contributing to miscues diminish so that this factor emerges as a more significant contributor to miscues. This becomes evident when upper grade readers of two stories show more peripheral field miscues in the easier story.

Insertions are very likely to be influenced by peripheral graphic cues, much more so than substitutions. This is increasingly true as proficiency increases. These insertions are very largely composed of function words which are often optional elements in the deep structure. Function word miscues are much more likely to involve the peripheral field than non-function words.

We can conclude that the influence of cues in the visual peripheral field is not a random one. Words are not likely to be pulled in from the peripheral field unless they fit in some ways with the semantic and syntactic cues the reader is processing and the predictions he is making.

> Sooner or later all attempts to understand language - its development and its function as the medium of communication - must confront linguistic reality. Theories, models, grammars, and research paradigms must predict and explain what people do when they use language and what makes it possible for them to do so. Researchers have contrived ingenious ways to make a small bit of linguistic or psycholinguistic reality available for examination. But then what they see is often out of focus, distorted by the design. Our approach makes fully available the reality of the miscues readers produce as they orally read whole, natural, and meaningful texts.

The message of this article, co-authored with Yetta Goodman and addressed to all those who study language, is that the study of oral reading miscues provides a unique window on cognitive and psycholinguistic processes because there is a continuous expectation, the predicted response to the text, to compare the actual response with. We can, through miscues, study language and thought *in process*.

14 LEARNING ABOUT PSYCHOLINGUISTIC PROCESSES BY ANALYZING ORAL READING

with Yetta M. Goodman

Over the past dozen years we have studied the reading process by analyzing the miscues (or unexpected responses) of subjects reading written texts. We prefer to use the word 'miscue' because the term 'error' has a negative connotation and history in education. Our analysis of oral reading miscues began with the foundational assumption that reading is a language process. Everything we have observed among readers from beginners to those with great proficiency supports the validity of this assumption. This analysis of miscues has been in turn the base for our development of a theory and model of the reading process.

In this paper we will argue that the analysis of oral reading offers unique opportunities for the study of linguistic and psycholinguistic processes and phenomena. We will support this contention by citing some concepts and principles that have grown out of our research.

We believe that reading is as much a language process as listening is. In a literate society there are four language processes: two are oral (speaking and listening), and two are written (writing and reading). Two are productive and two receptive. In the study and observation of productive language, we may analyze what subjects say or write; however, except for an occasional slip of the tongue, typographical error, or regression to rephrase, speech and writing offer no direct insight into the underlying process of what the speaker or writer intended to say. The study of receptive language - listening and reading - is even more difficult. Either we analyze postlistening or postreading performance, or we contrive controlled-language tasks to elicit reactions for analysis.

Reading aloud, on the other hand, involves the oral response of the reader, which can be compared to the written text. Oral readers are engaged in comprehending written language while they produce oral responses. Because an oral response is generated while meaning is being constructed, it not only is a form of linguistic performance but also provides a powerful means of examining process and underlying competence.

Consider how Peggy, a nine-year-old from Toronto, reads aloud. Peggy was chosen by her teacher as an example of a pupil reading substantially below grade level. The story she read was considered to be beyond her current instructional level. Peggy read the story hesitantly, although in places she read with appropriate expression. Below are the first fourteen sentences (S1-S14) from The Man Who Kept House (1964, pp.282-3). In this and other excerpts from the story the printed text is on the left; on the right is the transcript of Peggy's oral reading.

text	transcript
(S1a) Once upon a time there was a woodman who thought that no one worked as hard as he did.	(S1b) Once upon a time there was a woodman. He threw...who thought that no one worked as hard as he did.
(S2a) One evening when he came home from work, he said to his wife, 'What do you do all day while I am away cutting wood?'	(S2b) One evening when he ...when he came home from work, he said to his wife 'I want you do all day... what do you do all day when I am always cutting wood?'
(S3a) 'I keep house,' replied the wife, 'and keeping house is hard work.'	(S3b) 'I keep...I keep house,' replied the wife, 'and keeping...and keeping...and keeping house is and work.'
(S4a) 'Hard work!' said the husband.	(S4b) 'Hard work!' said the husband.
(S5a) 'You don't know what hard work is!	(S5b) 'You don't know what hard work is!
(S6a) You should try cutting wood!'	(S6b) You should try cutting wood!'
(S7a) 'I'd be glad to,' said the wife.	(S7b) 'I'll be glad to,' said the wife.
(S8a) 'Why don't you do my work some day?	(S8b) 'Why don't you...Why don't you do my work so... some day?
(S9a) 'I'll stay home and keep house,' said the woodman.	(S9b) I'll start house and keeping house,' said the woodman.
(S10a) 'If you stay home to do my work, you'll have to make butter, carry water from the well, wash the clothes, clean the house, and look after the baby,' said the wife.	(S10b) 'If you start house... If you start home to do my work, well you'll have to make bread, carry...carry water from the well, wash the clothes, clean the house, and look after the baby,' said the wife.
(S11a) 'I can do all that,' replied the husband.	(S11b) 'I can do that...I can do all that,' replied the husband.
(S12a) 'We'll do it tomorrow!'	(S12b) 'Well you do it tomorrow!'
(S13a) So the next morning the wife went off to the forest.	(S13b) So the next day the wife went off to the forest.

(S14a) The husband stayed home and began to do his wife's work.	(S14b) The husband stayed home and began to do his wife's job.

Peggy's performance allows us to see a language user as a functional psycholinguist. Peggy's example is not unusual; what she does is also done by other readers. She processes graphic information: many of her miscues show a graphic relationship between the expected and observed response. She processes syntactic information: she substitutes noun for noun, verb for verb, noun phrase for noun phrase, verb phrase for verb phrase. She transforms: she omits an intensifier, changes a dependent clause to an independent clause, shifts a 'wh-' question sentence to a declarative sentence. She draws on her conceptual background and struggles toward meaning, repeating, correcting, and reprocessing as necessary. She predicts grammar and meaning and monitors her own success. She builds and uses psycholinguistic strategies as she reads. In short, her miscues are far from random.

From such data one can build and test theories of syntax, semantics, cognition, comprehension, memory, language development, linguistic competence, and linguistic performance. In oral reading all the phenomena of other language processes are present or have their counterparts, but in oral reading they are accessible. The data are not controlled and clean in the experimental sense. Even young readers are not always very considerate. They do complex things for which we may be unprepared; and, not having studied the latest theories, they do not always produce confirming evidence. But they are language users in action.

MISCUES AND COMPREHENSION

If we understand that the brain is the organ of human information processing, that the brain is not a prisoner of the senses but that it controls the sensory organs and selectively uses their input, then we should not be surprised that what the mouth reports in oral reading is not what the eye has seen but what the brain has generated for the mouth to report. The text is what the brain responds to; the oral output reflects the underlying competence and the psycholinguistic processes that have generated it. When expected and observed responses match, we get little insight into this process. When they do not match and a miscue results, the researcher has a window on the reading process.

Just as psycholinguists have been able to learn about the development of oral-language competence by observing the errors of young children, so we can gain insights into the development of reading competence and the control of the underlying psycholinguistic processes by studying reading miscues.

We assume that both expected and unexpected oral responses to printed texts are produced through the same process. Thus, just as a three-year-old reveals the use of a rule for generating past tense by producing 'throwed' for 'threw' (Brown, 1973), so Peggy reveals her control of the reading process through her miscues.

We use two measures of readers' proficiency: *comprehending*, which shows the readers' concern for meaning as expressed through their miscues, and *retelling*, which shows the readers' retention of meaning. Proficient readers can usually retell a great deal of a story, and they produce miscues that do not interfere with gaining meaning. Except for S3, S8 and S9, all of Peggy's miscues produced fully acceptable sentences or were self-corrected. This suggests that Peggy's usual concern was to make sense as she read. In contrast, many nonproficient readers produce miscues that interfere with getting meaning from the story. In a real sense, then, a goal of reading instruction is not to eliminate miscues but to help readers produce the kind of miscues that characterize proficient reading.

Miscues reflect the degree to which a reader is understanding and seeking meaning. Insight can be gained into the reader's development of meaning and the reading process as a whole if miscues are examined and researchers ask: 'Why did the reader make this miscue and to what extent is it like the language of the author?'

Miscue analysis requires several conditions. The written material must be new to the readers and complete with a beginning, middle, and end. The text needs to be long and difficult enough to produce a sufficient number of miscues. In addition, readers must receive no help, probe, or intrusion from the researcher. At most, if readers hesitate for more than thirty seconds, they are urged to guess, and only if hesitation continues are they told to keep reading even if it means skipping a word or phrase. Miscue analysis, in short, requires as natural a reading situation as possible.

Depending on the purpose of the research, subjects often have been provided with more than one reading task. Various fiction and nonfiction reading materials have been used, including stories and articles from basal readers, textbooks, trade books, and magazines. Subjects have been drawn from various levels in elementary, secondary, and adult populations and from a wide range of racial, linguistic, and national backgrounds. Studies have been concluded in languages other than English: Yiddish (Hodes, 1976), Polish (Romatowski, 1972), and American Sign Language (Ewoldt, 1977). Studies in German and Spanish are in progress.

The open-ended retellings used in miscue analysis are an index of comprehension. They also provide an opportunity for the researcher or teacher to gain insight into how concepts and language are actively used and developed in reading. Rather than asking direct questions that would give cues to the reader about what is significant in the story, we ask for unaided retelling. Information on the readers' understanding of the text emerges from the organization they use in retelling the story, from whether they use the author's language or their own, and from the conceptions or misconceptions they reveal. Here is the first segment of Peggy's retelling:

> um...it was about this woodman and um...when he...he thought that he um...he had harder work to do than his wife. So he went home and he told his wife, 'What have you been doing all day.' And then his wife told him. And then, um...and then, he thought that it was easy work. And so...so...so his wife, so his wife, so she um...so the wife said, 'well so you have to keep,' no...the husband says that you have to go to the woods and cut...and have to go out in the forest and cut wood and I'll stay home. And the next day they did that.

By comparing the story with Peggy's retelling and her miscues, researchers may interpret how much learning occurs as Peggy and the author interact. For example, although the story frequently uses 'woodman' and 'to cut wood,' the noun used to refer to setting, 'forest,' is used just twice. Not only did Peggy provide evidence in her retelling that she knew that 'woods' and 'forest' are synonymous, but she also indicated that she knew the author's choice was 'forest.' The maze she worked through until she came to the author's term suggests that she was searching for the author's language. Although in much of the work on oral-language analysis mazes are not analyzed, their careful study may provide insight into oral self-correction and the speaker's intention.

There is more evidence of Peggy's awareness of the author's language. In the story the woodman is referred to as 'woodman' and 'husband' eight times each and as 'man' four times; the wife is referred to only as 'wife.' Otherwise pronouns are used to refer to the husband and wife. In the retelling Peggy used 'husband' and 'woodman' six times and 'man' only once; she called the wife only 'wife.' Peggy always used appropriate pronouns in referring to the husband and wife. However, when cow was the antecedent, she substituted 'he' for 'she' twice. (What does Peggy know about the sex of cattle?)

Comparing Peggy's miscues with her retelling gives us more information about her language processes. In reading, Peggy indicated twice that 'said' suggested to her that a declarative statement should follow: One such miscue was presented above (see S2); the other occurred at the end of the story and is recorded below.

text	transcript
(S66a) Never again did the woodman say to his wife,	(S66b) Never again did the woodman say to his wife,

'What did you do all day?'	'That he...what did you do all day?'

In both instances she corrected the miscues. In the retelling she indicated that after 'said' she could produce a question: 'And then, from then on, the husband did...did the cutting and he never said, "What have you been doing all day?"' Even though she had difficulty with the 'wh-' question structure in her reading, she was able to develop the language knowledge necessary to produce such a structure in her retelling.

It has puzzled teachers for a long time how a reader can know something in one context but not know it in another context. Such confusion comes from the belief that reading is word recognition; on the contrary, words in different syntactic and semantic contexts become different entities for readers, and Peggy's response to 'keep house' suggests this. In S3, where the clauses 'I keep house' and later 'and keeping house' occur for the first time, Peggy produced the appropriate responses but repeated each several times. In S9 she produced 'stay home and keep house' as 'start house and keeping house,' and she read the first phrase in S10 as 'If you start home to do my work.' The phrase 'keep house' is a complex one. First, to a nine-year-old 'keep' is a verb that means being able to hold on to or take care of something small. Although 'keeping pets' is still used to mean taking care of, 'keeping house' is no longer a common idiom in American or Canadian English. When 'stay home' is added to the phrase 'keep house,' additional complexities arise. Used with different verbs and different function words, 'home' and 'house' are sometimes synonyms and sometimes not. The transitive and intransitive nature of the verbs as well as the infinitive structure, which is not in the surface of a sentence, add to the complexity of the verb phrase.

Peggy, in her search for meaning and her interaction with the print, continued to develop strategies to handle these complex problems. In S14 she produced 'stayed home'; however, in S35 she encountered difficulty with 'keeping house' once again and read: 'perhaps keeping house...home and... is...hard work.' She was still not happy with 'keeping house.' She read the phrase as written and then abandoned her correct response. Throughout the story 'home' appears seven times and 'house' appears ten times. Peggy read them correctly in every context except in the patterns 'staying home' and 'keeping house.' Yet she continued to work on these phrases through her interaction with the text until she could finally handle the structure and could either self-correct successfully or produce a semantically acceptable sentence. Thus Peggy's miscues and retelling reveal the dynamic interaction between a reader and written language.

ORAL AND WRITTEN LANGUAGE

The differences between oral and written language result from differences of function rather than from any differences in intrinsic characteristics. While any meaning that can be expressed in speech can also be expressed in writing and vice versa, we tend to use oral language for face-to-face communication and written language to communicate over time and space. Oral language is likely to be strongly supported by the context in which it is used; written language is more likely to be abstracted from the situations with which it deals. Written language must include more referents and create its own context minimally supplemented by illustrations. Written language can be polished and perfected before it is read; therefore, it tends to be more formal, deliberate, and constrained than oral language.

For most people, oral-language competence develops earlier than written-language competence because it is needed sooner. But children growing up in literate societies begin to respond to print as language almost as early as they begin to talk. Traffic signs and commercial logos, the most functional and situationally embedded written language in the environment, are learned easily and early (Goodman and Goodman, 1979). Despite their differences and history of acquisition, oral- and written-language processes become parallel for those who become literate; language users can choose the process that better suits their purposes. Readers may go from print to meaning in a manner parallel to the way they go from speech to meaning.

Since the deep structure and rules for generating the surface structure are the same for both language modes, people learning to read may draw on their control of the rules and syntax of oral language to facilitate developing proficiency in written language. This is not a matter of translating or recoding print to sound and then treating it as a listening task. Rather, it is a matter of readers using their knowledge of language and their conceptualizations to get meaning from print, to develop the sampling, predicting, confirming, and correcting strategies parallel to those they use in listening. Gibson and Levin (1975) seem to agree with us that recoding print to sound is not necessary for adults, and Rader (1975) finds that it is not even necessary for children.

We are convinced that oral and written language differ much more in how they are taught than in how they are learned. Although most oral-language development is expected to take place outside of school, the expectation is that literacy development will take place in school programs under teachers' control. Attempts to teach oral language in school are not noted for being as successful as what children achieve outside school. Similarly, literacy instruction is not totally successful. Furthermore, capable readers and writers demonstrate the use and integration of strategies not included in the structured literacy curriculum. Although this paper is primarily concerned with the study of the reading process and not with reading instruction, we are convinced that a major error in many instructional programs has been to ignore or underestimate the linguistic competence and language-learning capabilities of children learning to read.

READING AND LISTENING: ACTIVE RECEPTIVE PROCESSES

A producer of language can influence the success of communication by making it as complete and unambiguous as possible. The productive process must carry through from thought to underlying structures to graphic or oral production. Written production, particularly, is often revised and edited to correct significant miscues and even to modify the meaning. The receptive process, however, has a very different set of constraints. Listeners and readers must go through the reverse sequence from aural or graphic representation to underlying structure to meaning. Receptive language users are, above all, intent on comprehending - constructing meaning.

Readers and listeners are *effective* when they succeed in constructing meaning and are *efficient* when they use the minimal effort necessary. Thus, through strategies of predicting, sampling, and confirming, receptive language users can leap toward meaning with partial processing of input, partial creation of surface and deep structures, and continuous monitoring of subsequent input and meaning for confirmation and consistency. Many miscues reflect readers' abilities to liberate themselves from detailed attention to print as they leap toward meaning. Consequently, they reverse, substitute, insert, omit, rearrange, paraphrase, and transform. They do this not just with letters and single words, but with two-word sequences, phrases, clauses, and sentences. Their own experiences, values, conceptual structures, expectations, dialects, and life styles are integral to the process. The meanings they construct can never simply reconstruct the author's conceptual structures. That every written text contains a precise meaning, which readers passively receive, is a common misconception detrimental to research on comprehension.

We have argued above that reading is an active, receptive process parallel to listening. Oral-reading miscues also have direct parallels in listening. Although listening miscues are less accessible, since listeners can only report those they are aware of, still these must be quite similar to reading miscues. Anyone who has ever tried to leave an oral message knows that listening miscues are surely not uncommon. In both reading and listening, prediction is at least as important as perception. What we think we have heard or read is only partly the result of sensory data; it is more the result of our expectations.

A major difference between reading and listening is that the reader normally can regress visually and reprocess when a miscue has led to a loss of meaning or structure. The listener, on the other hand, must reprocess mentally, await clarification, or ask a speaker to explain. Furthermore, the speaker may continue speaking, unaware of the listener's problem. Readers are in control of the text they process; listeners are dependent upon the speaker.

The receptive activity during the reading process is especially evident in two different types of miscues - those that are semantically acceptable with regard to the whole text and those that are semantically acceptable only with the prior portion of the text. A miscue may change the author's meaning; but, if it fits the story line, it can be considered semantically acceptable. For example, in S2 of the story Peggy read 'when I am always cutting wood?' for 'while I am away cutting wood?' These two miscues produced a sentence that fitted in with the meaning of the rest of the story. The more proficient a reader is, the greater the proportion of semantically acceptable miscues. The proportion and variety of high-quality miscues suggest that good readers constantly integrate their backgrounds with that of the author as if they are putting the author's ideas into their own language. This ability is often seen in oral language as a mark of understanding. 'Tell me in your own words' is a common request from teachers to discover whether a student has understood something.

Semantically acceptable miscues may be more complex than word-for-word substitutions. Many readers produce reversals in phrase structures such as 'said Mother' for 'Mother said' or other types of restructuring like the one Peggy produced in S12: 'Well, you do it tomorrow' instead of 'We'll do it tomorrow.' Although it seems that Peggy merely substituted 'well' for 'we'll' and inserted 'you,' the miscue is more complex at phrase and clause levels. Peggy inserted an interjection prior to the subject 'you' to substitute for the noun phrase. There was also a substitution of the verb phrase because the verb marker 'will,' indicated by the contraction of 'we'll,' was omitted, and the verb 'do' has been substituted for 'will do.' In addition, Peggy shifted intonation so that the wife rather than the husband says the sentence. Apparently Peggy thought the wife was going to speak, and her shifted intonation reflected changes in the grammatical pattern and meaning, although the sentence retained its acceptability within the story.

A reader's predicting strategies are also evident in those miscues that are acceptable with the prior portion of the text but that do not produce fully acceptable sentences. Such miscues often occur at pivotal points in sentences such as junctures between clauses or phrases. At such points the author may select from a variety of linguistic structures; the reader may have the same options but choose a different structure. Consider these examples from Peggy's reading:

text	transcript
(S38a) 'I'll light a fire in the fireplace and the porridge will be ready in a few minutes.'	(S38b) 'I'll light a fire in the fireplace and I'll... and the porridge will be ready in a flash...a few minutes.'
(S48a) Then he was afraid that she would fall off.	(S48b) Then he was afraid that the...that she would fall off.

Peggy's use of 'I'll' for 'the' in the second clause of the first example is highly predictable. Since 'and' generally connects two parallel items, it is logical that the second clause would begin with the subject of the first clause. The substitution of 'the' for 'she' in the second example occurs frequently in young readers' miscues. Whenever an author uses a pronoun to refer to a previously stated noun phrase, a reader may revert to the original noun phrase. The reverse phenomenon also occurs. When the author chooses a noun phrase for which the referent has been established earlier, the reader may use that pronoun. In the second example, Peggy was probably predicting 'the cow' which 'she' refers to. These miscues clearly show that Peggy is an active language user as she reads.

Readers' monitoring of their predictions is observed through their self-correction strategies. Clay's (1967) research and our own (Goodman and Burke, 1973) support the idea that a miscue semantically acceptable to the story line is less likely to be corrected than one that is not acceptable or is acceptable only with the immediately preceding text. For example, of the ten semantically acceptable miscues that Peggy produced in the first excerpt, she only corrected one ('all' in S11). However, of the six miscues that were acceptable only with the prior portion of the text, she corrected four. Such correction strategies tend to occur when the readers believe they are most needed: when a prediction has been disconfirmed by subsequent language cues.

Sentences that are fully unacceptable are corrected less than sentences with miscues acceptable with the prior portion of the sentence. Perhaps it is harder for readers to assign underlying structure to sentences in which fully unacceptable miscues occur. Without such a structure, they have difficulty unpacking the grammatical or conceptual complexity of a sentence and so are less able to self-correct. We believe that the two most important factors that make reading difficult are hard-to-predict grammatical structures and high conceptual load (Smith and Lindberg, 1973). What any particular reader finds hard to predict and difficult depends on the reader's background and experience.

The linguistic and conceptual background a reader brings to

reading not only shows in miscues but is implicit in the developing concepts or misconceptions revealed through the reader's retelling. Peggy added to her conceptual base and built her control of language as she read this story, but her ability to do both was limited by what she brought to the task. In the story, the husband has to make butter in a churn. Peggy made miscues whenever buttermaking was mentioned. For example, in S10 she substituted 'bread' for 'butter.' The next time 'butter' appears, in S15, she read it as expected. However, in S18, 'Soon the cream will turn into butter,' Peggy read 'buttermilk' for 'butter.' Other references to buttermaking include the words 'churn' or 'cream.' Peggy read 'cream' correctly each time it appears in the text but had trouble reading 'churn.' She paused about ten seconds before the first appearance of 'churn' and finally said it. However, the next two times 'churn' appears, Peggy read 'cream.'

text	transcript
(S25a) ...he saw a big pig inside, with its nose in the churn.	(S25b) ...he saw a big pig inside, with its nose in the cream.
(S28a) It bumped into the churn, knocking it over.	(S28b) It jumped...it bumped into the cream, knocking it over.
(S29a) The cream splashed all over the room.	(S29b) The cream shado... splashed all over the room.

In the retelling Peggy provided evidence that her miscues were conceptually based and not mere confusions:

> And the husband was sitting down and he poured some buttermilk and um...in a jar. And, and, he was making buttermilk, and then, he um...heard the baby crying. So, he looked all around in the room and um,...And then he saw a big, a big, um...pig. Um...He saw a big pig inside the house. So, he told him to get out and he, the pig, started racing around and um...he di...he um...bumped into the buttermilk and then the buttermilk fell down and then the pig, um...went out.

Peggy, who is growing up in a metropolis, knows little about how butter is made in churns. Although she knows that there is a relationship between cream and butter, she does not know the details of that relationship. According to her teacher, she has also taken part in a traditional primary-school activity in which sweet cream is poured into a jar, closed up tightly, and shaken until butter and buttermilk are produced. Although Peggy's miscues and retelling suggest that she had little knowledge about buttermaking, the concept is peripheral to comprehending the story. All that she needed to know was that buttermaking is one of the wife's many chores that can cause the woodman trouble.

Reading is not simply knowing sounds, words, sentences, and the abstract parts of language that can be studied by linguists. Reading, like listening, consists of processing language and constructing meanings. The reader brings a great deal of information to this complex and active process. Whenever readers are asked to read something for which they do not have enough relevant experience they have difficulty. That is why even proficient adult readers use such excuses as 'It's too technical' and 'He just writes for those inside the group.' For this reason, proficient readers go to pharmacists or lawyers, for example, to read certain texts for them.

ORAL AND SILENT READING

The basic mode of reading is silent. Oral reading is special since it requires production of an oral representation concurrently with comprehending. The functions of oral reading are limited. It has become a kind of performing art used chiefly by teachers and television and radio announcers. We have already explained why we use oral reading in miscue analysis. But a basic question remains: are oral and silent reading similar enough to justify generalizing from studies of oral-reading miscues to theories and models of silent reading?

In our view a single process underlies all reading. The cycles, phases, and strategies of oral and silent reading are essentially the same. The miscues we find in oral reading occur in silent reading as well. Current unpublished studies of non-identical fillers of cloze blanks (responses that do not match the deleted words) show remarkable correspondence to oral-reading miscues and indicate that the processes of oral and silent reading are much the same (Lindberg, 1977; Rousch, 1977).

Still, there are some dissimilarities between oral and silent reading that produce at least superficial differences in process. First, oral reading is limited to the speed at which speech can be produced. It need not, therefore, be as efficient as rapid silent reading. Next, superficial misarticulations such as 'cimmanon' for 'cinnamon' occur in oral reading but are not part of silent reading. Also, oral readers, conscious of their audience, may read passages differently than if they read them silently. Examples are production of nonword substitutions, persistence with several attempts at problem spots, overt regression to correct miscues already mentally corrected, and deliberate adjustments in ensuing text to cover miscues so that listeners will not notice them. Furthermore, oral readers may take fewer risks than silent readers. This can be seen in the deliberate omission of unfamiliar words, reluctance to attempt correction even though meaning is disrupted, and avoidance of overtly making corrections that have taken place silently to avoid calling attention to miscues. Finally, relatively proficient readers, particularly adults, may become so concerned with superficial fluency that they short-circuit the basic concern for meaning. Professional oral readers, newscasters for example, seem to suffer from this malady.

THE READER: AN INTUITIVE GRAMMARIAN

Recently, linguists have equated or blurred the distinction between deep structure and meaning. We, however, find this distinction useful to explain a common phenomenon in our subjects' reading. Moderately proficient readers are able to cope with texts that they do not understand by manipulating language down to a deep structure level. Their miscues demonstrate this. Readers may also correctly answer a question they do not understand by transforming it into a statement and then finding the sentence in the text with the appropriate structure. Thus, when confronted by an article entitled, 'Downhole Heave Compensator' (Kirk, 1974), most readers claim little comprehension. But they can answer the question, 'What were the two things destroying the underreamers?' by finding the statement in the text that reads, 'We were trying to keep drillships and semi-submersibles from wiping out our underreamers' (p.88). Thus it is dangerous for researchers and teachers to equate comprehension with correct answers obtained by manipulating and transforming grammatical structures. Our research may not prove the psycholinguistic reality of the deep structure construct as distinct from meaning, but it demonstrates its utility. In our research we judge syntactic acceptability of sentences separately from semantic acceptability, since readers often produce sentences that are syntactically, but not semantically, acceptable. In S10 Peggy read 'If you stay home to do my work' as a sentence which she finally resolved as 'If you start home to do my work.' This is syntactically acceptable in the story but unacceptable semantically since it is important to the story line that the woodman 'stay home.'

The first evidence used to separate syntactic from semantic acceptability came from research on the phenomenon of nonwords. Such nonsense words help give us insight into readers' grammatical awareness because sentences with nonwords often retain the grammatical features of English although they lose English meaning. Use of appropriate intonation frequently provides evidence for the grammatical similarity between the nonword and the text word. Nonwords most often retain similarities not only in number of syllables, word length, and spelling but also in bound morphemes - the smallest units that carry meaning or grammatical information within a word but cannot stand alone, for example, the 'ed' in 'carried.' The following responses by second, fourth, and sixth graders represent nonwords that retain the grammatical function of the text (Goodman and Burke, 1973). A different subject produced each response. Notice that 'surprise' and 'circus' are singular nouns and that, in producing the nonwords, the subjects did not produce 's' or 'z' sounds at the ends of the words as they would with plural nouns.

expected response	nonword substitutions
Second graders:	
The *surprise* is in my box.	supra, suppa
Then they will know the *circus* is coming.	ception, chavit
'Penny why are you so *excited*?' she asked.	excedled, encited
Fourth graders:	
He saw a little *fawn*.	frawn, foon, faunt
What queer *experiment* was it?	espressment, explerm, explainment
Sixth graders:	
Clearly and *distinctly* Andrew said 'philosophical.'	distikily, distintly, definely
A *distinct* quiver in his voice.	dristic, distinc, distet

There is other evidence in miscues of readers' strong awareness of bound morphemic rules. Our data on readers' word-for-word substitutions, whether nonwords or real words, show that, on the average, 80 percent of the observed responses retain the morphemic markings of the text. For example, if the text word is a non-inflected form of a verb, the reader will tend to substitute that form. If the word has a prefix, the reader's substitution will tend to include a prefix. Derivational suffixes will be replaced by derivational suffixes, contractional suffixes by contractional suffixes.

Miscue analysis provides additional data regarding the phenomenon of grammatical-function similarity. Every one of Peggy's substitution miscues in the portion of the text provided earlier had the same grammatical function as the text word. Table 14.1 (Goodman and Burke, 1973) indicates the percentage of miscues made by a sample of fourth and sixth graders that had the same grammatical function. These substitutions were coded prior to any attempt to correct the miscues.

Our research suggests that nouns, noun modifiers, and function words are substituted for each other to a much greater degree than they are for verbs. Out of 501 substitution miscues produced by fourth graders, only three times was a noun substituted for a verb modifier, and sixth graders made such a substitution only once out of 424 miscues.

Evidence from miscues occurring at the beginning of sentences also adds insight into readers' awareness of the grammatical constraints of language. Generally, in prose for children, few sentences begin with prepositions, intensifiers, adjectives, or singular common nouns without a preceding determiner. When readers produced miscues on the beginning words of sentences that did not retain the grammatical function of the text, we could not find one miscue that represented any of these unexpected grammatical forms. (One day we will do an article called 'Miscues Readers Don't Make.' Some of the strongest evidence comes from all the things readers could do that they do not.)

Table 14.1 Percent of miscues with grammatical function similarity

Identical grammatical function	4th graders	6th graders
Nouns	76%	74%
Verbs	76%	73%
Noun modifiers	61%	57%
Function words	67%	67%

Source: K.S. Goodman and C.L. Burke (1973), 'Theoretically Based Studies of Patterns of Miscues in Oral Reading Performance, Final Report,' Wayne State University, Detroit. (ERIC Document Reproduction Service No.ED 079 708), p.136.

Readers' miscues that cross sentence boundaries also provide insight into the readers' grammatical sophistication. It is not uncommon to hear teachers complain that readers often read past periods. Closer examination of this phenomenon suggests that when readers do this they are usually making a logical prediction that is based on a linguistic alternative. Peggy did this with the sentence (S35): 'Perhaps keeping house is harder than I thought.' As previously noted, Peggy had problems with the 'keeping house' structure. She resolved the beginning of this sentence after a number of different attempts by finally reading 'perhaps keeping home is hard work.' Since she has rendered that clause as an independent unit, she has nothing to which she can attach 'than I thought.' She transformed this phrase into an independent clause and read it as 'Then I thought.'

Another example of crossing sentence boundaries occurs frequently in part of a story (Moore, 1965) we have used with fourth graders: 'He still thought it more fun to pretend to be a great scientist, mixing the strange and the unknown' (p.62). Many readers predict that 'strange' and 'unknown' are adjectives and intone the sentence accordingly. This means that when they come to 'unknown' their voice is left anticipating a noun. More proficient readers tend to regress at this point and correct the stress patterns.

PARTS AND WHOLES

We believe that too much research on language and language learning has dealt with isolated sounds, letters, word parts, words, and even sentences. Such fragmentation, although it simplifies research design and the complexity of the phenomena under study, seriously distorts processes, tasks, cue values, interactions, and realities. Fortunately, there is now a strong trend toward use of full, natural linguistic text in psycholinguistic research. Kintsch (1974) notes:

> Psycholinguistics is changing its character.... The 1950s were still dominated by the nonsense syllables...the 1960s were characterized by the use of word lists, while the present decade is witnessing a shift to even more complex learning materials. At present, we have reached the point where lists of sentences are being substituted for word lists in studies of recall recognition. Hopefully, this will not be the end-point of this development, and we shall soon see psychologists handle effectively the problems posed by the analysis of connected texts. (p.2)

Through miscue analysis we have learned an important lesson: other things being equal, short language sequences are harder to comprehend than long ones. Sentences are easier than words, paragraphs easier than sentences, pages easier than paragraphs, and stories easier than pages. We see two reasons for this. First, it takes some familiarity with the style and general semantic thrust of a text's language for the reader to make successful predictions. Style is largely a matter of an author's syntactic preferences; the semantic context develops over the entire text. Short texts provide limited cues for readers to build a sense of either style or meaning. Second, the disruptive effect of particular miscues on meaning is much greater in short texts. Longer texts offer redundant opportunities to recover and self-correct. This suggests why findings from studies of words, sentences, and short passages produce different results from those that involve whole texts. It also raises a major issue about research using standardized tests, which utilize words, phrases, sentences, and very short texts to assess reading proficiency.

We believe that reading involves the interrelationship of all the language systems. All readers use graphic information to various degrees. Our research demonstrates that low readers in the sixth, eighth, and tenth grades use graphic information more than high readers. Readers also produce substitution miscues similar to the phonemic patterns of text words. Although such phonemic miscues occur less frequently than graphic miscues, they show a similar pattern. This suggests that readers call on their knowledge of the graphophonic systems (symbol-sound relationships). Yet the use of these systems cannot explain why Peggy would produce a substitution such as 'day' for 'morning' or 'job' for 'work' (S13). She is clearly showing her use of the syntactic system and her ability to retain the grammatical function and morphemic constraints of the expected response. But the graphophonic and syntactic systems alone cannot explain why Peggy could seemingly understand words such as 'house,' 'home,' 'ground,' and 'cream' in certain contexts in her reading but in other settings seemed to have difficulty. To understand these aspects of reading, one must examine the semantic system.

Miscue analysis shows that readers like Peggy use the interrelationships among the grammatical, graphophonic, and semantic systems. All three systems are used in an integrated fashion in order for reading to take place. Miscue analysis provides evidence that readers integrate cue systems from the earlier stages of reading. Readers sample and make judgments about which cues from each system will provide the most useful information in making predictions that will get them to meaning. S2 in Peggy's excerpt provides insight into this phenomenon. Peggy read the sentence as follows: 'One evening when h...he came home from work he said to his wife I want you [two second pause] do...all day [twelve second pause].' After the second pause, Peggy regressed to the beginning of the direct quote and read, 'What do you do all day when I am always cutting wood?' Peggy's pauses and regression indicate that she was saying to herself: 'This doesn't sound like language' (syntactically unacceptable); 'this doesn't make sense' (semantically unacceptable). She continued slowly and hesitatingly, finally stopping altogether. She was disconfirming her prediction and rejecting it. Since it did not make sense, she decided that she must regress and pick up new cues from which to make new predictions.

In producing the unacceptable language segment 'I want you do all day,' Peggy was using graphic cues from 'what' to predict 'want.' She was picking up the syntactic cues from 'he said,' which suggested that the woodman would use a declarative statement to start his conversation. From the situational context and her awareness of role relationships, she might have believed that, since the husband was returning home from working hard all day, he would be initially demanding to his wife. When this segment did not make sense to Peggy, she corrected herself. She read the last part of the sentence, 'when I am always cutting wood,' confidently and without hesitation. She was probably unaware that 'when' and 'always' are her own encodings of the meaning. She had made use of all three of the cue systems; her words fit well into the developing meaning of the story; therefore, she did not need to correct her miscues. We believe that both children and adults are constantly involved in this process during their silent reading but are unaware that it is taking place.

There are many times when the developing meaning of a

story is so strong that it is inefficient to focus on the distinctive graphic cues of each letter or each word. As long as the phrase and clause structure are kept intact and meaning is being constructed, the reader has little reason to be overly concerned with graphic cues. Peggy read 'day' for 'morning' in S13 and 'job' for 'work' in S14. These miscues have a highly synonymous relationship to the text sentence, but they are based on minimal or no graphic cues. In S38 Peggy indicated to an even greater extent her ability to use minimal graphic cues. Her prediction was strong enough; and she was developing such a clear meaning of the situation that 'in a flash' was an acceptable alternative to 'in a few minutes,' although she caught her miscue and corrected it.

Another phenomenon that exemplifies the interrelationships among the cuing systems is the associations readers develop between pairs of words. Any reader, regardless of age or ability, may substitute 'the' for 'a.' Many readers also substitute 'then' for 'when,' 'that' for 'what,' and 'was' for 'saw' in certain contexts. What causes these associations is not simply the words' look-alike quality. Most of these miscues occur with words of similar grammatical function in positions where the resulting sentence is syntactically acceptable. Differences in proficiency are reflected in the ways readers react to these miscues: the more proficient reader corrects when necessary; the less proficient reader, being less concerned with making sense or less able to do so, allows an unacceptable sentence to go uncorrected. This process can only be understood if researchers focus on how readers employ all the cues available to them. For too long the research emphasis on discrete parts of language has kept us from appreciating how readers interrelate all aspects of language as they read.

Sooner or later all attempts to understand language - its development and its function as the medium of human communication - must confront linguistic reality. Theories, models, grammars, and research paradigms must predict and explain what people do when they use language and what makes it possible for them to do so. Researchers have contrived ingenious ways to make a small bit of linguistic or psycholinguistic reality available for examination. But then what they see is often out of focus, distorted by the design. Our approach makes fully available the reality of the miscues readers produce as they orally read whole, natural, and meaningful texts.

Huey (1908/1968) once said:

> And so to completely analyze what we do when we read would almost be the acme of a psychologist's achievements, for it would be to describe very many of the most intricate workings of the human mind, as well as to unravel the tangled story of the most remarkable specific performance that civilization has learned in all its history. (p.6).

To this we add: oral reading miscues are the windows on the reading process at work.

REFERENCES

Brown, R. (1973), 'A First Language: The Early Stages,' Harvard University Press, Cambridge, Mass.

Clay, M.M. (1967), The Reading Behaviour of Five Year Old Children: A Research Report, 'New Zealand Journal of Educational Studies,' vol.2, pp.11-31.

Ewoldt, C. (1977), Psycholinguistic Research in the Reading of Deaf Children, unpublished doctoral dissertation, Wayne State University, Detroit.

Gibson, E., and H. Levin (1975), 'The Psychology of Reading,' MIT Press, Cambridge, Mass.

Goodman, K.S., and C.L. Burke, (1973), 'Theoretically Based Studies of Patterns of Miscues in Oral Reading Performance, Final Report,' Wayne State University, Detroit. (ERIC Document Reproduction Service No.ED 079 708).

Goodman, K.S. and Y. Goodman (1979), Learning to Read Is Natural, in L.B. Resnick and P. Weaver (eds), 'Theory and Practice in Early Reading,' (vol.1), Erlbaum Associates, Hillsdale, N.J.

Hodes, P. (1976), A Psycholinguistic Study of Reading Miscues of Yiddish-English Bilingual Children, unpublished doctoral dissertation, Wayne State University, Detroit.

Huey, E.B. (1908/1968), 'The Psychology and Pedagogy of Reading,' MIT Press, Cambridge, Mass. (Originally published, 1908).

Kintsch, W. (1974), 'The Representation of Meaning in Memory,' Erlbaum Associates, Hillsdale, N.J.

Kirk, S. (1974), Downhole Heave Compensator: A Tool Designed by Hindsight, 'Drilling-DCW,' June.

Lindberg, M.A. (1977), A Description of the Relationship between Selected Pre-linguistic, Linguistic, and Psycholinguistic Measures of Readability, unpublished doctoral dissertation, Wayne State University, Detroit.

The Man Who Kept House (1964), in J. McInnes, M. Gerrard, and J. Ryckman (eds), 'Magic and Make Believe,' Thomas Nelson, Don Mills, Ontario.

Moore, L. (1965), Freddie Miller: Scientist, in E.A. Betts and C.M. Welch (eds), 'Adventures Here and There' (Book V-3), American Book Co., New York.

Radar, N.L. (1975), 'From Written Words to Meaning: A Developmental Study,' unpublished doctoral dissertation, Cornell University.

Romatowski, J. (1972), A Psycholinguistic Description of Miscues Generated by Selected Bilingual Subjects during the Oral Reading of Instructional Reading Material as Presented in Polish Readers and in English Basal

Readers, unpublished doctoral dissertation, Wayne State University, Detroit.

Rousch, P. (1977), Miscues of Special Groups of Australian Readers, paper presented at the meeting of the International Reading Association, Miami, May.

Smith, L.A., and M.A. Lindberg (1973), Building Instructional Materials, in K.S. Goodman (ed.), 'Miscue Analysis: Application to Reading Instruction,' ERIC Clearinghouse on Reading and Comprehension Skills and National Council of Teachers of English, Urbana, Ill.

Part Three
APPROACHES TO RESEARCH

We have included Part Three because of the tremendous need to be aware of and to use appropriate methodologies if we want to get worthwhile answers from our research. Traditionally the reading field in the USA (where the bulk of the research has been conducted) has been preoccupied with narrow experimental studies devoid of sound theoretical bases. These studies have not always been helpful in furthering our understanding of the reading process as a whole. In more recent years it has been popular for some researchers to criticize the Goodman methodology from an experimental viewpoint. Chapter 15 is an excellent introduction for those not familiar with Goodman's views on traditional reading research and the need for operating from a sound theoretical base, while Cambourne's scholarly paper (Chapter 16), apart from providing an in-depth look at Goodman's work, provides much food for thought for those who would want to criticize (from a different research perspective) the Goodman Model of Reading and the research that led to the formulation of that model.

Knowledge of language and reading has reached a point where we must expect researchers to operate on a sound base of knowledge. That's the point of departure in this article which indicts research based on common sense, unexamined assumptions, and mindless empiricism. Goodman here examines where reading research has been, what factors continue to contribute to poor research and what ought to be the content, base, and methodology of contemporary and future research. Goodman foreshadows the major recent developments in research on comprehension of written discourse:

> A key example of an urgent unsolved problem is how to get at the competence underlying reading comprehension.... Probably breakthroughs will come from interdisciplinary teams, drawing on knowledge and methodology from linguistics, psychology and education.

15 LINGUISTICALLY SOUND RESEARCH IN READING

A PSYCHOLINGUISTIC VANTAGE POINT

Research in reading in the final quarter of the twentieth century has entered an age of science. A psycholinguistic vantage point has emerged based on a number of key premises.

These premises are simple, some will say self evident, yet they radically reorient and refocus research in reading.

Reading is now viewed as one of four language processes. Speaking and writing are productive, expressive processes. Reading, like listening, is a receptive process, no less active than writing, although the psycholinguistic activity is internal and not observable.

Readers, like listeners, speakers and writers are users of language. Communication of meaning is what language is used for. In productive language processes, speaking and writing, language is encoded; language users go from language to meaning. In receptive language processes, listening and reading, meaning is decoded; language users get meaning from language.

The new scientific premises require researchers also to see language in its social context. Language is both personal and social; it is the medium of communication and the main vehicle of human thought and learning.

Written language development in human societies comes after oral language development, at the point where communication must extend over time and space.

For individuals, written language almost always also comes after oral language development. It comes at the point where the individual in a literate society recognizes the personal need for moving beyond face-to-face communication to interact with unseen, perhaps unknown writers.

So far nothing I've said is either the result of research or profound theoretical insights. These premises represent a point of view in the most literal sense of that phrase. One need only look at reading to see them. They are in no need of scientific verification since they are so evident - that is, provided that one looks directly at reading.

Conventional Wisdom

Unfortunately many people, including researchers, have not begun consideration of reading from the simple direct vantage point that would lead to awareness of these premises. The study of language in general, in fact, has been plagued by the tendency to proceed from unexamined traditional beliefs about language. Conventional wisdom about language is so deeply rooted that even researchers committed to scientific method and logic often plunge into research on language and language learning with no attempt at consideration of the facts of linguistic reality.

The known and the unknowable
Many research studies are further hampered by use of one or two opposite but widely accepted views: In the first view, language is treated as being so well understood that it does not need examination. This translates to such statements as, 'Everybody knows that————.' This view in reading is one of the reasons the public is always so susceptible to attacks on current reading instruction. Since everybody knows that the way to teach reading is through phonics, it follows that programs that aren't phonics programs must be the work of idiots or a deliberate conspiracy to keep kids from learning to read.

On the other hand it is very popular for people speaking on reading to take the opposite view: Language is an unfathomable mystery. It is unknowable. This leads to justification of personal ignorance, by statements like, 'Nobody knows how reading works, therefore...' This then becomes a rationale for trial and error - particularly in methods and materials. If no one knows how reading works, anything is worth trying.

An obligation to be scientific
But language processes - reading included - are neither universally understood nor unknowable. This leads me to my final premise: Those conducting research in reading have an obligation to begin on a base of scientific insight and understanding. They must move to a clear unobstructed vantage point in looking at language, and they must become familiar with the best available theory and knowledge. Furthermore, they must use tools appropriate to psycholinguistic research.

LINGUISTIC INSIGHTS FROM THEORY AND RESEARCH

Research and scholarly thought have provided a number of insights about reading which expand on the base of the premises I've outlined. Both research and theory are in dynamic stages. That means that new knowledge is being produced at a rapid rate. It also means that there are competing theories and conflicting findings emerging. This condition is not justification for ignoring progress or reversion to a golden age when things seemed simpler. It is just such a dynamic state of affairs that opens up whole new directions in research - provided the research community can hang loose and remain open to innovation.

Some highly productive insights from scientific language study have emerged in the past decade and a half:

1 All children develop language competence. This development is so universal and rapid that some scholars have concluded that language is essentially not learned but innate. What is most remarkable is that children acquire not just a set of rules for generating new language; they can say things they've never heard.
2 Language acquisition relates to human need for communication. The mechanisms and motivation for acquisition of language operate in both written and oral language.
3 Language difference is to be expected. Language grows and changes to meet the changing needs of its users. Difference must never be confused with deficiency. Your dialect is not a funny way of speaking mine.
4 Language is learned in the context of its communicative use. Learners treat it like concrete learning if it is meaningful, and the meaning is relevant and significant to them. Language is only abstract when it is fragmented and/or divorced from meaningful use.
5 Language competence and language behavior are not the same. Competence results in behavior; it is the control over the process which results in behavior. Behavior reflects but is not equivalent to performance.
6 To infer the competence from behavioral indicators, it's useful to postulate a deep language structure and set of rules for generating the observable surface phenomena.
7 Research in reading must be process oriented, it must use behavioral indicators to infer underlying competence.
8 The human brain is the organ of information processing. As such, it directs the eye and ear and makes selective use of its input channels. Perception in reading is largely a matter of what we expect to see. In oral reading the mouth says what the brain directs it to say, not what the eye sees.
9 Effective reading is achieving coherent meaning. Efficient reading gets to meaning with the least amount of effort necessary, and uses minimal perceptual input.
10 Language processes, reading included, cannot be usefully studied by reducing them to manipulation of constituent units such as letters or words or distorting them by looking at them in highly limited and unusual circumstances.
11 Reading, like all language processes, must be studied in the personal and social contexts which give it purpose.

Even if researchers find it hard to accept some of these things I've labeled productive insights, they should still be generating exciting research if only in the attempt to reject them or demonstrate an alternative explanation of the phenomena involved.

POPULAR UNENLIGHTENED AND UNENLIGHTENING RESEARCH PRACTICE

I've suggested earlier some key reasons why reading researchers have not begun with an awareness of linguistic reality. I'd like to explore now some reasons intrinsic to popular research practice that might explain why so much research in reading is both unenlightened and unenlightening.

Narrow vision

Researchers frequently operate within very narrow frameworks. They often pluck a small item out of current practice or select a question of concern only within a specific program of reading instruction as the basis for their research. An example might be to study an experimental method of 'teaching consonant blends.' Such research not only suffers from being of value only within the narrow methodological context in which such instruction is used but it also suffers from the usual failure to examine the relationship of the item selected to the general question of children learning to read.

Restrictive models

Research on reading instruction has tended to be dominated by research design models which are of limited value in providing useful information on teaching and learning. This seems to stem from a desire to achieve 'rigor' and respectability without a sound theoretical base. Most common is the use of the *experimental-control group design*. An attempt is made to obtain significance, reliability, and validity through careful manipulation of data using statistics based on mathematical probability theory.

Some pitfalls in the use of *experimental methodology* are fairly well known:

* Variables are hard to control. Too much is happening in classrooms that can't be monitored and regulated.
* Control 'treatments' are usually poorly described and poorly controlled.
* Unwarranted assumptions are made that all experimental classrooms are equal and interchangeable as are all control classrooms.
* It isn't possible to control learning which takes place outside of school, planned and unplanned.
* Results of instruction may not show in any measurable sense until long after it is received. 'Results' of short term experimental studies are therefore unreliable.
* Some important aspects of reading are unassessable

in any quantifiable sense.
* Conclusions are usually based on performance on norm or criterion referenced tests. Such performances may not adequately represent gains in competence.

But there are more basic reasons for rejecting the experimental model as a basic tool in research on reading and reading instruction.

At best it can only 'prove' or 'disprove' a small set of hypotheses already believed to be true. It plows no new ground, provides no new insights.

The requirement for mass data and random samples causes a focus only on central tendencies in statistics, whereas individual variation and deviation may be most enlightening. We count 'right' answers instead of examining wrong ones.

Manipulation of data - however rigorously it's conducted - can never make up for the original poor quality of the data itself. Sound data can only come from a base of knowledge, sound assumptions, and a theoretical framework that give the data value.

Of what value is it to prove everyone does something if understanding *how* one person does it is what we really need to know?

Data worshipping

Sometimes it seems that research itself becomes confused with data collection and manipulation. There are so many elegant processes available, particularly with easy access to packaged computer statistical programs, that correlate, regress, factor analyze, and otherwise cause data to engage in impressive behavior, that meaningful results are lost.

Having produced tables, charts, arrays, and matrices, researchers engage in ex post datum speculation about why the statistical relationships exist, what to do about achieving them if they are good, or which should be eliminated because they are bad. Judgment as to whether they are good or bad is often made on a common sense level.

In reading and reading instruction with multitudes of texts, tests, workbooks, readability formulas, and management systems available, it's easy to generate great quantities of data. Making sense of the data, before or after statistical manipulation, requires some knowledge of what reading is and how it is learned.

Reifying tests

Tests are always developed to provide insights into phenomena not readily obtainable in the course of ongoing observation, teaching, or learning. A test maker builds a test which he hopes will reveal, through test performance, the competence he is seeking to examine. Building a valid test requires much more than administering it to various standardization groups to establish statistical norms as well as statistical reliability and validity. Building a test requires a theoretical model of the competence to be examined, based on adequate research and knowledge. Subtests, items, and tasks must relate to reality through this model. This requirement is as true for criterion referenced as for norm referenced tests.

When a researcher constructs his own test he is generally held responsible for demonstrating the validity both through theoretical and statistical means. But if he uses someone else's test - particularly one published and in wide use - he is absolved of such responsibility.

Researchers frequently equate performance on a test in reading with reading itself. Each subtest - 'vocabulary,' 'paragraph meaning,' 'word recognition' - is assumed to be a real isolatable competence or aspect of a general competence called 'reading,' and research data are reported not as test performance but as if the competence itself were being measured. Researchers rarely say 'The subjects had poor performance on the subtest on paragraph comprehension.' They simply say the subjects had poor paragraph comprehension. The reading test becomes reality itself, and the researcher often does not go beyond test performance in considering the significance of data. Too often in research reports *reading is performance on reading tests.*

Confusing science and technology

A contemporary madness results from the assumptions that all uses of mechanization, industrial organization, cybernetics, and other aspects of technology are scientific. Technology is treated as a synonym for science. It's as if people think that all that was necessary to get humans on the moon was to build a rocketship to get them there. Humanity couldn't have gotten there, as far as present science knows, without one; but science made both the trip and the needed technology possible. Furthermore, there are infinite numbers of uses of space technology that are possible which are worthless, absurd, or both.

In reading instruction and reading research, worthless and/or absurd uses of technology are frequently treated as scientific. Computer assisted instruction, computerized data gathering, instructional management systems are being built on wholly unscientific assumptions and views. They produce neat, manipulable data which are treated with unwarranted respect by researchers, who are awed by their technological trappings.

Technology can be, in fact must be, used to facilitate learning; but educational researchers are scientists who must control their tools and not become controlled by them. Nor can they retreat from their obligation to people into the impersonal comfort of the machine, the data, or the management system.

Recreating the world in the laboratory image
Researchers often create simplified versions of phenomena and experimental designs in their laboratories in order to study the world or some aspect of it which is too complex for direct study. Under special experimental conditions they can gain useful insights. The goal is then to test these insights against reality. But in reading and language research particularly, there has been a strong tendency to view reality as an extension of the laboratory and the narrow experimental view. Phenomena isolated for study are treated as unchanged from their occurrence in uncontrolled reality. This is a problem of great concern when researchers or others leap from research to development of reading methods and materials. There is a real world, and ideas - however cleverly tested in the narrow confines of the laboratory - must also be placed in the context of this real world.

Mindless empiricism
Objectivity in reading research is often construed to mean that only the tangible, measurable, directly observable aspects of things are legitimate concerns. Values, philosophical positions, theories are viewed as unnecessary, subjective, and dangerous.

What often results is a mindless empiricism of the sort demonstrated by the Blind Men of Hindustan. 'All we know is what we can measure' seems to be the motto of these researchers. They are content to stay on the surface of things, to add, but not to synthesize. They particularly reject consideration of values. In the name of scientific objectivity they disdain responsibility for the effects of their studies. No field of knowledge has been able to progress without theory to explain observational phenomena, to generate hypotheses, to predict behavior. Reading knowledge has tended not to move or build on research because of rigorously superficial, atheoretical research which has prevailed.

Atheoretical research often produces absurd conclusions which are apparently supported by empirical studies and are accepted even though they contradict the reality practitioners must deal with. Recent testing in California, for example, appeared to show that disproportionate numbers of Chicano and black school age children suffered from aphasia as compared to other populations. One must regard this conclusion as unlikely if not absurd, if these data are placed in the context of what is known about language development and language and cultural difference. In that context, we would do better to reconsider the tests than to group children and build curricula based on the results.

The dissertation process
Doctoral research ought to provide opportunities for scholars to explore the frontiers of reading. Yet one of the most conservative influences on reading research is the dissertation

process. The doctoral candidate often is up to date in his or her knowledge of research and thought. The student should select a current problem or issue and utilize innovative research methodology. He or she ought to know more about the topic and methodology than the chairman or the members of the committee of three to five faculty members, each of whom may view reading research from a somewhat outdated vantage point. By the time he or she has satisfied a committee and an archaic set of university requirements, the researcher may have been forced to compromise methodology, to touch irrelevant bases, to answer already answered questions. If he or she has built a background in linguistics and psycholinguistics, committee members may defend their ignorance by belittling the significance of the knowledge, insights, or vantage point being used. Often the effect is to push a student back to safe studies with traditional instruments. Sometimes the student perseveres, but the study is cluttered and weakened by conditions imposed by committee members. Universities and doctoral committees must give serious thought to opening up the dissertation process and liberating students from the yoke of tradition.

The funding process

Similarly, the process by which research gets funded works in a conservative manner. Proposals are read and judged by those who have made their mark and have vested interests in the status quo. Traditions of what 'good' research proposals look like grow up which make it difficult to tell the ingenious innovator from the crack pot. Official requests for proposals often are written in a language and conceptual framework which eliminates alternate, productive models.

Furthermore researchers must 'go where the money is' rather than deal with research that needs to be done and which they are competent to do. Sometimes research support goes to those who can include the right timely key words in their proposals.

Another problem is that money goes to money. New researchers with great ideas but no past funding find it hard to get that first grant. Universities and funding agencies both need to expand their support of high-risk research.

The research pecking order

Researchers like other human beings tend to be influenced in their attitudes toward others - by their perception of the status of those others relative to their own status. So psychologists are in awe of some linguists but show disdain for educational researchers and their work. This status-conscious view causes some researchers from disciplines other than education to be less careful in doing their homework when beginning research in reading. Sometimes they don't bother to find out what's already known. Sometimes they are unscholarly in the way they loosely interpret their data. Sometimes they state opinions authoritatively which have no basis in their research, particularly when extrapolating from data to methodological applications. Conversely, educational researchers sometimes show the up-tight, self-conscious behavior of the low-status group member who accepts the derogatory stereotype of his group. They become ever more conservative and narrow in theory, methodology, and research scope than the 'pure' scientists they emulate. Practical, applied research enjoys less status in many disciplines than pure research which pursues knowledge for its own sake.

Research oriented to the solution of real problems - illiteracy for example - is treated as unworthy. That view is reflected in promotion, salary, and research support policies of universities. It influences acceptance policies of research journals. It has even had effects on federally funded programs designed to deal with real problems.

It is becoming increasingly clear that sound research in reading is going to require an interdisciplinary base. But interdisciplinary teams will achieve their goals only if they can operate in a climate of mutual respect. Elitism in any form has no place in research planning, funding, or performance.

Broad jumps and other leaps

Reading has been particularly plagued by a tendency for 'methods' of instruction and sets of materials for instruction to be built by researchers or consumers of research on the basis of single conclusions from narrow or limited research. Researchers have the obligation to be cautious in generalizing from research conclusions to implications for practice. They also need to be careful when they change hats and become authors of basal reading texts that they consider all necessary inputs, become informed about all relevant concerns, and operate with the same scientific cautions which they employ in their research.

Early uses of linguistic concepts in reading research led to the so-called 'linguistic method' and a rash of 'linguistic readers,' all based on a single linguistic principle of minimal differences between phonemes. Phonics programs were renamed 'decoding' programs to capitalize on a popular misconception that learning to read was 'decoding' phonemes to graphemes. Better instruction will result from scientifically based research but not in a simple direct way. Research is needed on how reading works, how it is learned, how effective various programs for instruction are. The knowledge from such research must then be integrated with other practical knowledge to produce more effective instruction and more universal learning.

WHAT ARE THE REQUIREMENTS OF GOOD READING RESEARCH?

Some of the reasons for poor or nonproductive research have been explored above. In contrast, here are some of the requirements for linguistically sound reading research. Simply speaking, the more that's known about reading, the more necessary it is for researchers to base their studies on a wide understanding of what is known. Research must be consistent with modern insight into language and language learning.

Research studies of large numbers of subjects must give way to depth studies of small numbers, such as those popular in linguistics and developmental psycholinguistics. If a researcher can find through the study of a single subject how reading is used to comprehend a writer's message, an important contribution will be made to human knowledge.

Real people using real language in various real situations must be the objects of research if we are to understand reading as it really is. Research problems are being generated today from a variety of productive sources.

Theories and models

As we attempt to understand the phenomena observable in reading acquisition, models and theories are emerging. These models produce predictions and hypothetical explanations of reading phenomena. Very useful studies can emerge designed to support or reject these theories, models, and hypotheses. Studies that provide data which are consistent or inconsistent with a theoretical view will make clear whether any existing model is most useful in dealing with reading. The models become more powerful as they are tested against reality and our knowledge of the reading process grows at the same time.

Anomalies

Another base for generating useful research in reading is in the numerous unexplained anomalies which now exist. For example:

* Why do virtually all children acquire oral language without professional assistance yet some children don't seem to learn to read easily and well?
* Why do schools appear to be less successful in teaching reading to boys than girls, blacks than whites, poor kids than rich ones? Too often we start from the 'fact' of the difference in achievement and speculate on cause. We need to understand why and in what ways we're less successful with some groups of kids than others.
* Why, in a literate society with universal access to instruction, do some people remain functionally illiterate?

Rejected absurdity
As we come to understand more about the reading process, much useful research can come from reexamining the absurd findings of less enlightened research. Why do some groups have low norms on IQ and achievement tests? (We know it isn't a real difference.) Why has knowledge of the alphabet been a fair predictor of later performance on reading tests? Why do even ridiculous instructional programs succeed in helping some kids to learn to read?

Unsolved real problems
Bold new approaches to real problems in building the knowledge base necessary to achieve universal literacy are possible and necessary as the reality comes into focus.

A key example of an urgent unsolved problem is how to get at the competence underlying reading comprehension. In this, as in many other questions, it's easier to see what's wrong with current solutions and practice than to develop new approaches. We know that all current techniques try to infer comprehension competence from post reading performance. Such inference is never really adequate. It is always distorted.

Another major unsolved question is how much the silent reading process differs from the much more easily studied oral reading process.

These questions frustrate but they also tantalize. Probably breakthroughs will come from interdisciplinary teams, drawing on knowledge and methodology from linguistics, psychology, and education.

THE TIME HAS COME

It is not unreasonable to ask *now* that researchers bring a modern base of knowledge to their research. It is not unreasonable to expect them to conduct research worthy of time, effort, and expense - research that, whether big or small, contributes to some degree to movement toward the goal of universal literacy.

Brian Cambourne, an Australian researcher and teacher educator, spent a post-doctoral year at Harvard and Massachusetts Institute of Technology. This paper represents a distillation of his efforts to clarify for himself and his colleagues the issues that surround the Goodman reading model and the position on reading instruction that grows out of it.

> A model's validity is ... a function of the validity and logical consistency of the model-building process which lies behind it. It follows from this that any attempt to evaluate the model needs to be fully informed of the research activities which preceded the final form.

Cambourne places Goodman's research at the naturalistic pole of a research continuum which has as its opposite pole manipulative research.

He argues that one can not evaluate Goodman's work on the basis of findings from research in which the researcher was more manipulative or intruded more. Instead he suggests evaluation must be on the basis of: 1 examining the internal consistency and validity of Goodman's data generation process; 2 examining the validity of any assumptions that are critical to the Goodman position.

16 GETTING TO GOODMAN

Brian Cambourne

It's at least a decade now since Kenneth Goodman and his colleagues started investigating children's oral reading miscues. During this time they have published many articles and reports describing the results of their investigations. A consequence of this research has been the gradual building and refining of a 'model' or 'theory,' which is typically referred to as 'the Goodman Model of Reading.' The impact of this work has been significant, a fact that can be confirmed in several ways. For example, it is difficult to find recent journals and/or volumes concerned with the domain of reading that do not directly or indirectly refer to Goodman's work. Similarly, reading conferences - whether local, national, or international - typically include a section, or at least a paper, which is addressed to Goodman's work. And this year (1976), the National Council of Teachers of English acknowledged the impact that Goodman's work had made in the realm of English teaching by awarding him the David H. Russell award 'for services to the teaching of English,' an award that is not lightly given and which accords the recipient a high honor.

Although these facts are evidence to the effect that Goodman's work is not being ignored by his research peers, it is perhaps more important from a pedagogical point of view that Goodman's ideas are not being confined to discussion among researchers. Goodman perceives himself to be engaged more in an 'applied' than a 'pure' discipline, and therefore much of his published work appears in teachers' journals and is aimed specifically at a teacher audience. If accepted by teachers, many of Ken Goodman's ideas will have a profound effect on their teaching behavior and thus on the subsequent learning experiences of many children. Thus it seems that not only is his an interesting theoretical position which generates argument and controversy among researchers in academe, but it has, via the teachers' journals, pedagogical relevance as well. The ultimate beneficiaries (or victims) of the outcome of the debate surrounding the Goodman model are the raw materials of future society - its children. In this sense an analysis and subsequent evaluation of the model becomes a more urgent enterprise than merely resolving an interesting and controversial academic argument. Rather, it becomes one aspect of a larger series of questions concerned with literacy and the development of curricula designed to facilitate its attainment.

It is the notion of evaluation that raises the dilemma that

motivated this article. Specifically, how ought a model of reading such as Goodman's be evaluated? One possibility would be to study the past and current research literature which is relevant to the position he adopts in order to seek both counter and confirming evidence, and then after 'weighing' any pro's and con's that might emerge, make a judgment. Another possibility would be to test the model empirically, for example in a longitudinal study with experimental and control groups, pretests and post tests, random sampling, blind and double-blind strategies, and all the other accoutrements of traditional experimental design.

Although both the 'historic' and 'empirical' are tried and legitimate methods of evaluating theoretical models, the major thrust of this article will argue that neither is appropriate for Goodman's model. Rather it will be shown that Goodman chose to employ a relatively rare orientation (for reading) from which to direct, frame, and interpret his research and that because of this, an alternate form of evaluation is more appropriate. In order to pursue this argument, this article is divided into three sections. The first is essentially descriptive and should serve to acquaint the reader with the most salient features of the Goodman model, and with some of the areas of controversy that are associated with it. The second section revolves around a single question - 'How did Goodman develop the model that bears his name?' In this section the processes that lie behind the ultimate form which the model takes are examined in detail. Then finally, having described Goodman's research orientation and stripped down the model-building process which he employed to its component parts, the third and last section argues for the necessity of a special approach to evaluating Goodman's work and suggests some likely places to begin.

THE GOODMAN MODEL OF READING: 1 CONTENT AND CONTROVERSY

Goodman describes the act of reading as a 'psycholinguistic guessing game,' a description that aptly and succinctly summarizes the theory which he and his co-workers have developed. In his own words he describes it thus:

> Three kinds of information are available to the reader. One kind, the graphic information, reaches the reader visually. The other two, syntactic and semantic information, are supplied by the reader as he begins to process the visual input. Since the reader's goal is meaning, he uses as much or as little of each of these kinds of information as is necessary to get to the meaning. He makes predictions of the grammatical structure, using the control over language structure he learned when he learned oral language. He supplies semantic

> concepts to get the meaning from the structure. In turn his sense of syntactic structure and meaning make it possible to predict the graphic input so he is highly selective, sampling the print to confirm his prediction. In reading, what the reader thinks he sees is partly what he sees, but largely what he expects to see. As readers become more efficient, they use less and less graphic input.
>
> Readers test the predictions they make by asking themselves if what they are reading makes sense and sounds like language. They also check themselves when the graphic input they predict is not there. In all this it is meaning which makes the system go. As long as readers are trying to get sense from what they read, they use their language competence to get to meaning. The extent to which a reader can get meaning from written language depends on how much related meaning he brings to it. That is why it is easier to read something for which the reader has a strong conceptual background.
>
> Readers develop sampling strategies to pick only the most useful and necessary graphic cues. They develop prediction strategies to get to the underlying grammatical structure and to anticipate what they are likely to find in the print. They develop confirmation strategies to check on the validity of their predictions. And they have correction strategies to use when their predictions do not work out and they need to reprocess the graphic, syntactic, and semantic cues to get to the meaning. (Goodman, 1973a, p.9)

According to this view, reading is a process in which information flows essentially in an 'inside-out' direction - that is, from 'inside' the reader's head to the 'outside' where it meets the graphic display. The only 'outside-in' flow of information involves processing the graphic array of printed symbols, and in the fluent reader (according to Goodman) this is minimal and just sufficient to set in motion the 'inside-out' flow of previously learned and stored syntactic and semantic information.

The similarity of this view to the model of sentence comprehension developed by psycholinguists working with spoken language (Garrett, Bever, and Fodor, 1966; Wanner, 1973) is important, for it highlights one major critical assumption on which the Goodman model rests. The assumption is this: Written text and oral speech are merely alternate forms of the same language process, not, as some researchers assert, a case of one (written text) being a secondary, more abstract representation of the other (oral speech). In terms of the ultimate form which Goodman's model takes, this assumption has some far-reaching and controversial consequences.

For example, this assumption allows Goodman to argue that a child who has learned to process language in the oral mode by the age of five or six (when he comes to school) has already learned a great deal about getting information through language.

Therefore, as the task of getting meaning from print is an almost identical process (the only difference being the necessity to develop 'an alternate parallel mode of doing it' - Goodman, 1975, p.627), then (the argument goes) learning to extract meaning from print ought not to be very much more difficult nor mystical than the process by which one learns the oral mode of language. That is, provided that the same principles of relevance, meaningfulness, and motivation for communication that characterized the learning of oral language have been adhered to.

At this point, one of the major controversies associated with the Goodman model emerges - the 'hierarchy of subskills' controversy. Goodman's model argues that there is no hierarchy or sequence of subskills which needs to be 'taught.' Rather the assertion is made that 'in learning to talk one must use all the skills at the same time' (1974, p.18). Thus, according to Goodman's model, reading instruction ought not to begin with subparts of language, but with 'whole, real, relevant language' (1974, p.18) going from 'the general to the precise, from the whole to a clear kind of information processing that makes it possible to handle very fine kinds of differences' (1975, p.628).

The ramifications of this controversy spill over into other areas of reading instruction. For example, Goodman extends the argument thus: As written and oral language are alternate rather than sequentially related modes of the same entity, there is little necessity to assume that the reading act necessarily requires the reader to convert print to oral language prior to processing it. In other words, by pursuing this line of argument, Goodman is strongly de-emphasizing the role of decoding from print to sound, arguing that the 'preoccupation with grapheme-phoneme correspondence or sound correspondence or phonics in any form in reading instruction is but a peripheral concern' (1975, p.627).

This stance is one that brings the Goodman model into conflict with other theories of the beginning reading process. Not only does it deny the conclusions of one of the most painstaking analyses of research literature on beginning reading (Chall, 1967), but also it denies both the notion of distinct stages in reading development and the notion of decoding to speech or speech sounds. Despite the controversy and the conflict, Goodman is quite adamant about this aspect of his work:

> as long as we continue to use terms like 'decoding' to mean, not going from language to meaning, but from one language representation to another, we're missing the basic point. That's not 'decoding'; that's a kind of recoding. There are lots of kinds of recoding you can do, but they don't get you to meaning. This misuse of decoding began from two sources: the work of early linguists who believed oral language to be the most universal form of language experience, and an old

> preoccupation with the idea that when you read you have to somehow say everything to yourself before you can process it, a very inefficient process and one that no reader really does, though some of them try because that's what they've been taught to do. (1975, p.628).

This is a clear and strongly worded position that Goodman has adopted and is one which is likely to have effects on reading instruction. What is the basis of these strong claims? Are they valid? How did Goodman arrive at this position? This last question is not a trivial one, for in the final analysis a model's validity is, to a large degree, a function of the validity and logical consistency of the model-building process which lies behind it. It follows from this that any attempt to evaluate the model needs to be fully informed of the research activities that preceded the final form. Accordingly, the next section of this article will examine just this aspect of Goodman's work. Before doing so, however, it may be helpful to summarize the issues relating to the Goodman model - one which warrants our analysis and evaluation because of its impact on the domain of reading.

1 One critical assumption that underlies the Goodman model is that oral and written modes of language are alternate modes of the same entity and are not more or less abstract interdependent representations of each other. This assumption has led to a series of controversial assumptions about beginning reading.
2 The major controversies seem to center on the following aspects of the model:
   * A de-emphasis on decoding to speech or sound as a necessary intermediate step between grapheme and comprehension of meaning;
   * A denial of the notion that a hierarchy of subskills is a necessary aspect of beginning instructions;
   * Support for the encouragement of making fullest use of the internalized knowledge that the speakers of a language have;
   * A de-emphasis on the teaching of phonics in any form and a denial that such analysis is either a useful or necessary method of getting meaning.

THE GOODMAN MODEL OF READING: 2 HOW DID GOODMAN ARRIVE AT THE MODEL?

To answer this question - even at a superficial level - it is necessary to locate Goodman's research within some kind of model-building framework, and then by 'stripping down' the process that he employed to a sequence of discrete stages, to attempt to describe the finer details and thereby gain insights that will assist in evaluating the model as a whole. Such a strategy is employed in this section of the article. First, an attempt is made to identify and describe the research orientation that Goodman employed. This is followed by a closer examination and description of the finer details that such an orientation entails.

Orientation

Goodman asserts that his research differs from the mainstream of research in reading in at least one important way: in its attempts to generate data in settings which approach the 'real' reading situation as closely as possible. His claim that 'we worked with real kids reading real books in real schools. Everything we learned we learned from kids' (1973a, p.3) is an important one which is usually glossed over by both fans and critics of his work. It is important because it assigns a 'naturalistic' viewpoint to his research methodology, and as will be argued later on in this article, this viewpoint has important ramifications for any attempted evaluation.

For purposes of simplification, a 'naturalistic' viewpoint to research can be contrasted to a laboratory-centered, manipulative, 'experimental' viewpoint. The two viewpoints can be imagined as extremes on a bipolar continuum of research activities. At one extreme, research activities would be characterized by a technique with which the researcher imposes a high degree of control over the stimulus input and response output aspects of his research. In such a research situation, a setting (usually a laboratory) has been specially prepared by the researcher, and as many as possible of all the antecedent conditions of the experimental situation have been arranged by him. Research at the other extreme would be characterized by techniques that exhibit zero imposition or intrusion by the researcher. Rather than being an active manipulator and stager of behavioral events, he is a docile, passive, non-interfering recorder and coder of behavioral events as they occur 'in situ.'

These two extremes are idealized representations. Rarely does any research enterprise fulfill *all* the characteristics of being either absolutely and totally 'manipulative' or 'naturalistic.' However, neither does research cluster around the center of the hypothetical continuum; and it is possible to place research activities along it. The main distinction between research activities which do locate themselves as more toward either end is to be found essentially in the underlying purposes of each. Any research that happens to be located at the 'manipulative' end of the continuum is concerned with finding answers to questions about cause-effect relationships between rigorously controlled antecedent (input) conditions and subsequent output (response) conditions. On the other hand, the concern of the researcher whose activities place him more toward the opposite end of the continuum is with quite different questions. His concern is with questions of the distribution of phenomena in real-world situations. His research answers questions like 'What goes on here?', 'How are phenomena distributed?', 'How are they related?', and 'Can any patterns of relationship among the distribution be discerned?'

With these distinctions in mind, it is not difficult to imagine a continuum such as that depicted in Figure 16.1, along which reading research could be plotted.

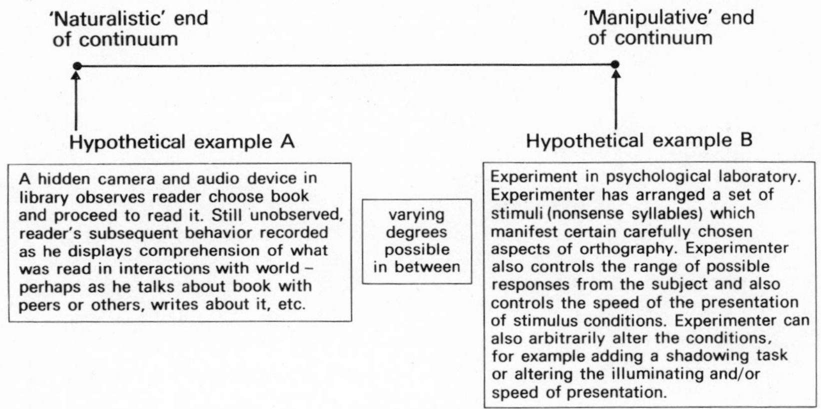

Figure 16.1 A continuum of reading research activities

At the 'naturalistic' end of the continuum, the hypothetical example A depicts reading research that is carried out under conditions which do not interfere with the subject's ongoing 'natural' behavior. In fact, the particular example chosen in Figure 16.1 suggests that great pains were taken to avoid any intrusion at all. At the other end of the continuum (example B) the opposite occurs, while differing degrees of 'manipulation' and/or 'naturalness' can be plotted in between. Although not absolutely 'natural,' as is the hypothetical example in Figure 16.1, Goodman's research methodology places his work closer to that end of the continuum.

Consider how Goodman approached the research situation. He visited children in classroom settings and asked them to read aloud complete stories from children's story books. He first of all informed them that they would not be helped with any difficulties they encountered, but that they were to guess at words that they could not recognize. He also tried to encourage them to read for understanding by informing them that they would be expected to retell the stories as fully as possible when they finished reading them. Using subjects from beginning through high school levels, he asked their teachers to classify them as low, average, or high readers in terms of their perceived 'proficiency.' He further relied on teacher judgment to choose stories in such a way that each grade would have tasks of 'comparable' difficulty. The tasks were such that, although not at the frustration level for each group, they were difficult enough to produce 'errors' in the oral reading. These 'errors,' or 'miscues' as Goodman prefers to call them, comprised deviations between what was actually said by the reader and what was actually written in the text.

To attempt to argue that the classroom as Goodman set it up for his research purposes represents a more 'natural' than 'contrived' situation may raise objections when considered in the light of the 'natural' versus 'artificial' distinction which was made above. After all, aren't the physical and temporal boundaries of a classroom highly artificial, contrived limits which are not 'natural' ones that children typically choose to cross? Not only this, but Goodman adds a researcher and a tape recorder - doesn't this add more and more imposition? How could reading aloud to a researcher in a classroom setting be perceived as a 'natural' situation? This is an interesting, almost paradoxical state of affairs, similar to that faced by Raush (1968) when he attempted to defend the typical clinical interview situation as a type of 'natural' situation. He argued thus:

> The structure of the clinical situation is an artificial one, created for those who are suffering and who are seeking a very special form of help in the alleviation of their suffering. The paradox here, as Bordin (1965) notes, is that the clinic, an artificial creation, is a natural habitat for those who need and seek the kind of help it may offer. A schoolroom is similarly an artificially created structure and similarly a natural habitat for certain forms of teaching and learning. (p.125)

A similar kind of logic applies to Goodman's research process. In terms of the everyday stream of classroom behavior, his research situation is a relatively natural one. By choosing books rather than passages from standardized tests and by relying on teacher judgment for estimates of pupil ability and text readability, the actual data collection conforms very closely to the typical 'read-aloud-to-teacher' lesson found in most classrooms. If, for the moment, we grant one of Goodman's assumptions - that oral reading accurately reflects the silent reading process (an issue to be taken up later in the paper) - then the situation also conforms to the 'reading-for-pleasure/information' behavior that readers typically engage in. That is, they read real, whole, complete stories/articles and attempt some form of comprehension. All that is different is that they read aloud. In short, it can be argued that the one big intrusion into the research situation that Goodman made is the researcher with his tape recorder, which, in the everyday ebb and flow of classroom life, is a minimal intrusion.

By locating Goodman's research at this end of the 'naturalistic-manipulative' continuum, some of the model-building processes from which the model developed become more transparent. For example, the general questions that are typical of naturalistic research can be applied to the specific context of Goodman's research: 'What goes on when someone reads?' 'What are the phenomena that comprise the reading act?' 'How are they distributed and how do they relate?' More importantly, however, certain critical stages in the evolution from raw data to finished model become more apparent and thus more accessible to fuller description.

Figure 16.2 attempts to illustrate this point. It represents, in a combination of pictographic and flow chart form, the various stages of model building based on a naturalistic viewpoint. A researcher with a strong motivation to answer questions which interest him, with a well developed set of ideas, prejudices, and mini-theories about the domain which interests him (usually the result of exposure to and immersion in a conceptual milieu which relates to his interests) approaches the complex, apparently chaotic world of human behavior. He has a strong desire to build a theory which explains some of the complexity that confronts him. He therefore captures a piece of this complexity *as it is*, and stores it ('freezes it') in some retrievable form without reducing the complexity of it at all - it's merely a smaller slice of the same complexly organized world. As it is in its raw form, this slice of reality is much too difficult to work with; so he 'chops it up' in a very systematic way into 'bits' (units) which are more manageable. However, the bits, although systematically chopped up, are still chaotically organized; so the researcher 'pushes' these meaningfully sized bits through a specially devised 'grid' which rearranges and orders the whole complex of bits and pieces. The grid reorders them in ways that relate to the researcher's original problem (or set of ideas, prejudices, and mini-theories) and permits patterns of relationship to be seen/inferred, tested if appropriate (sometimes statistically), refined if necessary, until finally a theory or model emerges.

Although an oversimplification of the model-building process, this is a reasonably accurate representation of the stages through which Goodman proceeded in the evolution of his model. For example, the mini-theories brought to the research situation (top left-hand box of Figure 16.2) would be represented in Goodman's case by the influences of the research literature and activities which were contemporaneous with his own interests. The recording stage corresponds to Goodman's actual taping of reading behavior, while the 'chopping-up' and 'rearranging' stages correspond, respectively, to the decision to make miscues the unit of analysis, and to the decisions that culminated in the taxonomy. Other correspondences are self-evident. With the process laid bare like this it becomes possible to examine and describe in more detail the path that Goodman

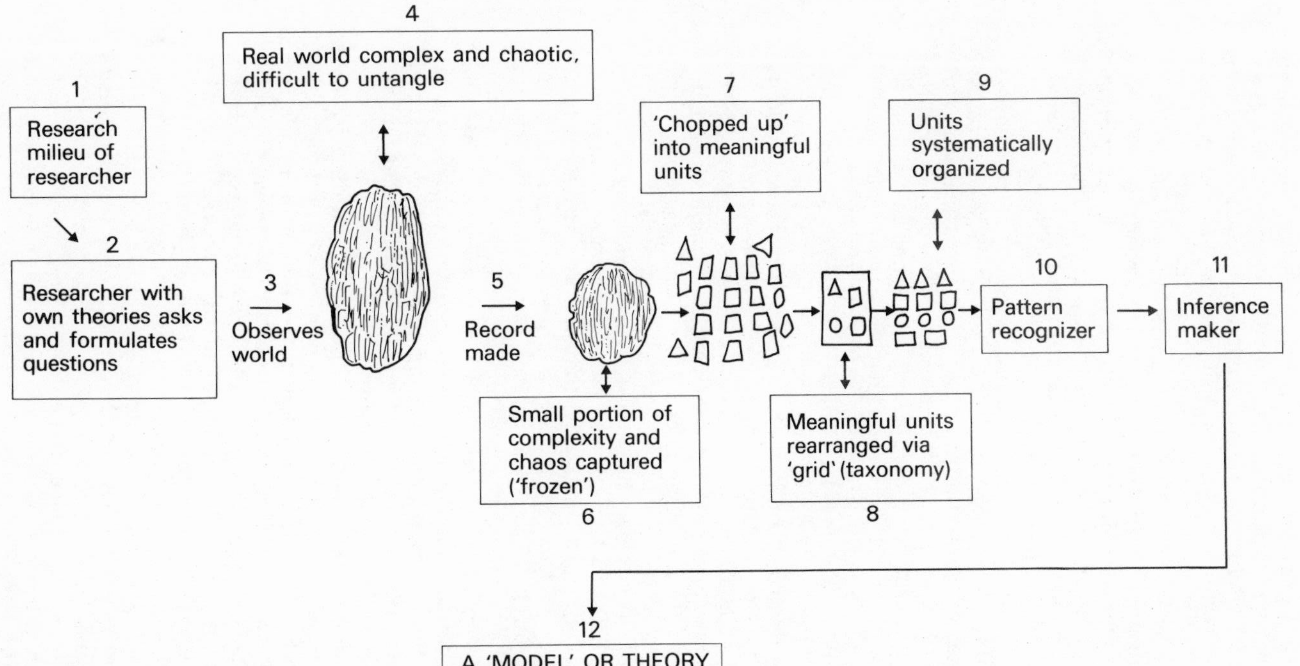

Figure 16.2 A schematic representation of the model-building process using a naturalistic research orientation (sequence of numbers 1-12 indicate 'steps' or 'stages')

followed in order to arrive at his theory. This is, in fact, what the next section of this article will focus on.

Origins and ontogeny
As Weber (1968) points out, studying the reading process by analyzing errors which are made during oral reading is not a new paradigm; the practice has had a long history. However, Goodman's incursion into the error analysis domain was different from others in that he began researching his model during a period in which new and powerful insights were being developed in linguistics, psycholinguistics, and cognitive psychology.

The early publications containing reference to his model of reading seem to have been written by Goodman in the early and middle 1960s. This was a period during which the change which Noam Chomsky had wrought in linguistics had spilled over into psychology. A new discipline, 'experimental psycholinguistics,' had emerged and was on the brink of a vigorous research era. One of the main thrusts of experimental psycholinguistics in this period was the attempt to provide a performance model of sentence comprehension that would match the competence model described by Chomsky in 1957.

During this period (1960-6), there was a great deal of interest in developing a theory that would explain the nature of the processes underlying the listener's ability to comprehend spoken sentences. Did the comprehension process involve a 'passive' kind of pattern recognition or analysis which relied wholly on the physical characteristics of the incoming speech waveform to carry all the cues that were necessary and sufficient for comprehension? Or was there more to sentence comprehension than a simple correlation between the physical properties of the acoustic signal and subsequent comprehension? Several important yet independent lines of research that were pertinent to this problem were being carried out at this time.

One line of research that dealt with this question began much earlier with the now classic experiment of Miller, Heise, and Lichten (1951). They compared the intelligibility of words in two conditions. In one condition the words were parts of well-formed sentences; in the other they were spoken in isolation. By introducing background noise to the situation and systematically varying the signal to noise ratio over both conditions, Miller et al. showed that sentential context made words easier to identify. Their conclusion was that information, in the form of context - and thus outside the region of the sound wave that is local and specific to any individual word - played a significant role in its identification (and subsequent comprehension). In a related experiment, the same researchers demonstrated that the listener's ability to recognize a word in isolation could be improved by letting him know beforehand the details of the set from which the text words could be drawn.

In a different (but conceptually related) experiment of the

same era, Pollack and Pickett (1964) arrived at similar conclusions concerning the nature of the comprehension process. They recorded conversations in an anechoic chamber (free from ambient noise) so that they could be assured of the high fidelity of their resultant tapes. Selections of varying length were systematically chosen from the corpus of conversational material and played to listeners who knew nothing of the context of the recorded conversations. Each selection was scored in terms of words correctly identified by the listeners. Despite the fact that the physical signals were clear and undistorted, and despite the fact that the listeners were permitted repeated exposures to the recordings, comprehension performances were relatively poor. Why? The conclusion arrived at was that conversational speech is simply not 'clear' enough to permit the listener to recognize one word at a time using only the specific sounds in the acoustic signal. In the same vein, Lieberman (1963) produced evidence that the quality of speakers' pronunciations deteriorate as contexts become more informative.

Other, different lines of research concerning the comprehension process were also being carried out during this period. Taking the 'click migration' research paradigm which was pioneered by Ladefoged and Broadbent (1960), Fodor and Bever (1965) hypothesized that the click locations noted by Ladefoged and Broadbent could be accounted for by the listener's tendency to recognize sentences a phrase at a time. In a series of experiments, Fodor and Bever (1965) and later Garrett, Bever, and Fodor (1966) attempted to disentangle the questions surrounding the phenomenon of click mislocation. In the process they established a theory of sentence comprehension (for the speech mode) which has obvious similarities to Goodman's account of comprehension of written material. Assuming that their original hypothesis that clicks migrate to phrase boundaries of sentences was valid, they asked, 'Are the phrases which appear to displace the clicks determined by the listener on the basis of syntactic knowledge, or are there physical cues which determine the phrasing and attract the click to boundaries?' Taking into account the fact that any number of physical attributes (pauses, temporal junctures, stress, intonation, word length) could cue phrase boundaries, Garrett et al. managed, in an ingenious way, to control all these possibilities; and they demonstrated that click migration will change direction when the phrase boundary shifts, even though the shift changes none of the cues which are local to the boundary. The implications of this kind of research were significant for the theories of sentence comprehension which were being worked on at the time. Primarily this kind of research enabled conclusions to be reached about the unconscious and unobservable processes underlying any listener's ability to understand the spoken sentences of his language, and it upset some widely held 'common-sense' notions about both the way language is used and about the nature of the language user.

For example, one implication of the research was that understanding a sentence or discourse was not entirely contingent upon the recognition of all the component speech sounds which made up the acoustic sound wave. It implied that the listener made an active contribution to what he heard and that his ability to understand speech sounds depended to a large extent on his ability to understand meanings first of all rather than vice-versa. In other words, in the act of comprehension of spoken words, the process is not exclusively an outside-in flow of information, but has a major inside-out flow as well, the listener bringing to bear, among other things, his knowledge of the regularities of his language and his background conceptual knowledge of the topic of discourse. In this way, he builds up a set of expectations of what is going to be said next by his interlocutor as he listens.

The similarities with Goodman's model are obvious. If one substitutes 'eye' for 'ear,' 'seeing' for 'listening,' 'graphic display' for 'acoustic waveform,' and so on, then one is left with a description of language processing in the written mode that is virtually identical with Goodman's model of reading. Goodman's model of reading appears to be a 'visual-written' analogue of the 'auditory-spoken' comprehension model which grew out of the kind of psycholinguistic research typical of the era. It is of interest to note that in the dozen or so years since Miller, Fodor, and their colleagues developed their model of speech comprehension, few changes have been made to it.

However, the point to be made here is that Goodman's model of reading has an historical relationship with a respectable tradition of psycholinguistic research. It is reasonable, therefore, to suggest that this relationship was more than an historical coincidence, but rather that Goodman's thinking during the formative stages of his model-building was influenced by the psychological research milieu of the time. This is not to mean that Goodman slavishly 'took over' an already established model of speech comprehension and merely modified it to include reading within its ambit. Goodman's insistence that he and his colleagues worked 'with real kids reading real books in real schools' (1973,p.3) is evidence that he was at least sensitive to one of the criticisms levelled at psycholinguists of that era - that by using a highly atypical group of subjects (students) and by asking them to perform tasks in highly structured laboratory settings, perhaps the processes which are relevant to the 'real' world of speech communication and comprehension were not being tapped. To avoid the same criticism, Goodman adopted a less structured viewpoint and researched the phenomena which interested him quite differently, but obviously with the same theoretical guidelines influencing him.

Apart from its historical origins, Goodman's model has an interesting ontogenetic history, which can be studied by examining his taxonomy. The taxonomy that Goodman developed is one of the critical components of the model-building process which contributed to the form that his model took. It is critical because it is at this point in the model-building process that the first major transformation of raw data occurs. Therefore, it seems reasonable that in addition to some knowledge of the influences to which Goodman was exposed during the formative stages of his theory building, it is also necessary to examine the mechanism through which Goodman transformed his observations to data. Accordingly, in what follows, Goodman's taxonomy will be described from two points of view: its structure and the assumptions underlying some of the coding decisions which are made (how it functions).

Structure The basic unit of the taxonomy is a 'miscue,' operationally defined as any 'variation from the expected response (any variation in the actual text) that the listener has been able to detect' (Goodman, 1973, p.3). The variations that Goodman typically detected manifested themselves in five different categories of miscue:

1 Insertions: Items added to those already in text.
2 Omissions: Items deleted from those which appear in the text.
3 Substitutions: An item is substituted for one in the text.
4 Reversals: The relative position(s) of a (some) text item(s) is (are) altered.
5 Regression: A portion of the text is repeated.

Categories 1 through 4 are mutually exclusive forms of variation, whereas category 5 can co-occur with the other categories and is coded in relationship to them. In schematic form, the structure of the taxonomy with respect to these five major categories of miscue is relatively straightforward and simple, as depicted in Figure 16.3.

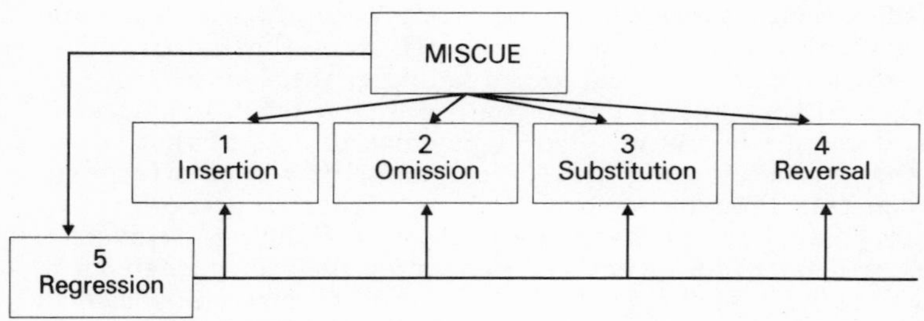

Figure 16.3 Schematic representation of five manifestations of miscues

However, the structural complexity of the taxonomy increases considerably. The rest of the taxonomy comprises a set of eighteen categories which are based on eighteen questions that are asked about each miscue. Each question is actually a category on the taxonomy and corresponds to an aspect of the miscue. The answer to each of these eighteen questions indicates whether or not the aspect of the miscue being examined is present or absent, and if present, to what degree. An analogy may make the idea a little clearer. Instead of hundreds of miscues, imagine instead a large box of stamps which are randomly and haphazardly arranged. The owner of these stamps decides to classify them according to some orderly scheme he has in mind. One possible method of ordering them would be according to 'country of origin.' Thus the stamp classifier would draw up a set of categories based on national boundaries. Each stamp would be classified according to the presence or absence of certain markings which indicate its country of origin. This would require a simple 'yes-no' decision because the stamp would either possess or not possess the requisite markings. Suppose, however, that instead of 'country of origin,' our stamp classifier decided that 'monetary value' was the aspect of the stamp which interested him. This is a feature which has a dimensional quality to it. In this case there would be a need first to decide on certain levels of value - say, 'high,' 'moderate,' and 'low,' and second to draw up rules for allocating each stamp to each of the three categories. The stamps could then be classified according to the degree of 'value' that each possessed.

Although not identical, the Goodman taxonomy is similarly structured with both kinds of decisions being made. However, the Goodman taxonomy is much more complex. The complexity of the taxonomy is reflected in the number and range of coding decisions which need to be made for each miscue. Note how the same format is followed for each decision. A simple binary 'yes-no' decision is made to the question about the presence or absence of a particular feature of the miscue which is currently being examined. If the answer to the question is 'no,' then no further decision about that particular question is made and the next feature of the miscue is examined (the next question on the taxonomy is asked). If, however, the answer to the first 'yes-no' question is 'yes,' then further questions and further decisions need to be made. Figure 16.4 describes this format in flow chart form.

As the eighteen questions that form the basis for the taxonomy and the coding decisions made with respect to each one are crucial determinants of the process by which observations are transformed to data, it is helpful to examine them in toto. Table 16.1 sets them out in simplified form.

Function Given the structure depicted in Table 16.1 and Figure 16.4, how does the taxonomy function? To understand this aspect of the model-building process, it is necessary to be aware of two important features of the taxonomy. One is an assumption that underlies the whole miscue paradigm:

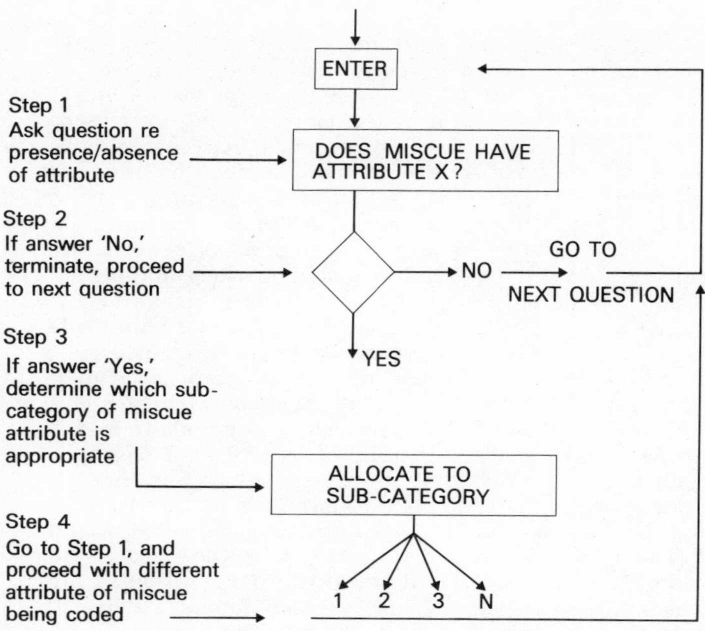

Figure 16.4 Schematic representation of process of miscue coding decisions

that the miscues which occur during oral reading are not random, coincidental occurrences, but rather reflect the systematic, covert information-processing strategies by which the reader extracts meaning from print when reading silently as well. Goodman on occasion has referred to miscues as 'windows on the reading process' (1972, p.2). The second relates to the kinds of inferences that are made about the processes which are implied to underlie or be reflected by the categories of the taxonomy, both individually and in various combinations.

Some examples may help clarify what is meant here by the second feature. The occurrence of a 'correction' or correction attempt (category 1 in Table 16.1) prompts the inference by Goodman that this behavior reflects that the reader is aware that he has made a miscue and is therefore monitoring at least some, and possibly all, of the meaning-bearing aspects of what he is reading. Another example is the category 'degree of semantic acceptability' (category 5 of taxonomy in Table 16.1). Degree of semantic acceptability is assumed to reflect the reader's ability to make use of his semantic knowledge and the degree to which he comprehends the on-going story line and/or content of what he is reading. Thus, if a reader's miscues display 'low semantic acceptability' and his reading is character-

Table 16.1 Taxonomy questions and sub-categories

Category number*	Question asked	Sub-categories if answer is 'yes'
1	Is the miscue self-corrected by the reader?	3
2	Is the reader's dialect involved in the miscue?	5
3	How much graphic similarity between ER and OR?	9
4	How much phonemic similarity is there?	9
5	Is the OR an allolog of ER?	7
6	Does the miscue produce a syntactically acceptable text?	4
7	Does the miscue produce a semantically acceptable text?	4
8	Does a grammatical retransformation result from the miscue?	4
9	If the miscue is syntactically acceptable how much syntax is changed?	9
10	If the miscue is semantically acceptable how much meaning is changed?	9
11	Is intonation involved in miscue?	6
12	Does miscue involve submorphemic language level?	5
13	Does miscue involve bound morpheme level?	7
14	Does miscue involve phrase or free morpheme level?	8
15	Does the miscue involve the phrase level?	4
16	Does miscue involve clause level?	4-6
17	What is grammatical category of ER and OR?	5 main categories, further sub-divided into 2 Sub-Sub-Categories
18	What influence has the surrounding text (peripheral visual field) on miscues?	3

*Based on Goodman and Burke's 1973 study. As the taxonomy is always being refined and developed, so some categories are altered, some deleted, some added.

ized by few 'corrections,' the inference drawn is that he is not aware of the meaning of what he is reading and is certainly not monitoring it. If the same hypothetical reader had a high 'graphemic proximity score,' it would be inferred that the reason that he was not attending to meaning was that he was too intent on the graphic display and was attending to the task of getting as close a match as possible to the graphic shape of the words in the text. Although these are superficial and hypothetical examples, they do illustrate the nature of the inferential processes that relate to the major categories of the taxonomy. In reality, the manner in which the taxonomy functions is at least as complex as its structure. This complexity is hinted at in Table 16.2 where it can be seen that the range of covert reading behaviors assumed to be reflected by individual categories and the number of ways they can be combined, are considerable.

It is out of the possible permutations and combinations of reading behaviors which the various categories of the taxonomy are inferred to represent that patterns start to emerge. The patterns that emerge become the data on which the model of reading developed by Goodman is based. When patterns of miscues emerge, it is not difficult to understand how Goodman makes theory from them. Basically what he does is to relate the emerging patterns of miscue behavior with the grade and proficiency levels of the readers who produced them. Figure 16.5 illustrates the nature of this step in the process.

		Grade level		
		Beginner	Elementary	Secondary
Proficiency Level	Low	A	B	C
	Average	D	E	F
	High	G	H	I

Examples of 'Mini-theory building':

Patterns of miscue phenomena in cells A,D,G = Mini-theory of beginning reader

Patterns of miscue phenomena in cells G, H, I = Mini-theory of fluent reader

and so on.

Figure 16.5 Possible patterns of miscue phenomena

Figure 16.5 corresponds to Goodman and Burke's 1973 study (which supplied much of his data for model building). In that study, the data were collected from ninety-four readers who varied in two fundamental ways (grade level and proficiency level), such that the group could be placed unambiguously into one of the nine cells represented in Figure 16.5. The

Table 16.2 Sample of some inferences made about miscue behavior

Category	Question	Inference Made About Process Reflected by Miscue
1	Is miscue corrected?	If no self-correction, reader is either a) unaware of miscue, b) making a silent correction, or c) conscious of miscue but unable to correct. If there is self-correction, reader is aware of miscue and therefore is attending to meaning.
2	Is dialect involved?	If dialect is involved and no meaning is lost, reflects reader's ability to retranslate to own dialect. Reader is, therefore, attending to meaning.
3 and 4	How much graphic/phonemic similarity between ER and OR?	High score with high degree of semantic acceptability reflects ability to use graphic, phonemic, semantic cues from text efficiently. High score with low degree semantic acceptability reflects inability to use semantic system – apparently overcome by graphic (or phonemic) elements that are present. Low score with high degree semantic acceptability. Concentrating on meaning, using very little of graphic/phonemic display. Low score with low degree semantic acceptability; guessing – not making any use of any systems available – a non-reader.
5	Is the OR an allolog of ER?	Allolog substitution indicates ability to get to meaning, as well as ability to use syntactic/semantic cues.
6 and 7	Does miscue produce syntactically (semantically) acceptable text?	High degree of acceptability indicates awareness that written text must be as syntactically/semantically acceptable as spoken language. High degree also indicates ability to monitor reading so that syntactic/semantic acceptability results. Low degree of either indicates either lack of awareness that written text has same syntactic/semantic expectations as oral speech, or, lack of ability at monitoring own reading, or loss of story line or meaning of concepts or all three.
8	Does a grammatical retransformation result from the miscue?	If no change then reader is anticipating author's deep structure. If there is a change without loss of meaning, reader is not anticipating author's deep structure but is able to grasp meaning and is able to use another syntactic option to express it. Reader is syntactically and semantically well developed or text is sufficiently 'easy' to permit no loss of meaning. If there is change as well as a loss of meaning, reader is not anticipating author's deep structure and is unable to recover meaning using alternate syntactic option. Texts conceptually too difficult.
9	Is intonation involved in miscue?	If yes, as intonation is based on access to deep structure, indicates reader possibly allocating incorrect phrase structure or semantic interpretation to text.

resulting subgroups (low-beginners, etc.) consequently produced patterns of miscue attributes from which certain interpretations were made. Hence patterns of miscues that emerged from the 'high' proficiency cells G, H, I became the basis of a mini-theory which attempted to account for the reading process in the fluent and accomplished reader. In the same way, the patterns that emerged in the 'beginning-school' cells A, D, and G formed the basis for a mini-theory which attempted to account for reading in the early stages. A mini-theory concerned with explaining the non-proficient reader would likewise be based on the miscue patterns in the 'low' cells, and so on. In other words, given a taxonomy for classifying miscues plus a group of readers of varying age and proficiency who are engaged in reading tasks which are of comparable difficulty, patterns of miscues will emerge. The interaction of these miscue patterns, grade levels, and levels of proficiency are the materials out of which Goodman developed his model.

To sum up the argument thus far: An examination of the factors that give the Goodman Model of Reading its form revealed, among other things, the following:

1 The data-gathering process rests on at least one critical assumption, namely that the oral reading process reflects ('is a window to') the silent reading process.

2 In answer to the question 'How did Goodman arrive at the model which bears his name?', it has been shown that it is the result of a combination of diverse historical and methodological factors, including:

a) A tradition of psycholinguistic research in speech comprehension;

b) A rarely used research viewpoint that imposes certain constraints on evaluation;

c) A data-transformation mechanism (a taxonomy) which has the potential for affecting the inferences and conclusions made about the original observations;

d) A set of inferences made on the basis of both miscue patterns and assumptions about the covert processes that these patterns represent.

THE GOODMAN MODEL OF READING: 3 ADVOCATING APPROPRIATE ASSESSMENT

Having described in some detail the processes by which Goodman derived his model of reading, one can turn to the question of a rationale or framework from which the model might be evaluated. The question of evaluation is an important one, especially when, in Goodman's case, the impact of his work has been and will continue to be significant. This article will proceed by advocating that in evaluating Goodman's work, some strategies are appropriate ones while others are inappropriate and could therefore lead to false or invalid judgments being made. Finally it will outline some aspects of Goodman's work that are likely candidates for evaluation and suggest criteria on which an evaluation might be based.

Inappropriate evaluative strategies

A frequently occurring evaluative strategy in the reading research literature (indeed in most research literature) seems to be one in which the evaluator attempts to support or reject a position (theory, model, idea, etc.) by describing and/or citing research evidence which purports to support or detract from the theory being considered. For example, in the opening paragraph of Mattingly (1972), the following appears:

> The possible forms of natural language are very restricted; its acquisition and functions are biologically determined (Chomsky, 1965). There is good reason to believe that special neural machinery is intricately linked to the vocal tract and the ear, the output and input devices used by all normal human beings for linguistic communication ((Lieberman, Cooper, et al., 1967, p.133[2]) emphasis added).

Mattingly uses a strategy, which - as well as being a tempting and seductive method of marshalling support for one's position - has an intuitive logic about it that goes something like this:

1 The studies that are cited/described are scientific enterprises;
2 Therefore they have a powerful aura of 'truth' about them;
3 They support/reject the position being considered;
4 Therefore the position is true/false, supported/rejected, etc.

The logic of this kind of strategy is deceptive and holds up only under certain conditions. One of these conditions is that the data-generation systems of the research being evaluated and the research being cited/described to support/reject it must be very similar. When any degree of dissimilarity occurs, then it is futile to adopt it as an evaluative strategy. A famous example of this kind of futility is that described by Barker (1965):

> Some years ago, when I was a student of Kurt Lewin, he and Tamara Dembo and I carried out some experiments upon frustration (Barker, Dembo and Lewin, 1941). The findings of these experiments have been verified by others, and they have become part of the literature of scientific psychology. The experiments provided basic information about the consequences for children of frustration, as defined in the experiments, and about the processes that produce these consequences. Time passed. In due course *I* had a student,

and he undertook to study frustration. So far, so good. All in the grand tradition! My student, Clifford L. Fawl, did not replicate the earlier study; he did not *contrive* frustration for his subjects; he pioneered, and extended the investigation from children *in vitro*, so to speak, to children *in situ*. He searched our specimen records of children's everyday behavior for instances of this allegedly important phenomenon without psychologists as operators. Here are the words of his report (Fawl, 1963):

> The results...were surprising in two respects. First, even with a liberal interpretation of frustration fewer incidents were detected than we expected....Second... meaningful relationships could not be found between frustration...and consequent behavior such as...regression...and other theoretically meaningful behavioral manifestations. (p.99)

In other words, frustration was rare in the children's days, and when it did occur it did not have the behavioral consequences observed in the laboratory. It appears that the earlier experiments simulated frustration very well as we defined and prescribed it for our subjects (in accordance with our theories); but the experiments did not simulate frustration as life prescribes it for children.

Fawl's results made us wonder, and worry![9] (p.5)

The footnote from Barker's long quote is another more interesting example:

> 9 Such wonders and worries are not infrequently expressed; here is a recent instance: George A. Miller wrote in the introduction to a study of the spontaneous speech of an infant (Weir, 1962), 'After many years of reading...about the environmental events that strengthen or weaken various stimulus-response associations, I was completely unprepared to encounter a two-year-old boy who - all alone - corrected his own pronunciations, drilled himself on consonant clusters, and practiced substituting his small vocabulary into fixed sentence frames (p.15)'.

This is not an isolated or exaggerated example. Menzel (1968) describes a similar occurrence in primate behavior research, in which two groups of researchers examined the same behavioral phenomena in the same organisms (monkeys). Taken separately, the two studies were 'scholarly, sound, and deservedly successful'; however, taken together, 'it is difficult to conceive of two more different pictures of primate behavior than seen in these books. Even the primates themselves looked different, and there is little apparent overlap in the research questions, techniques or theories' (p.78).

Again, in some research involving language performance of first-grade children in Australia (Cambourne, 1972), language performance collected under laboratory-type conditions and under experimenter-free conditions (using a wireless transmitter) revealed significantly different patterns of language from the same children. Looking at the data separately, one would easily be led to assume that they represented quite distinctly different levels of ability and not data collected from the same children. Other examples of quite different explanatory accounts of the same phenomena are plentiful in the literature (see Willems and Raush, 1968).

How can equally scholarly research efforts of the same phenomena produce such different explanatory theories? How can two respected and capable researchers in any domain of concern carry out a study of the same thing(s) and arrive at such different conclusions? The answer lies in the data-generating techniques employed, especially with respect to the relative position of the data-generation techniques on the hypothetical 'naturalistic-manipulative' dimension referred to in Figure 16.2.

The intention here is to suggest that the data generated by approaches that are widely separated on this dimension are not analogous and that they differ in fundamental ways because they represent totally different situations. The facts are that in each case the researcher intrudes himself differentially into the research situation, and subsequently this affects the generalizing power of any conclusions which might be reached. The problem is one of the degree to which the 'artificial tying and untying' of variables occurs (Brunswick, 1955). Just as one cannot confidently map conclusions drawn from research paradigms that lie at the extreme manipulative end of the continuum described in Figure 16.1 into the world of everyday events,[3] so one cannot call upon research findings and conclusions from one end of the continuum to support or reject findings and conclusions based on research which employs methods of data generation lying closer to the opposite end. This is not to imply that either kind of research is any 'better' or more 'worthwhile' than the other. Both kinds are essential if progress in any domain of research is to result. Rather, the question is one of an awareness of the limits of generalization that are inherent in any research paradigm; not only must one be aware of such limits, but one must pay more than lip service to them.

In terms of evaluating Goodman's model, this line of argument implies that an evaluation strategy which cites conclusions from other research into the reading process to either support or reject the model needs to be carefully screened. For example, it would be useless to focus on models of the reading process developed from reaction-time, tachistoscopic research paradigms in order to evaluate Goodman's model. Whether such research involved letter, word, or sentence recognition; whether it used adults, children, college students; whether it measured syntactic, semantic, or letter characteristics - the results and conclusions are non-transferable to Goodman's work, either to support or reject his model. Thus to cite Sperling's (1963) finding - that subjects presented with a random display of letters followed by a pattern mask can recognize letter-by-letter at a rate of about 10 msecs per letter - is not a valid refutation of Goodman's claim that reading is *not* a letter-by-letter process.

The same argument holds for research, which, although not structured to the degree that the typical reaction-time experiment is, nevertheless involves more experimenter intrusion into the research situation than was evident in Goodman's work. Thus research that involves intruding into the experimental situation to the degree that administering standardized tests of reading comprehension, or the skills of structural analysis, or any other kind of standardized test or instrument intrudes, is just as incongruous a base from which to evaluate Goodman's work. Stated briefly, the argument is that, as a strategy for evaluating Goodman's work, the method of seeking an evaluative base in conclusions drawn from other researchers' work is fraught with many (epistemological) pitfalls and as such ought to be avoided.

Are there any alternate strategies that might be adopted? It may be suggested that there are at least two which are useful and interesting. The first is a strategy that examines in detail the internal consistency and validity of the data generation process which Goodman employed. This entails focussing on the process at those points where observations are transformed to data and also where data are built into theory. The second is a strategy that involves examining the validity of any assumptions that are critical to the Goodman position. To elaborate on the first of these alternatives, consider three main questions. How does one proceed? What does one evaluate? By what criteria?

First one could examine the structural logic of the code (the taxonomy) by which Goodman transforms raw behavior into data. There are a number of aspects of code structure that are crucial in research of the kind which collects data using naturalistic methods. Some questions which might be asked are:

Is the code theoretically based? A negative answer would considerably weaken the power of the code to arrange systematically the phenomena that have been 'frozen' for analysis. If the assumptions that underlie the code are totally atheoretical, then the data that emerge as a result of coding will be totally unsystematic, lacking any axiomatic anchorage or grounding at all.

If, on the other hand, the assumptions underlying the code are theoretically based, but the theory is wrong or weak, then the resulting data will be correspondingly uninteresting and/or trivial. The stamp sorting analogy used earlier will clarify this point. Suppose one took the same large set of unsorted stamps and merely threw them in the air and let them fall. If the resulting aggregates were assigned category names that corresponded to the names of large cities (or animals, or football players, etc.), then the resulting set of categories would be totally atheoretical and without meaning. If, however, the decision was made to sort the stamps according to, say, initial cost as printed on the stamp, then we would have a theoretical base to arrange them, and it would be a better base than the haphazard aggregates that result from throwing them up in the air. However, if after arranging them carefully by initial cost, we start generating theories about 'country-of-origin' of the stamps, then it would be a weak base. What would result in this case would be irrelevant conclusions that were based on weak theory. As Goodman claims that his taxonomy *is* based on sound linguistic and psycholinguistic principles, then this aspect of his work is a candidate for evaluation.

Does the code facet? That is, are the categories in the taxonomy mutually exclusive and are the rules for mapping the phenomena to each of the categories clear and unambiguous? If not, then the assignment of phenomena to categories in the code becomes less precise and the resultant data might distort or conceal certain features of the phenomena being studied. Using the stamp-sorting analogy again, if one were sorting by color and two of the categories were 'blue' and 'purple,' then unless very clearly defined rules for allocating various shades of 'mauve' or other 'bluish-purplish' possibilities were spelled out, some might be allocated 'blue' on some occasions and 'purple' on others.

In terms of Goodman's work, this is an important characteristic of his code, as again and again fine distinctions need to be made. One example is the allocation of miscue phenomena to categories that range from 'total semantic acceptability' through varying degrees of 'less-than-totally-acceptable semantically' to 'not acceptable.' Another example is 'phonemic proximity' and 'graphemic proximity,' both of which also involve fine degrees of judgment and therefore require highly specific rules for allocation. The point is that for Goodman to make the claims that he makes, his coding procedures must be such that the possibility of ambiguous categorization of miscue phenomena are minimized. So far as this author is aware, no critic of Goodman's work has examined this aspect of his work. There are, of course, other aspects of the taxonomy that could be examined, but those just discussed seem to be the two most critical.

As well as features of the code that could be examined, there are other possible areas of evaluation. For example, a second point in the data generation process that Goodman used warrants serious evaluation - the point at which the transformed data undergo interpretation and emerge as theory. This is the 'inference making' or 'searching-for-pattern' stage. All the covert 'knowledge' and 'information processing' which is inferred from certain miscue behavior should be carefully evaluated, for it is these kinds of inferences that shape the ultimate form that the theory takes. For example, does a 'high' score in the 'phonemic proximity' category reflect the degree of 'phonics' skill/knowledge that a reader possesses? Or is there an alternate explanation? Do 'regressions' reflect a kind of 'back-up' procedure and can they be interpreted as indices of the degree to which the reader is monitoring the story-line and/or the syntax? Given the logical and theoretical structure of the code, are these inferences reasonable? Are they leaps of faith? Are there other equally strong and valid inferences which might be drawn?

Evaluating the inferences that Goodman has drawn about covert processes which underlie miscue behavior can be extended a stage further to include an interpretation of the patterns of miscue data that emerge after coding. This would mean taking the claims that the Goodman model makes about beginning reading - or about fluent reading, reading and dialect, or whatever aspect of the model might be of interest - and in granting the theoretical, logical, and inferential validity of the data processing to this stage of the enterprise, ask the question, 'What patterns of miscue data support this (these) claim(s)?' For example, one ought to be able to transfer the claim that 'Low proficiency readers are using the same processes as high proficiency readers but less well' (Goodman and Burke, 1973b, p.ii) or the statement that 'the analysis revealed no hierarchy of skills in reading development' (p.ii) back into patterns of miscues in the samples of reading of the children Goodman used. If this can't be done, then that fact must detract from the power of the model; for it suggests that in the transition from data to theory, something that only the model builders can account for has been added. If it can be done (and an initial exploration of Goodman's data suggests that, in the main, it can), then the patterns ought still to be examined just in case alternate accounts of what they mean can be offered and then compared from the point of view of 'reasonable explanation.'

As well as the code and the coding decisions, there is another area of Goodman's model that lends itself to evaluation - namely, the two critical assumptions that underpin everything he claims. These are

1 The assumption that the written mode of language is an independent, alternate form of language and not a more abstract representation of speech; and
2 The assumption that the oral reading process is a 'window' through which the covert information processing strategies in reading can be observed.

While the first is essential to the stance that Goodman takes on beginning reading, the second is necessary to his research paradigm. Without the first, he would be hard pressed to support the claim that learning to extract meaning from print is no more cognitively difficult than learning to comprehend speech. If in fact print could be shown to be a secondary, more abstract form of speech, his argument about naturalness of learning to read is difficult to sustain. Without the second, he can make no claims about the most common form of reading (silent reading); for it means that his data merely reflect reading aloud, which except for news broadcasters, teachers, and actors, seems to have little to do with pedagogy or a theory of reading. These assumptions then are axiomatic to the Goodman model, and as such need to be assessed and accounted for in any evaluation of his work.

CONCLUDING STATEMENT

The form that this article finally took was motivated by two experiences. First, as this author read into the various criticisms and judgments of the Goodman model and talked with colleagues about it, he became aware of great diversity of opinion about what it was that the Goodman model actually represented. With an enormous egocentric leap of faith it was assumed that others would find tracing the development of Goodman's model from raw observations to finished theory illuminating. The second experience had less egocentric overtones, but was perhaps more evangelistic in its motivation. At about the time this article was taking shape, the author received Farr, Weintraub, and Tone's little book 'Improving Reading Research' (1976). He was struck by the following remark in the introduction:

> Most of the papers in this volume deal with but one type of research - the classical empirical design. This emphasis seems valid because the vast preponderence of research literature that has been done and that continues to be produced follows the classical model. Research, however is - or ought to be - more broadly defined than the classical model. It seems crucial that we look at other types of research and recognize them as valuable. (p.3)

Being totally in agreement with this comment, this author seized upon an opportunity to publicize the details of a research model which is 'more broadly defined than the classical type model.' He was, however, aware of a more mundane possibility. If the 'vast preponderance of research literature that has been done and continues to be done' follows the classical model, then it was likely that the techniques and strategies of evaluation would also be those of the classical model. Thus, this article was structured as it is in the hope that it would fulfill the purposes implied by its title and that some enthusiastic and energetic evaluator would find it useful in 'getting *to*' rather than 'getting *at*' Goodman.

NOTES

1 The taxonomy is constantly being modified and refined. The number eighteen is based on Goodman's 1973 study (Goodman and Burke, 1973).

2 This example has been chosen randomly. It should not be seen as detracting from Mattingly's paper in any way. On the contrary, Cambourne is an avid fan of his work.

3 Raush (1968) suggests an interesting example of this lack of confidence. 'For example the conditions of operant conditioning can be stated and tested with precision, but whether the operant model represents a modal, optimal, or trivial form of learning, is obscure' (Willems and Raush, 1968, p.131).

REFERENCES

Barker, R.G. (1965), Explorations in Ecological Psychology, 'American Psychologist,' vol.20, pp.1-14.

Brunswick, E. (1955), Representative Design and Probabilistic Theory in Functional Psychology, 'Psychological Review,' vol.62, no.3, pp.193-217.

Cambourne, B.L. (1972), A Naturalistic Study of Language Performance in Grade 1 Rural and Urban School Children, doctoral dissertation, Faculty of Education, James Cook University of Nth. Qld. (Australia).

Chall, J.S. (1967), 'Reading: The Great Debate,' McGraw-Hill, New York.

Chomsky, N. (1957), 'Syntactic Structures,' Mouton, The Hague.

Farr, R., S. Weintraub and B. Tone (1976), 'Improving Reading Research,' International Reading Association, Newark, Delaware.

Fodor, J., and T. Bever (1965), The Psychological Reality of Linguistic Segments, 'Journal of Verbal Learning and Verbal Behavior,' vol.4, pp.414-21.

Garrett, M., T. Bever, and J. Fodor (1966), The Active Use of Grammar in Speech Perception, 'Perception and Psychophysics,' vol.1, pp.30-2.

Goodman, K.S. (1972), Miscues: Windows on the Reading Process, in 'Miscue Analysis,' Urbana, Ill.

Goodman, K.S. (1973), Miscues: Windows on the Reading Process, in K.S. Goodman (ed.), 'Miscue Analysis: Application to Reading Instruction,' ERIC Clearinghouse on Reading and Communication, NCTE, Champaign, Urbana, Illinois.

Goodman, K.S. (1974), Miscue Analysis: Theory and Reality in Reading, address given at IRA World Reading Conference, Vienna.
Goodman, K.S. (1975), Do You Have to Be Smart to Read: Do You Have to Read to Be Smart? 'Reading Teacher,' vol.28, no.7, pp.625-32.
Goodman, K.S., and C. Burke (1973), Theoretically Based Studies of Patterns of Miscues in Oral Reading Performance, final report Project No.9-0375, Grant No. OEG-O-9-320375-4269, US Dept of Health, Education and Welfare.
Ladefoged, P., and D. Broadbent (1960), Perception of Sequence in Auditory Events, 'Quarterly Journal of Experimental Psychology,' vol.12, pp.162-70.
Lieberman, P. (1963), Some Effects of Semantic and Grammatical Context on the Production and Perception of Speech, 'Language and Speech,' vol.6, p.172.
Mattingly, I.C. (1972), Reading: the Linguistic Process and Linguistic Awareness, in J.F. Kavanagh and I.C. Mattingly (eds), 'Language by Eye and Ear,' MIT Press, Cambridge, Mass, pp.133-49.
Menzel, E.Q. (1968), Naturalistic and Experimental Approaches to Private Behavior, in E.P. Willems and H. Raush (eds), 'Naturalistic viewpoints in psychological research,' Holt, Rinehart & Winston, New York, pp.78-121.
Miller, G., A. Heise, and W. Lichten (1951), The Intelligibility of Speech as a Function of the Context and Test Materials, 'Journal of Experimental Psychology,' vol.40, pp.329-35.
Pollack, I. and J. Pickett (1964), The Intelligibility of Excerpts from Conversation, 'Language and Speech,' vol.6, pp.165-71.
Raush, H. (1968), Naturalistic Method and the Clinical Approach, in E.P. Willems and H. Raush (eds), 'Naturalistic Viewpoints in Psychological Research,' Holt, Rinehart & Winston, New York; pp.122-46.
Sperling, G. (1963), A Model for Visual Memory Tasks, 'Human Factors,' vol.5, pp.19-31.
Wanner, E. (1973), Do We Understand Sentences from the Outside-in or the Inside-out? 'Daedalus,' Summer, vol.102, no.3, pp.163-74.
Weber, R. (1968), The Study of Oral Reading Errors: a Review of the Literature, 'Reading Research Quarterly,' Fall, vol.4, pp.96-119.
Willems, E.P. and H. Raush (eds), (1968), 'Naturalistic Viewpoints in Psychological Research,' Holt, Rinehart & Winston, New York.

APPENDIX: The Goodman Taxonomy of Reading Miscues

A Note on the Taxonomy: As Kenneth Goodman explains in his article, "What We Know about Reading," the Taxonomy through which miscue researchers explore the reading process has already been revised several times to take into account new findings. Its evolution is continuing with another major revision, now in process.

The version reproduced here appeared in 1973 as part of a government research project report (Goodman, K. S. and Burke, C. L. *Theoretically based studies of patterns of miscues in oral reading performance.* [U.S.O.E. Project No. 90375] Grant No. OEG-0-9-320375-4269. Washington, D.C., U.S. Department of Health, Education, and Welfare, March, 1973.) This manual and its revisions utilize established computer programs. If teachers or researchers wish to use the manual in research, they may obtain information on the computer programs by querying Dr. Kenneth Goodman, College of Education, University of Arizona, Tucson, Arizona 85721.

On the following pages each of the eighteen categories of the taxonomy are briefly outlined and examples are given. There are some limitations placed on the examples used.

1 There is no consistent way of representing the intonation which has caused us to make specific keying decisions. In some cases punctuation markings and/or the changing grammatical function of the ER items will serve as partial indicators.

2 All of the examples presented contain only one miscue per sentence. While this situation does not always exist in continuous text, it does serve to focus attention within the examples.

3 All of the examples (with the exception of those in the correction category) are presented as if they were not corrected. This is the state in which the ER sentence must be read to answer the taxonomy questions.*

4 All of the examples represent miscues made by children studied in the research. In the instance of a couple of subcategories we have been unable to supply examples.

1 CORRECTION

A reader can produce a miscue and be totally unaware that he has varied from the text. In such instances the reading will continue uninterrupted.

When the reader does become aware of a miscue, he can choose to correct either silently or orally, or he can choose to continue without correcting.

Uninterrupted reading at the point of a miscue can be related to the reader's lack of awareness of the miscue, his use of silent correction or his conscious awareness that he is unable to handle the variation. We have no consistent method devised for distinguishing between these possibilities.

It is possible to note some silent corrections by paying attention to pauses in the reading, by checking miscues made during repeated occurrences of the same word in text, and by comparing miscues made during the reading with successful usage during the oral retelling.

Because our proficiency in identifying silent miscues is sufficient to substantiate their existence but not to accurately tally their occurrences the correction category is used only to tally oral correction occurrences.

The occurrence of a correction or correction attempt is evidence that the reader feels he has made a miscue. In order to correct a reader must repeat material which has already been read. The length of the repetition (whether it involves one or several words) can provide a cue to when the reader became conscious of the miscue and/or the point at which he was able to determine the word.

It is possible for the correction attempt to occur further on in the text either due to repeated occurrences of the word or to the developing semantic context of the reading. Corrections that occur across structures and not with near immediacy to the miscue occurrence will not be coded in this category.

In no time at all Sven's pet was everybody's pet. [*pup* written above *pet*]

pup for *pet* is coded 1.0 (not corrected)

When a complex miscue is involved, the correction category must be keyed on the main line of the miscue only.

He had a smile on his face. [*small* above *smile*, *one* above *on*; ©]

The miscue is *small one* for *smile on* and is coded 1.9 (unsuccessful correction).

0 *No attempt at correction is made.*

She pounded the young tree into (long) strings.

Then he picked up the fawn and carried it home.

When warm weather came, ^ the Whitemoons moved to their summer camp. [*to* inserted]

1 *The miscue is corrected.*

Not
No one had ever heard Billy's songs.

canberry
One of the things he liked most was cranberry picking in the fall.

the
Then he noticed that his one leg was broken!

We
He will make a good pet.

2 *An original correct response is abandoned in favor of an incorrect one.*

"You can't prove it!" the hunter said.

9 *An unsuccessful attempt is made at correcting the miscue.*

crawled
crowned
Then they crowded into the car.

creeped
cr–
Then they crowded into the car.

Additional Notes: Terminal punctuation can be assumed to be corrected when the reader adjusts the intonation of the following structure.

We had just never had any pets until Sven Olsen decided he wanted one.

Freddie nodded sadly. Sometimes he thought that a scientist's life was filled with disappointments.

2 DIALECT

Dialects of a language vary from each other through phonemes, intonation, vocabulary and structure. Phonemic and intonation variation almost never result in any meaning or structural changes. Only dialect miscues which involve vocabulary or structural changes will be coded in this category.

For specific substudies phonemic dialect variations can be coded on the Multiple Attempts Taxonomy and under the secondary dialect influence and doubtful subheadings of the general taxonomy.

In substudies which record phonemic variations use a spelling which approximates what was said while retaining as much as possible of the ER spelling. This representation is preceded by a dollar sign ($).

In all other studies, the general rule of thumb is to accept the wide range of phonological variants found in communities as within the limits of the expected response and hence not miscues.

When a miscue has been marked DIALECT it can not be coded under ALLOLOG.

0 *Dialect is not involved in the miscue.* The OR is not recognizable as a distinguishing feature of a specific group of speakers.

1 *Dialect is involved in the miscue.* The OR is recognizable as a vocabulary item or structure which is a distinguishable part of the speech system of an identifiable group of speakers.

ER But the woman said to him, "Do not go."
OR But *the woman, she,* took him, "Do not go."

ER I don't have *any* pennies.
OR I don't have *no* pennies.

ER He *is* a funny pet.
OR He a funny pet.

ER Neither of us *was* there.
OR Neither of us *were* there.

Bound morpheme differences of inflected words. Dialect miscues involving bound morphemes will be treated graphically as having a standard spelling; /help/ and /helpt/ are both spelled *helped* and morphonemically as having null forms of the inflectional endings. The absence of an ending is itself a signal. Hence, *help* ( ) for *help (ed)* is a substitution rather than an omission.

ER helped	ER Freddie's	graphic 3.9
OR help	OR Freddie	bound & combined morpheme 13.11
		word & free morpheme 14.18

Bound morpheme differences of noninflected words. Some words register tense or number changes internally (woman/women) while others have neither inflectional nor internal changes (sheep/sheep). It is possible for the reader to become confused over what constitutes the root word (present tense of a verb, singular form of a noun). Where this confusion is habitual to a particular reader it will be marked idiolect (2.2). Where it is habitual to a group of people, it will be marked dialect (2.1). In these instances the reader does not change tense or number by his miscue.

ER sheep	ER women	dialect 2.1 or .2
OR sheeps	OR womens	bound & combined morpheme 13.17

In other instances the reader is not confused over what the root word is, but simply applies alternate rules in order to produce tense or number changes.

ER women	ER men	ER drew	dialect 2.1
OR woman (pl.)	OR mans	OR drawed	bound & combined morpheme 13.12

2 *Idiolect is involved in the miscue.* The OR is recognizable as a vocabulary item or structure which is a distinguishable part of the speech system of the reader. It is an example of his own personal dialect but will not be a part of the patterns of his speech community.

ER Elizabeth	ER library	ER refrigerator
OR $Lizabit (phonemic)	OR $liberry (phonemic)	OR $frigerator (morphemic)

3 *A supercorrection is involved in the miscue.* In some instances a reader intentionally uses a word pronunciation which he views as being acceptable regardless of the pronunciation he habitually uses in speech situations. This can be a reflection of what he hears or thinks he hears in others' dialects. It can be a school-taught pronunciation which is an attempt to use a reading dialect or a supposed literate form.

ER kitten	ER frightened	ER a tree
OR kit+ten	OR frighten+ed	OR ā tree
ER started	ER the man	
OR start+ted	OR thē man	

This category will be used on the Multiple Attempts Taxonomy for substudies which include phonemic dialect variations. It will also be used on the general taxonomy if an example of supercorrection which includes structural changes can be identified.

4 *There is a secondary dialect involvement in the miscue.* The OR which the reader produces involves a variation which can be identified as dialect, idiolect or supercorrection.

ER . . . learning the ways of the range and the work of a sheep dog.
OR . . . learning the ways of the range and the work of *coming* a sheep dog. (*coming* is an idiolect variation for *becoming*)

ER Why were there no coyote fires at night?
OR Why were *not no* coyote fires at night? (*not no* is a dialect form)

ER I could see he was watching to make sure his whispering wasn't disturbing the thing that lay there.
OR I could see he was watching to make sure his *whispers* wasn't disturbing the thing that lay there. (*whispers wasn't* is a dialect form)

Additional Notes: This category is used on the general taxonomy only for substudies which include phonemic dialect variations or if an example of secondary dialect involvement which includes structural changes can be identified.

5 *A foreign language influence is involved in the miscue.* The reader applies to an English word the phonological rules of an alternate language which he speaks.

ER chair
OR $shair (French influence)

ER busy
OR $bissy (French influence)

This subcategory will be used on the Multiple Attempts Taxonomy for substudies which include phonemic dialect variations. It will also be used on the general taxonomy if an example of foreign language influence which includes structural changes can be identified.

9 *Dialect involvement is doubtful.* There is a lack of conclusive information on which to make a definite decision, but dialect involvement is suspected. When "doubtful" is marked the rest of the taxonomy categories are coded as if there is no dialect involvement.

This category is generally marked only for suspected dialect involving vocabulary substitutions or structural changes. Phonemic variations are included only for specifically designated substudies.

3 & 4 GRAPHIC AND PHONEMIC PROXIMITY

A reader must anticipate the structures and meanings of the author. In so doing both the graphemes and related phonemes of the ER are available to him as cues. The physical shape and/or the sound patterns related to the ER function in determining the reader's choice of the OR.

The two categories are scored using a zero through nine scale of increasing similarity. The points on the scales are intended to have equal weight across the two categories. Only word level substitutions are keyed.

3 GRAPHIC PROXIMITY

Blank *This category is inappropriate.* The miscue involves:

a An omission or an insertion of a word.

ER "Here *take* one," said the man.
OR "Here one," said the man.

ER The herder patted Chip and gave an arm signal toward the flock.
OR The herder patted Chip and gave *him* an arm signal toward the flock.

b A phrase level substitution in which the two phrases can not be broken down into submiscues.

ER You *do not have to stay home.*
OR You *may go and have fun.*

Or, a phrase level substitution for a single word (or the reverse.)

ER ...is quite a *businessman.*
OR ...is quite a *busy man.*

ER do not
OR don't

c Phrase or clause level intonation changes only. The specific word involved might change its grammatical category but not its spelling or its pronunciation.

ER ...that grew under *water, snails,* and...
OR ...that grew *underwater snails,* and...

ER He still thought it more fun to pretend to be a great scientist, mixing the *strange* and the *unknown.*
OR He still thought it more fun to pretend to be a great scientist, mixing the *strange* and the *unknown*⊙——→

ER It was fun to go to *school. When* he wasn't in *school, he* skated with his friends.
OR It was fun to go to *school when* he wasn't in *school. He* skated with his friends.

d Reversal miscues that involve no substitution of ER items.

ER suck the venom out
OR suck out the venom

ER look first
OR first look

0 *There is no graphic similarity between ER and the OR.*

ER the OR a	ER too OR very	ER so OR but	ER huddle OR moving
ER looking OR $intellate	ER coyote OR fighting	ER urged OR only	ER had OR been

1 *The ER and the OR have a key letter or letters in common.*

ER for OR of	ER under OR ground	ER be OR keep	ER accident OR instead
ER with OR this	ER enough OR often	ER ledges OR glen	ER made OR read

2 *The middle portions of the ER and OR are similar.*

ER zoom OR cook	ER took OR looked	ER touch OR would	ER explode OR $imploy
ER Elizabeth OR Isabel	ER bold OR glow		

3 *The end portions of the ER and OR are similar.*

ER don't OR needn't	ER voice OR face	ER sharply OR deeply	ER uncles OR friends
ER taking OR checking	ER vegetate OR $invirate		

4 *The beginning portions of the ER and OR are similar.*

ER perceive OR perhaps	ER may OR might	ER have OR hadn't
ER queer OR quick	ER out OR of	ER experiment OR $exmotter

5 *The beginning and middle portions of the ER and OR are similar.*

ER chloroform OR chlorophyll	ER walk OR walked	ER went OR wanted
ER narrowed OR $nearow	ER morally OR normal	ER vapid OR rapidly

6 *The beginning and end portions of the ER and OR are similar.*

ER twitching OR twinkling	ER pets OR puppies	ER lamps OR lights
ER library OR liberty	ER uncle OR once	ER must OR might

or, the middle and end portions of the ER and OR are similar.

ER eternal OR internal	ER cough OR enough	ER glanced OR danced

7 *The beginning, middle and end portions of the ER and OR are similar.*

ER chemist OR $chemisist	ER quickly OR quietly	ER preconception OR preoccupation
ER thought OR through	ER exclaimed OR explained	ER calibrations OR celebrations

or, there is reversal involving three or more letters.

ER was OR saw	ER spot OR stop	ER elbow OR below

8 *There is a single grapheme difference between the ER and the OR.*

ER squirting OR squinting	ER batter OR butter	ER stripes OR strips	ER A OR I

ER sister's OR sisters	ER cloudy OR $cloudly	ER made OR make	ER when OR then

or, a reversal involving two letters.

ER on OR no	ER stick OR ticks	ER girl OR grill

9 *The ER and the OR are homographs.*

ER read (present tense) OR read (past tense)	ER live (adjective) OR live (verb)
ER tear (noun) OR tear (verb)	ER record (noun) OR record (verb)

Additional Notes: For numbers 0 through 6, one extra point is added when:

a the ER and OR have similar configuration

ER tab OR tip	ER dig OR dip	ER plug OR play

b or when the ER and OR are two letter words which might have no other points of graphic similarity.

ER to OR in	ER he OR it	ER at OR in

When the OR is a nonword, a spelling is created for it by using the spelling of the ER as a base.

ER caperings OR $camperings	ER scabbard OR $scappard	ER vegetate OR $venget

Dialect miscues involving phonemic variations are treated as having standard spelling.

ER	get	ER	with	ER	this
sounds like	/git/	sounds like	/wif/	sounds like	/dis/
OR	get	OR	with	OR	this

4 PHONEMIC PROXIMITY

Blank *This category is inappropriate.* The miscue involves:

a An omission or an insertion of a word.

ER Soon he returned *with* two straight sticks.
OR Soon he returned two straight sticks.

ER Her hunger made her sniff hopefully under rocky ledges and along the small trails in the sage.
OR Her hunger made her sniff hopefully under *the* rocky ledges and along the small trails in the sage.

b A phrase level substitution in which the two phrases are not broken down into submiscues.

ER You *do not have to stay home.*
OR You *may go and have fun.*

Or, a phrase level substitution for a single word.

ER businessman — ER don't
OR busy man — OR do not

c Phrase or clause level intonation changes only. The specific word involved might change its grammatical category but not its spelling or its pronunciation.

ER . . . that grew under *water, snails*, and . . .
OR . . . that grew *underwater snails*, and . . .

ER He still thought it more fun to pretend to be a great scientist, mixing the *strange* and the *unknown.*
OR He still thought it more fun to pretend to be a great scientist, mixing the *strange* and the *unknown* ⟶

ER It was fun to go to *school. When* he wasn't in *school, he* skated with his friends.
OR It was fun to go to *school when* he wasn't in *school. He* skated with his friends.

d Reversal miscues that involve no substitution of ER items.

ER suck the venom out — ER look first
OR suck out the venom — OR first look

0 *There is no phonemic similarity between the ER and the OR.*

ER huddled — ER so — ER find — ER have
OR moving — OR but — OR allow — OR use

ER had — ER urged — ER sage
OR been — OR only — OR shack

1 *The ER and the OR have a key sound or sounds in common.*

ER keep — ER under — ER often
OR pick — OR around — OR enough

2 *The middle portion of the ER and OR are similar.*

ER tight — ER his — ER knolls
OR lightly — OR with — OR stroll

ER explode — ER ran
OR $imploy — OR had

3 *The ER and OR have the end portions in common.*

ER higher
OR anger

ER voice
OR face

ER made
OR head

ER choked
OR caught

ER taking
OR checking

ER had
OR did

4 *The ER and OR have the beginning portion in common.*

ER stood
OR still

ER before
OR because

ER have
OR hadn't

ER kite
OR cap

ER experiment
OR $exmotter

ER lamp
OR light

ER who
OR he

5 *The ER and OR have common beginning and middle portions.*

ER should
OR shouldn't

ER smiling
OR smile

ER needn't
OR needed

ER setting
OR settle

ER neighbor
OR $neighnew

6 *The ER and OR have common beginning and end portions*

ER twitching
OR twinkling

ER poured
OR pushed

ER being
OR beginning

ER must
OR much

ER tearful
OR $teareeble

ER while
OR well

ER library
OR liberty

or, they have common middle and end portions.

ER calibrations
OR celebrations

ER eternal
OR internal

ER moisture
OR posture

ER cellar
OR curler

ER expressed
OR impressed

7 *The beginning, middle and end portions of the ER and OR are similar.*

ER dissidents
OR descendents

ER crowded
OR crowned

ER Maximilian
OR $Maxiymilan

ER exclaimed
OR explained

8 *The ER and OR differ by a single vowel or consonant or vowel cluster*

ER grow
OR grew

ER A
OR I

ER stripes
OR strips

ER sighed
OR said

ER round
OR around

ER Tom
OR Tommy

ER when
OR then

ER cloudy
OR $cloudly

or, there is a morphophonemic difference

ER went	ER pen
OR $wint	OR $pin

or, there is an intonational shift (including the schwa).

ER a	ER contract (v)
OR ā	OR contract (n)

9 *The ER and OR are homophones.*

ER read	ER too	ER heir
OR red	OR two	OR air

5 ALLOLOGS

Allologs are considered to be alternate representational forms for the same item. Unlike synonyms there is no meaning change involved in the substitution of allolog forms. Both forms are generally available to the same language user; he uses them in different settings.

0 *An allolog is not involved in the miscue.*

a The miscue is coded under DIALECT. (The only exception to this rule is 5.4—long and short form or syllable deletion/insertion.)

b The miscue is coded under SEMANTIC WORD RELATIONSHIPS.

1 *The OR is a contracted form of the ER.*

ER can not	ER that is	ER you have
OR can't	OR that's	OR you've

2 *The OR is a full form of the ER contraction.*

ER won't	ER haven't	ER let's
OR will not	OR have not	OR let us

3 *The OR is a contraction which is not represented in print.*

ER He will not go.
OR He willn't go.

4 *The OR is either a long or short form of the ER.* This must be an alternatve available form within the dialect of the reader,

ER airplane	ER Tom	ER because	ER into
OR plane	OR Tommy	OR 'cause	OR in
ER toward	ER round	ER trouser pocket	
OR towards	OR around	OR trousers pocket	

or the OR involves a syllable deletion or insertion. This must be an alternative available form within the idiolect of the reader.

ER regardless	ER refrigerator
OR irregardless	OR frigerator

5 *The OR involves a shift to idiomatic form.*

ER The sheep were spreading *over* the sides.
OR The sheep were spreading *all over* the sides.

ER . . . reading the words *aloud.*
OR . . . reading the words *out loud.*

6 *The OR involves a shift from idiomatic form.*

ER The boss *took in* the camp at a glance.
OR The boss *took* the camp at a glance.

ER He is going *on* nine.
OR He is going *to be* nine.

7 *The OR involves a misarticulation.* This is an inadvertent production of a form for which the reader has another acceptable form.

ER Aluminum	ER strings	ER brother	ER soft-soled
OR $Alunimum	OR $shtrings	OR $brothy	OR $soft-sholed

In instances where the reader has an articulation difficulty and is unable to produce the acceptable form, 2.2 'idiolect' is marked.

6 & 7 SYNTACTIC AND SEMANTIC ACCEPTABILITY

A sentence can be viewed as involving both a syntactic organization and a semantic organization. The effects that a miscue has upon these two systems can be analyzed both in terms of acceptability and of change.

The following two categories are concerned only with whether the OR produces structure and/or meaning which is acceptable within the context of the material.

A reader reacts to the correctness and the expectedness of material in terms of his own dialect. In both of the acceptability categories, the reader's dialect is the norm by which the material is judged.

6 SYNTACTIC ACCEPTABILITY

The grammatical structures forming the sentence must be viewed apart from any semantic meaning which they carry. The view is an abstract one involving possible grammatical function organization. The sentence: "*Canaries* are very vicious dogs." involves a grammatical organization.

Subject pl. noun	be present tense pl.	intensifier	adjective	subject complement common pl.

which is completely acceptable while *canaries* does not fit semantically with the rest of the sentence.

The test for the syntactic acceptability of any word is that an acceptable English sentence be able to be produced with that word in the specified position.

the
ER Did you see my little monkey?

The grammatical function has been changed from possessive pronoun to determiner, but the resulting structure is fully acceptable.

It is possible for the miscue to produce a significant change in grammar which is still acceptable within the context. This category is meant to register only the acceptability of the OR to the rest of the material.

As a reader processes a sentence, it is possible for an initial miscue to cause the need either for a regression correction or for additional changes in the structure in order to maintain its acceptability. Whether or not a reader chooses to make these adjustments provides a cue to his processing of grammatical structure. In determining syntactic acceptability, the entire sentence is read with all uncorrected miscues intact.

Ⓒthat Ⓒwas Ⓡ
The quick eyes of the boss found what Jacob saw, and he shouted, "Don't shoot!
Ⓒ I
That's Peggy."

In coding *that* the sentence must be read:

The quick eyes of the boss found that Jacob saw, and he shouted, "Don't shoot! That's Peggy."

In coding *was* the sentence must be read:

The quick eyes of the boss found what Jacob was and he shouted, "Don't shoot! That's Peggy."

In coding *I* the sentence must be read:

The quick eyes of the boss found what Jacob saw, and he shouted, "Don't shoot! I Peggy."

The structure which is treated as an "entire sentence" is defined by Kellogg Hunt's concept of "minimal terminable unit."

It had been a long day for the dogs/and Peggy limped heavily as she approached the camp. (2 minimal terminable units)

The rays of the setting sun lingered over the high Arizona desert, touching the rocky tip of Badger Mountain and tinting the bold face of Antelope Rim. (1 minimal terminable unit)

0 *The miscue results in a structure which is completely syntactically unacceptable.* The miscue disrupts the structure of the sentence and does not have any possible grammatical relationship with either prior or succeeding portions of the sentence.

ER I couldn't *help* feeling proud.
OR I couldn't feeling proud.

ER My blue airplane *is* not here.
OR My blue airplane *look* not here.

ER *Look* for the red train.
OR *The* for the red train.

1 *The miscue results in a structure which is syntactically acceptable only with the prior portion of the sentence.* It would be possible to complete this segment and produce an acceptable grammatical structure.

ER Billy was delighted that *the* roots had made such beautiful colors.
OR Billy was delighted that *he*/roots had made such beautiful colors.

ER I stood still beside him watching. Harry was watching too and sweating all over his face so it shone like it was smeared thick with face cream.
OR I stood still beside him watching Harry./was watching too and sweating all over his face so it shone like it was smeared thick with face cream.

ER He had *the* blue airplane.
OR He had blue/airplane.

ER The shallow basin of Salt Creek Wash became a gathering pool of darkness where a band of eight hundred sheep with their lambs were bedding down for the night on a small patch of meadow.
OR The shallow basin of Salt Creek Wash became a gathering pool of darkness where a band of eight hundred sheep *were*/with their lambs were bedding down for the night on a small patch of meadow.

2 *The miscue results in a structure which is syntactically acceptable only with the following portion of the sentence.* It would be possible to complete this segment and produce an acceptable grammatical structure.

ER He pulled the kitchen stepladder *out* into the hall.
OR He pulled the kitchen stepladder/*walked* into the hall.

ER Both of us *together* can open the door.
OR Both of us/*Tommy* can open the door.

ER "Is my little monkey here?" said the man.
OR "Is my little/the monkey here?" said the man.

3 *The miscue results in a structure which is syntactically acceptable only within the sentence.* The OR sentence is a completely acceptable structure. However, it does not fit within the structural restraints that are operating within the larger context of the material.

ER *Where* did you get your pretty hat?
OR Did you get your pretty new hat?

(The plot of the story revolves around a number of people commenting on a new hat which Mrs. Duck is unaware of wearing. The question must reflect the person's awareness of the hat.)

ER Every year they *give* a prize to the student with the most original outside project.
OR Every year they *gave* a prize to the student with the most original outside project.

(The plot involves the author's attempt to win the prize. The action must be continuing.)

4 *The miscue results in a structure which is syntactically acceptable within the total passage.* The OR sentence is a completely acceptable structure which fits within the structural restraints operating within the larger context of the material.

ER He *wanted* to see what was inside.
OR He *went* to see what was inside.

ER He was making an electric bell *as a surprise* for his mother.
OR He was making an electric bell *to surprise* his mother.

ER He started to go *quickly* across the room.
OR He started to go *quick* across the room.

Additional Notes: When a miscue is an omission, the word following (preceding) must be included in the reading for the miscue to be syntactically acceptable with prior portion of sentence (6.1),

ER Mrs. Duck looked *here* and there.
OR Mrs. Duck looked and/there.

ER The expression *was* in the eyes and around the mouth.
OR The expression in/the eyes and around the mouth.

or syntactically acceptable with following portion of sentence (6.2).

ER "He did not stop here," said Sue.
OR "He did/not here," said Sue.

ER "If it bothers you *to* think of it as baby sitting," my father said, . . .
OR "If it bothers/you think of it as baby sitting," my father said, . . .

When either the first or the last word of a sentence is involved in a miscue, the possible structural relationships to the rest of the sentence are limited to "total acceptability," (either 6.3 or 6.4)

ER *Then* one day Freddie made an interesting mixture.
OR One day Freddie made an interesting mixture.

ER From the strings she made beautiful *baskets*.
OR From the strings she made beautiful *blankets*.

ER *Where* did you get your pretty hat?
OR Did you get your pretty hat?

or to "total unacceptability" (6.0).

ER *A* policeman stared at them.
OR *I* policeman stared at them.

ER *His* eyes caught sight of a red jacket.
OR *He* eyes caught sight of a red jacket.

ER I'll be back *soon*.
OR I'll be back *so*.

7 SEMANTIC ACCEPTABILITY

The acceptability of the meaning involved in the OR sentence is the concern. Multiple miscues can occur within a sentence. The reader has the option of correcting them or of altering the material. When determining semantic acceptability, the entire sentence will be read with all uncorrected miscues intact. (An "entire sentence" will be defined as being a Minimal Terminable Unit.)

He was speaking slowly and trying to think the thing out while he talked.

The omission of *the* is unacceptable with any portion of the sentence and will be marked 7.0. Because of this first miscue the substitution of *we* for *he* will only be marked acceptable with following, 7.2.

The structural organization of a sentence forms the basis for semantic relationships. Meaning, as a language system, is dependent upon syntax. It is the order of items and the use of inflection that indicate the meaning relationships of the items. The syntactic order is separate from and can precede the meaning but the meaning can not exist without the order. Semantic acceptability can never be scored higher than syntactic acceptability.

She was a small yellow canary.

syntactic acceptability 6.4
semantic acceptability 7.0

0 *The miscue results in a structure which is completely semantically unacceptable.* The miscue disrupts the meaning of the sentence and does not have any possible semantic relationship with either prior or following portions of the sentence.

ER One of the things he liked most was *cranberry* picking in the fall.
OR One of the things he liked most was *$carberry* picking in the fall.

ER Kitten Jones would not have changed her white *fur* coat for anything.
OR Kitten Jones would not have changed her white *few* coat for anything.

ER Billy liked to take part in the work of *his* tribe.
OR Billy liked to take part in the work of tribe.

1 *The miscue results in a structure which is semantically acceptable only with the prior portion of the sentence.* It would be possible to complete this segment and produce an acceptable grammatical structure.

ER I thought I would faint. I thought the refrigerator would explode. I knew *it* was Freddie's fault.

OR I thought I would faint. I thought the refrigerator would explode. I knew *I*/was Freddie's fault.

ER "You're just like your Uncle August—never *letting* well enough alone."
OR "You're just like your Uncle August—never *lifting*/well enough alone."

ER It helps me to remember the word definitions *if* I read them out loud.
OR It helps me to remember the word definitions I/read them out loud.

2 *The miscue results in a structure which is semantically acceptable only with the following portion of the sentence.* It would be possible to complete this segment and produce an acceptable grammatical structure.

ER His Uncle Maximilian was a real *chemist* with a company in Switzerland.
OR His Uncle Maximilian was a real/*chemistry* with a company in Switzerland.

ER At *once* Freddie set to work seriously.
OR At /*only* Freddie set to work seriously.

ER Suddenly I jumped from the chair, a wonderful idea *implanted* in my brain.
OR Suddenly I jumped from the chair, a wonderful idea/*implant* in my brain.

3 *The miscue results in a structure which is semantically acceptable only within the sentence.* The OR sentence is completely semantically accept-

able. However, it does not fit within the semantic restraints that are operating within the larger context of the material.

ER Danny had to hold up the wires for him.
OR Danny had to hold up the *telephone* wires for him.
(Telephone wires are not in the story, nor do they fit in.)

ER She taught him to know the kind of *roots* used by Winnebago Indians for many years.
OR She taught him to know the kind of *roofs* used by Winnebago Indians for many years. (They lived in tepees.)

4 *The miscue results in a structure which is semantically acceptable within the total passage.* The OR sentence is completely semantically acceptable and fits within the semantic restraints that are operating within the larger context of the material.

ER He *wanted* to see what was inside.
OR He *went* to see what was inside.

ER Freddie tried, with all his strength, but he couldn't open the *closet* door.
OR Freddie tried, with all his strength, but he couldn't open the *closed* door.

ER He started to go *quickly* across the room.
OR He started to go *quick* across the room.

ER "I've been waiting for *you.*" *He* raised his eyes and looked at me.
OR "I've been waiting for *you,*" *he* raised his eyes and looked at me.

Additional Notes: As with Syntactic Acceptability, when the miscue is an omission, the word following (preceding) must be included in the reading for the miscue to be semantically acceptable with prior portion of sentence (7.1).

ER But he still thought *it* more fun to pretend to be a great scientist . . .
OR But he still thought more/fun to pretend to be a great scientist . . .

ER You haven't told me *what* the idea is yet.
OR You haven't told me the/idea is yet.

or semantically acceptable with following portion of sentence (7.2).

ER When 200 million Americans sign a Sunday New York Times ad opposed *to* the Vietnam War, the Pentagon will retreat.
OR When 200 million Americans sign a Sunday New York Times ad/opposed the Vietnam War, the Pentagon will retreat.

ER There two men were signaling to each other, and *one* was pointing to the clock.
OR There two men were signaling to each other,/and was pointing to the clock.

When either the first or the last word of a sentence is involved in a miscue, the possible semantic relationships to the rest of the sentence are limited to "total acceptability," (either 7.3 or 7.4)

ER *He* will make a good pet.
OR *We* will make a good pet.

ER He and the fawn would race together through the *forest*.
OR He and the fawn would race together through the *field*.

or to "total unacceptability" (7.0).

ER *All* of them were living in Switzerland.
OR *Any* of them were living in Switzerland.

ER She made her own paints from the roots that Billy gathered from the *swamps*.
OR She made her own paints from the roots that Billy gathered from the *stamps*.

8 TRANSFORMATION

A reader works with already generated and transformed grammatical structures. His miscues reflect his anticipation of the deep structure, surface structure and the meaning with which he is dealing. It is possible for a miscue to cause a change in either or both.

Syntactic changes which the reader institutes can occur at either the deep or surface structure level. In this sense, he recreates the generative process of the author and transforms the material.

0 *A grammatical transformation is not involved.* The syntactic structure of the sentence is unchanged.

a A change involving only surface-level morphophonemic rules.

ER an	ER can not
OR a	OR can't

b A change involving meaning only.

ER It *sounded* like a fire siren.
OR It *shouted* like a fire siren.

ER He *taped* the batteries end to end.
OR He *tapped* the batteries end to end.

c Changes occurring within the noun and noun modifier category.

1 Distinctions between masculine and feminine in nouns and titles.

ER Mr.	ER boy
OR Mrs.	OR girl

ER John
OR Joan

ER aviator
OR aviatrix

2 Substitutions of one noun type for another.

ER The *surprise* is in my box. (common noun)
OR The *five* is in my box. (word as word name)

3 Changes occurring between noun modifier fillers.

ER ... during the *television* program. (noun adjunct)
OR ... during the *televised* program. (verb derived noun)

ER ... the ears of the *larger* dog. (comparative)
OR ... the ears of the *large* dog.

4 Some changes between pronouns.

ER he (she)
OR it

When the noun referred to is an animal or object.

d An omission or insertion within a grammatical function.

ER "Look at me," said *Yellow Bird*.
OR "Look at me," said *Bird*.

Both *Yellow* and *Bird* are keyed as noun phrasal unit, so that the word omission does not cause the omission of the grammatical function.

e Movements of adverbs or particles within a sentence.

ER Take your shoes *off*.
OR Take *off* your shoes.

ER He ran *happily*.
OR *Happily* he ran.

f Variations not involved in the sentence structure.

ER The words "*corrals*" and "boss" meant things to Peggy.
OR The words "*corral*" and "boss" meant things to Peggy.

1 *A transformation occurs which involves a difference in deep structure between the ER and OR.* In some instances both syntax and meaning are changed, in others, the syntax changes while the meaning is retained.

a Differences in tense or number.

ER As they approached the tent, the thin wail of coyotes reached *her* ears from upstream.
OR As they approached the tent, the thin wail of coyotes reached *their* ears from upstream.

ER He saw *the* spring flowers.
OR He saw *a* spring flowers.

Determiner substitutions do not usually involve a transformation, but in this case, the determiner substitution causes a move from singular to plural.

b Omissions or insertions of a grammatical function.

ER All of them were living in Switzerland.
OR All of them were living in *about* Switzerland.

ER His father *usually* called him Tinker.
OR His father called him Tinker.

ER She put on a *bright* cotton dress.
OR She put on a cotton dress.

ER He was straining to get the *words* out.
OR He was straining to get out.

ER We have many goals for tomorrow.
OR We have *made* many goals for tomorrow.

c Changes in the relationship of phrases and/or clauses.

ER I'm going to give you an injection. Serum.
OR I'm going to give you an injection of serum.

ER It went in smooth as into cheese.
(as if it were going into cheese)
OR It went in smooth as cheese.
(as cheese is smooth)

ER Here, take one. (*you* take one)
OR Here's one. (one *for you*)

ER Typical, that's it, typical. (*that* as a pronoun)
OR Typical, that is, typical. (*that* as a clause marker)

ER On nights when the fires were burning, she often heard coyotes singing *a protest* from distant ridges.
OR On nights when the fires were burning, she often heard coyotes singing *to protest* from distant ridges.

ER He said to keep *quite* still.
OR He said to keep *quiet*, still.

ER I switched off the headlamps of the car so the beam wouldn't swing in through the window of the side bedroom and *wake* Harry Pope.
(*The beam* wouldn't swing in and *the beam* wouldn't wake)

OR I switched off the headlamps of the car so the beam wouldn't swing in through the window of the side bedroom and *woke* Harry Pope. (*I* switched off and *I woke*)

2 *A transformation occurs in which the deep structure of the ER and the OR remains the same while the surface structure of the OR is generated by a different set of compulsory rules.* The author and the reader have a different set of obligatory transformations in their grammars.

a Regional or social dialect variations are involved.

ER She tore *bunches* of fur from his back.
OR She tore *bunch* of fur from his back.

ER He *has* gone to the store.
OR He gone to the store.

b The author has produced a structure which is either unusual for the situation or not entirely correct.

ER Billy knew that fawns *were* very shy.
OR Billy knew that fawns *are* very shy.

The shyness of fawns is a continuing situation and need not be past tense because of the verb *knew* in the sentence.

ER Knew I mustn't move. (This is not a usual surface level deletion.)
OR *I* knew I mustn't move.

c Compulsory rule shifts have become involved due to a change in terms.

ER After *school* one day Ted went for a walk in the park.
OR After *the show* one day Ted went for a walk in the park.

3 *A transformation occurs in which the deep structure of the ER and the OR remains the same while the surface structure of the OR is generated by alternate available rules.* The reader has available, in his grammar, the transform rules for both ER and OR surface structures.

ER This senseless, futile debate between *the* obstetrician and the mortician will end.
OR This senseless, futile debate between obstetrician and the mortician will end.

To be fully syntactically acceptable *the* before *mortician* would also need to be omitted.

ER One of them tore chunks of fur and hide from her neck *while* the other slashed a hind foot.
OR One of them tore chunks of fur and hide from her *neck. The* other slashed a hind foot.

ER When Freddie told how he *had fixed* the clock Mrs. Miller said, "You're just like Uncle Charles."
OR When Freddie told how he *fixed* the clock Mrs. Miller said, "You're just like Uncle Charles."

The variation in forms of the past tense does not alter the meaning.

ER He started to go *quickly* across the room.
OR He started to go *quick* across the room.

An alternate acceptable adverbial form.

ER ... counting each step carefully in the dark so I wouldn't take an extra *one* which wasn't there ...

OR ... counting each step carefully in the dark so I wouldn't take an extra *step* which wasn't there ...

Involves the same antecedent.

ER The building of coyote fires was not new to her ...
OR The building of *the* coyote fires was not new to her ...

ER The herder patted Chip and gave an arm signal ...
OR The herder patted Chip and gave *him* an arm signal ...

4 *The deep structure has been lost or garbled.* Sometimes the reader is completely unsuccessful in handling the grammatical structure produced by the author because it is new to him, or he fails either to recognize or anticipate it. He does not produce the structure used by the author and he fails to produce any recognizable portion of an alternate structure. (The coding of Phrase—15—and Clause—16—is optional when Transformation is coded "lost or garbled.")

a The structure has been lost.

ER "*A doctor*. Of course. That's it. I'll get Ganderbai."
OR "Of course. That's its. I'll get Ganderbai."

ER ... "I'm going to give you an injection. *Serum.* Just a prick but try not to move."
OR ... "I'm going to give you an injection. Just a prick but try not to move."

b The structure has been garbled. (Syntactic Acceptability has been coded "not acceptable"—6.0)

ER What his mother called him *depended* on what he had done last.
OR What his mother called him *$dipedee* on what he had done last.

Neither the use of an inflectional ending or of intonation made it possible to assign a grammatical function to this non-word.

ER *None* of the chemicals in his set was harmful.
OR *Known* of the chemicals in his set was harmful.

ER They were not likely to *explode.*
OR They were not likely to *employed.*

9 *There is some question of whether or not a transformation is involved in the miscue.* Sometimes there might be a doubt as to whether the change which has occurred falls within the parameters of the transformation category. This confusion can be due either to the OR containing a very limited portion of structure or to some confusion concerning the limits of the parameters themselves.

In such situations the Transformation category should be marked "doubtful" (8.9) and the miscue should be keyed, in the rest of the taxonomy categories, as if no transformation is involved.

9 & 10 SYNTACTIC AND SEMANTIC CHANGE

In two previous categories, the syntactic and semantic acceptability of the OR has been measured. The question now becomes one of evaluating how extensive a change the miscue has caused in both the structure and the meaning of the ER.

Like the Graphic Proximity and Phonemic Proximity categories, Syntactic Change and Semantic Change are scored using a zero through nine scale of increasing similarity. The points on the scales are intended to have equal weight across the two categories.

When a miscue produces a sentence which is syntactically acceptable (6.3 or 6.4), the degree of syntactic change between the ER and the OR is measured.

Because syntax can be examined with ever increasing finiteness, the following set of parameters is used for this category.

a In coding Syntactic Change, phrase structure is considered to consist of a surface level NP and VP so that changes involving adverbial phrases are treated as changes within the verb phrase and not as changes in phrase structure.

b The surface structure of a sentence is treated as being composed of independent, dependent and embedded clauses.

independent	*He ran home.* *The dog bit the man* when he entered the cage.
dependent:	The girl screamed *when the cars hit.* *After the game ended,* the team celebrated.
embedded:	The *yellow* bird . . . (adjective) *His* house . . . (possessive pronominal) He wanted *to buy* a toy. (infinitive)

c Conjunctions are not treated as a part of either the phrase or clause structure when connecting two independent units.

ER	He ran and he jumped.	clause—no involvement
OR	He ran. He jumped.	phrase—no involvement
ER	It was blue and green.	phrase —substitution
OR	It was blue-green.	clause—omission
ER	He ran and then he sat.	clause—no involvement
OR	He ran, then he sat.	phrase—no involvement

When reading the text sentence to determine Syntactic Change all uncorrected miscues made previous to the miscue being keyed must be read intact.

9 SYNTACTIC CHANGE

Blank *This category is inappropriate.* The miscue involves either no or partial syntactic acceptability (Syntactic Acceptability "0," "1" or "2").

0 *The syntax of the OR and the ER are unrelated.* They retain no single common element of a particular phrase structure.

ER Where'd it bite you?
OR A bite?

1 *The syntax of the OR and the ER have a single element in common.*

2 *The syntax of the OR has a key element which retains the syntactic function of the ER.*

ER *You* do not have to stay home.
OR *You* may go and have fun.

Retention of the noun phrase.

3 *There is a major change in the syntax of the OR.*

ER "Sue," said the man. "He did have it."
OR Sue said. "The man, he did have it."

All of the phrases remain present but their basic relationships are altered.

ER He was lying there very still and tense *as though* he was holding onto himself hard because of sharp pain.
OR He was lying there very still and tense *as he thought* he was holding onto himself hard because of sharp pain.

Addition of a clause.

ER "Oh, I like it here."
OR "Go. I like it here."

Addition of a clause.

4 *There is a minor change in the syntax of the OR.*

ER When summer *ended, the* Whitemoons packed their belongings again.
OR The summer *ended. The* Whitemoons packed their belongings again.

Move from dependent to independent clause.

ER He was speaking more slowly than ever *now and* so softly I had to lean close to hear him.
OR He was speaking more slowly than ever *and now* so softly I had to lean close to hear him.

Change in dependency of adverb.

ER Soon he returned *with* two straight sticks.
OR Soon he returned two straight sticks.

Move from prepositional phrase to direct object.

ER "Well, he's home a lot, " *I said.*
OR "Well, he's home a lot."

Omission of the dialogue carrier.

ER He was wearing a pair of pajamas *with blue, brown* and white stripes.
OR He was wearing a pair of pajamas, *blue and brown, with* white stripes.

Move from adjectives embedded in prepositional phrase to subject complements.

5 *There is a major change within the structure of the phrase.* This includes the insertion, deletion or substitution within the phrase of any structure having more than one constituent.

ER I want you to save half your allowance *for it* each week.
OR I want you to save half your allowance each week.

Omission of a prepositional phrase.

ER He had a carriage.
OR He had a *horse-drawn* carriage.
(that was drawn by a horse)

Insertion of an embedded clause.

ER I will tell it *all over* Green Hills.
OR I will tell it *all on* Green Hills.

With the substitution of one preposition for another (*over* for *on*), *all* moves from being a function word quantifier to the direct object. Yet the basic structural outlines of the sentence have not changed.

ER He is going *on* nine.
OR He is going *to be* nine.

A verb particle is replaced by an infinitive form.

ER "Then I will find work," said Ted.
OR "Then I will work," said Ted.

The direct object replaces the verb.

6 *There is a minor change within the structure of the phrase.* This includes the insertion, deletion or substitution of any single constituent within the phrase structure.

ER He did see the fires.
OR He did *not* see the fires.

Insertion of the negative.

ER She pounded the young trees into *long* strings.
OR She pounded the young trees into strings.

Omission of embedded adjective.

ER I leaned on the *baby* bed.
OR I leaned on the *baby's* bed.

Move from adjective to possessive noun modifier.

ER ... most of them came from *jungle rivers* where ...
OR ... most of them came from *Jungle River* where ...

Move from common to proper noun.

ER He raised his eyes and looked *at me*.
OR He raised his eyes and looked *now*.

Move from prepositional phrase to adverb.

ER I *could see* he was awake.
OR I *could have seen* he was awake.

Move from past tense to past perfect.

7 *There is a change in person, tense, number or gender of the OR.*

ER How he *wanted* to go back.
OR How he *wants* to go back.

ER Billy sang for all the *tribe*.
OR Billy sang for all the *tribes*.

ER *I* made a special mixture.
OR *He* made a special mixture.

ER *You* not in bed yet?
OR *You're* not in bed yet.

The move away from the question does not alter the relationship of the sentence to the rest of the text.

8 *There is a change in choice of function word or another minor shift in the OR.* This includes changes within subcategories of a function word and the omission or insertion of optional surface structure. No miscues which cause a change in either dependency or modification will be coded in this subcategory.

a Changes in choice of a function word.

ER There was *a* dinosaur.
OR There was *one* dinosaur.

ER Young dissidents have been widely berated for lacking an alternative *to* the present system.
OR Young dissidents have been widely berated for lacking an alternative *in* the present system.

ER . . . and the generation now in power will widen *into* a new national fault line.
OR . . . and the generation now in power will widen *to* a new national fault line.

b Omission or insertion of optional surface structure.

ER He heard the rustling of leaves.
OR He heard the rustling of *the* leaves.

ER It is impossible to grow, change, mature or expand, . . .
OR It is impossible to grow, change *and* mature or expand, . . .

ER I saw *that* my mother was smiling broadly.
OR I saw my mother was smiling broadly.

ER Knew I mustn't move.
OR *I* knew I mustn't move.

ER "Quickly Timber, *but* take your shoes off."
OR "Quickly Timber, *you* take your shoes off."

ER I swear *it*.
OR I swear.

9 *The syntax of the OR is unchanged from the syntax of the ER.* Only form class (noun, verb, adjective, adverb) substitutions will be marked here. Included are all null forms for tense or number which are dialect variations.

ER The windows were full of *puppies* and kittens.
OR The windows were full of *pets* and kittens.

ER What *queer* experiment was it this time?
OR What *queen* experiment was it this time?

ER What his mother called him *depended* on what he had done last.
OR What his mother called him *depend* on what he had done last.

10 SEMANTIC CHANGE

When a miscue produces a sentence which is semantically acceptable (7.3 or 7.4) the degree of semantic change between the ER and the OR is measured.

In reading the text sentence to determine Semantic Change all uncorrected miscues made previous to the miscue being keyed must be read intact.

Blank *This category is inappropriate.* The miscue involves either no or partial semantic acceptability (Semantic Acceptability marked 0, 1 or 2).

0 *The OR is completely anomalous to the rest of the story.* A concept, action or relationship is introduced which is totally incongruous to the rest of the story.

ER The bulb began to *glow.*
OR The bulb began to *grow.*

The bulb is an electric light.

ER He came out of his *slump* and looked around.
OR He came out of his *slum* and looked around.

The reference was to how a TV producer was sitting.

ER She turned questioning eyes to the coughing herder and then to the sheep and the shadowy figure of *Chip* moving about the band.
OR She turned questioning eyes to the coughing herder and then to the sheep and the shadowy figure of *the chimp* moving about the band.

The story involves a sheep herder, two dogs, and a herd of sheep.

1 *There is a change or loss affecting the plot in basic sense or creating major anomalies.*

ER It was no less than an hour before *dawn.*
OR It was no less than an hour before *dark.*

The coyotes in the story become a danger to the sheep during the late hours of the night.

ER *Just* like your Uncle Maximilian!
OR *I* like your Uncle Maximilian!

This line is repeated throughout the story as the mother compares her son to his uncles.

ER We're two days out from the *corrals* and a day late on the drive.
OR We're two days out from the *quarrel* and a day late on the drive.

The possibility of help hinges on their expected arrival at the corrals.

2 *There is a change or loss involving key aspects of the story or seriously interfering with subplots.*

ER "*Oh*, I like it here."
OR "*Go*. I like it here."

The character who is speaking likes her locale because of the other characters. She does not want them to leave.

ER This is the *last* day of Fair Week.
OR This is the *light* day of Fair Week.

This was the main character's only chance to earn money and see the fair.

ER Then her eyes caught a movement in the *sage* near the top of the knoll.
OR Then her eyes caught a movement in the *same* near the top of the knoll.

The plot hinges on the dog successfully picking up the cues of a coyote attack.

3 *There is a change or loss resulting in inconsistency concerning a major incident, major character or major sequence.*

ER Freddie tried with all his strength, but he couldn't open the closet door *either*.
OR Freddie tried with all his strength, but he couldn't open the closet door *enough*.

If the door had opened at all the sister would have had light and Freddie would not have had to construct a flashlight to keep her from being frightened until help came.

ER In one corner of the kitchen, *Freddie* was busy working on an experiment.
OR In one corner of the kitchen, *mother* was busy working on an experiment.

Mother, and the rest of the family, object to Freddie's experimenting.

ER "*Find* the toys!" said the man.
OR "The toys!" said the man.

The hunt for the missing toys is the main action of the story.

4 *There is a change or loss resulting in inconsistency concerning a minor incident, minor character or minor aspect of sequence.*

ER We have to buy *feed* for the *horse.*
OR We have to buy *rugs* for the *house.*

The main point is that the family must spend their money on things other than tickets to the fair.

ER Then it stopped moving and now it's lying there in the warmth.
OR Then it stopped moving and now it's *probably* lying there in the warmth.

There is no doubt in the character's mind that a snake is lying there.

5 *There is a change or loss of aspect which is significant but does not create inconsistencies within the story.*

ER He had been experimenting with his *chemistry* set.
OR He had been experimenting with his set.

This is the first mention of the chemistry set in the story and the omission limits information on a significant aspect.

6 *There is a change or loss of an unimportant detail of the story.*

ER One of the things he *liked* most was cranberry picking.
OR One of the things he *got* most was cranberry picking.

This is just one of a number of jobs which the boy in the story does for the tribe.

ER I want *you* to save half your allowance for it each week.
OR I want to save half your allowance for it each week.

There is a change in detail concerning whether the mother or the boy will be responsible for saving the money.

ER Next he placed the bulb so that it touched the cap on the *top* battery.
OR Next he placed the bulb so that it touched the cap on the battery.

There is a change in the number of batteries the boy uses in making his flashlight.

7 *There is a change in person, tense, number, comparative, etc. which is non-critical to the story.*

ER Andrew *had* made a very favorable impression.
OR Andrew made a very favorable impression.

ER "Where are you?" *he* shouted.
OR "Where are you?" *she* shouted.

8 *There is a slight change in connotation.*

ER Then he noticed *that this one's leg* was broken.
OR Then he noticed *that one leg* was broken.

ER Then they all *crowded* into the car.
OR Then they all *crawled* into the car.

ER Ganderbai took a piece of *red* rubber tubing from his bag and slid one end under and up and around Harry's bicep.
OR Ganderbai took a piece of rubber tubing from his bag and slid one end under and up and around Harry's bicep.

or, substitution of a similar name which doesn't confuse the cast.

ER Billy Whitemoon was a *Winnebago* Indian boy.
OR Billy Whitemoon was a *$Wonniebago* Indian boy.

ER I went across to the door of *Harry's* room, opened it quietly, and looked in.
OR I went across to the door of *Henry's* room, opened it quietly, and looked in.

9 *No change has occurred involving story meaning.*

ER They covered it* with deer *hides* to keep the family dry in rainy weather.
OR They covered it with deer *hide* to keep the family dry in rainy weather.

(* a summer house)

ER He heard the rustling of leaves.
OR He heard the rustling of *the* leaves.

ER *When* summer ended, *the* Whitemoons packed their belongings again.
OR *The* summer ended. *The* Whitemoons packed their belongings again.

ER "I've been waiting for you." *He* raised his eyes and looked at me.
OR "I've been waiting for you," *he* raised his eyes and looked at me.

11 INTONATION

Changes in intonation are involved in almost all miscues. This category attempts to register only those situations where the intonation change is part of the direct cause of the miscue and not only a result of other changes.

0 *Intonation is not involved in the miscue.* Within these miscues the intonation shifts which occur result from other changes which the reader has made.

ER "You *are* too little," said Father.
OR "You *is* too little," said Father.

ER Here is something *you can do.*
OR Here is something *to get down.*

ER Come, Peggy.
OR Come *on*, Peggy.

1 *An intonation shift within a word is involved.* The shift in intonation creates either a nonword or a different lexical item.

ER "*Philosophical!*" I yelled.
OR "*Philoso=phical!*" I yelled.

ER ... lingered over the high Arizona *desert,* ...
OR ... lingered over the high Arizona *de=sert,* ...

ER ... the tendon above one hind leg was *severed,* ...
OR ... the tendon above one hind leg was *se=vered,* ...

2 *An intonation shift is involved between words within one phrase structure of the sentence.* The shift does not cause changes which cross phrase structure boundaries.

ER ... came from *jungle rivers* where ...
OR ... came from *Jungle River* where ...

Jungle moves from an adjective position to a part of a proper name (noun phrase).

ER ... that grew *under water, snails*, and ...
OR ... that grew *underwater snails*, and ...

Snails moves from being the first in a list of items that grow under water to being a specifically modified kind of snail.

3 *Intonation is involved which is relative to the phrase or clause structure of the sentence.* The intonation shift causes changes which cross phrase and/or clause boundaries.

ER Tomorrow we must crown a Miss America who has buck teeth, *cash in Las Vegas*, abandon our calling cards and list everyone in Who's Who.
OR Tomorrow we must crown a Miss America who has buck teeth, *cash* in Las Vegas, abandon our calling cards and list everyone in Who's Who.

In the ER sentence *cash in* is a verb plus particle meaning "to turn in." The reader anticipated a noun meaning "money" plus a prepositional phrase.

ER ... a last look assured her that all was well *and* that her mate was patrolling the far side.
OR ... a last look assured her that all was well, that her mate was patrolling the far side.

ER The dogs' *uneasiness, growing* for the past few days, now became more acute.
OR The dogs' *ungreasy growl* for the past few days, now became more acute.

4 *A shift in terminal sentence intonation is involved.*

ER It was fun to go to *school. When* he wasn't in *school, he* skated with his friends.
OR It was fun to go to *school when* he wasn't in *school. He* skated with his friends.

ER And bring serum for a krait bite.
OR And bring serum for a krait bite?

ER Her muscles *tensed. As* she started *forward, Chip* wheeled to face the knoll.
OR Her muscles *tensed as* she started *forward. Chip* wheeled to face the knoll.

5 *The intonation change involves a substitution of a conjunction for terminal punctuation or the reverse.*

ER The boys fished *and* then they cooked their catch.
OR The boys fished. Then they cooked their catch.

ER She pounded the young trees into long strings. From the strings she made beautiful baskets.
OR She pounded the young trees into long strings *and* from the strings she made beautiful baskets.

6 *The intonation change involves direct quotes.*

ER "Tom," said mother.
OR Tom said, "Mother."

ER Mr. Miller sighed. "*Seriously, Tinker,* sometimes I wish you didn't want to be a scientist."
OR Mr. Miller sighed *seriously.* "*Tinker* sometimes I wish you didn't want to be a scientist."

LEVELS 12 THROUGH 16

Previous categories have registered the occurrence of any syntactic change. The following set of categories records these changes for both surface and deep structure in relation to the varying structural constituents.

Language constituents are interrelated so that a change within one can also mean a change in another. Where possible, these compulsory relationships are indicated.

In many ways, change at one structural level causes changes at all of the succeeding levels. For this reason, the categories in this section become increasingly selective of the phenomena which they record as they incorporate subsequent categories.

The kind and level of miscue can restrict the possible involvement of structural constituents. When a category is either not involved or restricted from involvement zero will be marked.

12 SUBMORPHEMIC

Sound differences between the ER and the OR are recorded. These differences are limited to one and two phoneme sequences and bound morphemes which are composed of a schwa plus a consonant.

0 *The submorphemic level is not involved.*

a There is a difference of a two phoneme sequence which is either co-terminus with the morpheme or within a three to four phoneme sequence.

ER an	ER of	ER the
OR ā	OR it	OR this

ER bigger	ER had
OR better	OR made

b The miscue is a word level substitution with a difference greater than a two phoneme sequence.

ER Maximilian	ER explode	ER cranberry
OR $Maxmil	OR employed	OR $canderberry

c The miscue involves a whole word omission/insertion, or a phrase level miscue.

ER It's very dark *in* here.
OR It's very dark here.

ER I can't get out.
OR I can't get *it* out.

ER He put it *aside.*
OR He put it *to the side.*

1. *There is a substitution of phonemes.* This can include a substitution between a one and two phoneme sequence.

ER bit	ER then	ER none
OR bat	OR when	OR known

ER weakened	ER hunger	ER rocky
OR widened	OR hungry	OR rocks

A one phoneme sequence can be co-terminus with the morpheme.

ER I
OR A

2 *There is an insertion of a phoneme(s).*

ER tanks	ER Tom	ER your
OR $tranks	OR Tommy	OR yours
ER a	ER high	
OR the	OR higher	

3 *There is an omission of a phoneme(s).*

ER tracks	ER quickly	ER feasted
OR tacks	OR quick	OR feast
ER midst	ER noses	
OR mist	OR nose	

4 *There is a reversal of phonemes.*

ER pilot	ER Spot	ER girl	ER split
OR polite	OR stop	OR grill	OR slipped

5 *There are multiple minor phonemic variations.* This involves the occurrence of more than one substitution, insertion, or omission of a one or two phoneme sequence within a longer morpheme.

ER dinosaur	ER Winnebago	ER experimenting
OR $dine+oh+staur	OR $Wonniebag	OR $espairamenteeng

13 BOUND & COMBINED MORPHEME LEVEL

Miscues involving bound or combined morphemes are marked first for the physical qualities of the miscue—substitution, insertion, omission, reversal—and then for the kind of morphemic involvement. The examples are presented from the perspective of the morphemic involvement.

Included here are all miscues involving inflectional, derivational or contractional morphemes.

Irregularly formed bound morphemes which involve spelling changes internal to the root word (come/came, woman/women, ox/oxen) are included within the category.

Also included are variant base forms which cause the use of bound morpheme allomorphs (breakfas, breakfases). (See Word and Free Morpheme categories also.)

00 *This category is not involved:*

a There is a word level substitution which does not involve bound or combined morphemes.

ER when	ER and	ER cranberry
OR then	OR had	OR $canberry
ER backward	ER toward	ER tucked
OR backwards	OR towards	OR stuck

b The miscue involves an irregularly formed bound morpheme which does not involve internal spelling changes.

ER read	ER lead
OR read	OR lead

c The miscue involves either the omission or insertion of a whole word or phrase.

ER Billy smiled *shyly*. Then he began to sing.
OR Billy smiled. Then he began to sing.

ER All of them were living in Switzerland.
OR All of them were living in *about* Switzerland.

d There is a change in phrase or sentence level intonation.

ER It was fun to go to *school. When* he wasn't in *school, he* skated with his friends.
OR It was fun to go to *school when* he wasn't in *school. He* skated with his friends.

_1 *The miscue involves an inflectional suffix.*

11 substitution

ER frighten*ed*	ER help	ER horse
OR frighten*ing*	OR help*ed*	OR houses
ER walk*ed*	ER girl	ER Freddie's
OR want*ing*	OR girls	OR Teddie (dialect)

All miscues involving tense and number changes through inflectional endings will be treated as substitutions.

Dialect related miscues involving a null form of the possessive will be treated as substitutions.

21 insertion

ER Freddie	ER small	ER high
OR Freddie's	OR smallest	OR higher
ER hurt		
OR hunt*ing*		

31 omission

ER quickly	ER growing	ER cooking
OR quick	OR growl	OR cook

41 reversal

ER coyote's walk
OR coyote walks

_2 *The miscue involves a noninflected form.* This is restricted to situations in which both the ER and OR are words which indicate inflection through internal spelling changes.

12 substitution

ER woman	ER men	ER come
OR women	OR woman	OR came

This subcategory will never involve insertions, omissions, or reversals.

_3 *The miscue involves a contractional suffix.*

13 substitution

ER you've	ER I'm
OR it's	OR I'll

23 insertion

ER you	ER could	ER I
OR you've	OR couldn't	OR I'll

33 omission

ER couldn't	ER he's
OR could	OR he

43 reversal

ER needn't have
OR needed hadn't

_4 *The miscue involves a derivational suffix.*

14 substitution

ER hopefully
OR hopelessly

24 insertion

ER Tom	ER hunger
OR Tommy (diminutive)	OR hungry

ER reassure
OR reassurance

34 omission

ER sunn*y* beach
OR sun beach

ER meaning*less*
OR meaning

ER herd*er*
OR herd

44 reversal

_5 *The miscue involves a prefix.*

15 substitution

ER *ex*ternal
OR *in*ternal

ER *pre*conception
OR $reconception

ER *im*partial
OR $*un*partial

25 insertion

ER usual
OR *un*usual

ER regardless
OR *ir*regardless

ER urgently
OR *un*gently

35 omission

ER *pre*determined
ER determined

ER *de*scendant
OR $scendant

45 reversal

ER *pre*determined requisition
OR determined $*pre*requisition

_6 *The miscue crosses affix types.*

16 substitution

ER televis*ed* program
OR televis*ion* program

ER use*less*
OR *un*less

ER need*n't*
OR need*ed*

46 reversal

ER small work*er*
OR small*er* work

This subcategory will never involve omissions or insertions.

_7 *The miscue involves the base.* There is some confusion over what constitutes the root word.

17 substitution

ER sheep (pl.)
OR sheeps

ER women
OR womens

ER drowned
OR $drownd*ed*

This subcategory will never include insertions, omissions, or reversals.

Additional Notes: In some instances a single miscue involves two or more changes which fall with the Bound and Combined Morpheme category. In such instances submiscues are used and all of the changes noted.

34 34 34 31
ER institutionalizing
OR institute

ER tight
24 21
OR tightened

14 WORD AND FREE MORPHEME LEVEL

Free morphemes are oral meaning bearing units within the language which can function independently or in combination with other free or bound morphemes. Words are graphic representations of free morphemes, and free and bound morpheme combinations.

Miscues involving words and/or free morphemes are marked first for the physical qualities of the miscue—substitution, insertion, omission, reversal—and then for the kind of morphemic involvement. The examples are presented from the perspective of the morphemic involvement.

00 *This category is not involved.*

a The miscue involves either a misarticulation,

ER *sickly* whisper
OR *$slicky* whisper

ER soft-*soled* shoes
OR $soft-*sholed* shoes

or, a morphophonemic variant of a word.

ER little
OR $lit+tle

ER just
OR $jus

ER reassuring
OR $resuring

b The word involved in the miscue is not physically changed but its grammatical function and/or meaning is altered.

ER He went *in* the house. (preposition)
OR He went *in*. (proadverb)

ER He was a *criminal* lawyer. (noun adjunct)
OR He was a *criminal*. (noun)

c The miscue is at the phrase level.

ER You *do not have to stay home.*
OR You *may go and have fun.*

ER He is going *on* nine.
OR He is going *to be* nine.

ER I *haven't.*
OR I *have not.*

_1 *The ER and/or the OR involve a multiple morpheme word.*

11 substitution

ER He *looked* at the doll.
OR He *looks* at the doll.

ER She *thumped* the camera . . .
OR She *climbs* the camera . . .

ER It was *useless.*
OR It was *unless.*

ER They packed their *belongings.*
OR They packed their *belonging.*

ER Mr. Jones *finished* the pictures . . .
OR Mr. Jones *fishing* the pictures . . .

21 insertion

ER All of them were living in Switzerland.
OR All of them were living in *about* Switzerland.

ER I suspect that the gap between . . .
OR I suspect that the *generation* gap between . . .

ER We'll just have to build fires again.
OR We'll just have to build *bigger* fires again.

31 omission

ER He heard a little *moaning* cry.
OR He heard a little cry.

ER The chicken pecked *rapidly.*
OR The chicken pecked.

ER The *helpless* animal at her feet . . .
OR The animal at her feet . . .

40 reversal

Any reordering of already existing elements within the text will be treated as a word reversal. Word level reversals are not marked according to the number or kind of morphemes contained within the two words involved in the miscue.

ER *I can* do it.
OR *Can I* do it?

ER A *first look*.
OR A *look first*.

ER He was taking *the shoes off*.
OR He was taking *off the shoes*.

_2 *The ER and/or the OR involve a single morpheme word.*

12 substitution

ER The *train* was . . .
OR The *toy* was . . .

ER The *women* came. (irregularly formed plural)
OR The *woman* came.

ER He *came*. (irregularly formed past tense)
OR He *went*.

ER . . . to accept *a* future they want and . . .
OR . . . to accept *the* future they want and . . .

22 insertion

ER He heard the rustling of leaves.
OR He heard the rustling of *the* leaves.

ER The boy ran.
OR The *young* boy ran.

ER . . . we have many goals for tomorrow.
OR . . . we have *made* many goals for tomorrow.

32 omission

ER The owner of the store explained *that* the fish . . .
OR The owner of the store explained the fish . . .

ER He returned *with* two sticks.
OR He returned two sticks.

ER . . . wandered away from its mother, *and* she raced to it . . .
OR . . . wandered away from its mother, she raced to it . . .

_3 *The ER is a single morpheme word and the OR is a multiple morpheme word.*

13 substitution

ER How do I know he is *your* deer?
OR How do I know he is *yours*, dear?

ER He sang for all the *tribe*.
OR He sang for all the *tribes*.

ER Yet by *accident* he might discover something.
OR Yet by *accidently* he might discover something.

ER ... that maturity will *force* the young to stop fighting ...
OR ... that maturity will *enforce* the young to stop fighting ...

This subcategory will never involve insertions, omissions or reversals.

_4 *The ER is a multiple morpheme word and the OR is a single morpheme word.*

14 substitution

ER One of the things he *liked* most was cranberry picking.
OR One of the things he *got* most was cranberry picking.

ER This *one's* leg was broken.
OR This *one* leg was broken.

This subcategory will never involve insertions, omissions, or reversals.

_5 *The miscue involves a free morpheme within a longer word.*

15 substitution

ER They *crowd*ed into the car.
OR They *crawl*ed into the car.

ER He *look*ed.
OR He *jump*ed.

ER ... and *tint*ing the bold face of Antelope Rim.
OR ... and *tilt*ing the bold face of Antelope Rim.

ER His hold *weak*ened.
OR His hold *wide*ned.

25 insertion

ER He was being quiet.
OR He was be*com*ing quiet.

35 omission

ER He was be*com*ing quiet.
OR He was being quiet.

_6 *The miscue involves one or both of the free morphemes in a compound or hyphenated word.*

16 substitution

ER He must smash his *shock*-proof gold watch, . . .
OR He must smash his *stock*-proof gold watch, . . .

ER . . . when our *sputnik-obsessed* teachers began clobbering us with homework . . .
OR . . . when our *$sprutnik-observed* teachers began clobbering us with homework . . .

ER . . . to the *saddle*bag home of her five puppies, . . .
OR . . . to the *sand*bag home of her five puppies, . . .

ER His mother was making a *headband*.
OR His mother was making a *handbag*.

26 insertion

ER . . . on a small patch of meadow.
OR . . . on a small patch of meadow*land*.

ER She scampered up the hill.
OR She scampered up the hill*side*.

36 omission

ER . . . gave her attention to her left *fore*paw . . .
OR . . . gave her attention to her left paw . . .

ER . . . spilled the contents of a saddlebag *on*to the ground.
OR . . . spilled the contents of a saddlebag to the ground.

ER The *air*plane landed safely.
OR The plane landed safely.

46 reversal

ER The anchor was in the *boathouse*.
OR The anchor was in the *houseboat*.

_7 *The OR is a nonword.*

ER Inside there was usually a *parrot* or a monkey.
OR Inside there was usually a *$partroot* or a monkey.

ER . . . the rocky tip of *Badger* Mountain . . .
OR . . . the rocky tip of *$Bagger* Mountain . . .

ER . . . and send them to the *contest*.
OR . . . and send them to the *$consate*.

This subcategory will never involve insertions, omissions or reversals.

-8 *The OR is a phonemic or morphophonemic dialect alternate of the ER.*

ER She suddenly *wanted* a drink . . .
OR She suddenly *want* (past tense) a drink . . .

ER The water *spilled* all over the floor.
OR The water *$spilleded* all over the floor.

ER . . . *laying* the book on the bed.
OR . . . *lying* the book on the bed.

This subcategory will never involve insertions, omissions, or reversals.

15 PHRASE

Within this category, the surface structure of a sentence is treated as being composed of possible noun and verb phrases with the verb phrase consisting of possible verb and adverb phrases. Recognizable structural changes within any of these three phrases are recorded. Any of the three phrases can be represented by a single constituent.

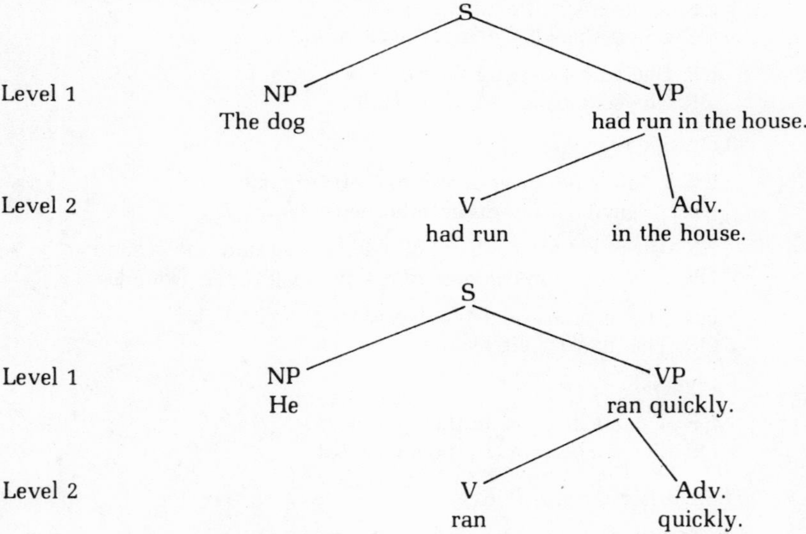

0 *This category is not involved.*

a An OR word for which a grammatical function can not be assigned.

to
"You see," I said, "it helps . . ."

To could be either a verb marker or a preposition.

b A phonemic or word level substitution dialect miscue is involved in which there is no change of grammatical function.

ER He *went*.
OR He *goed*.

ER Penny and Sue Jones *liked* to wear pretty colored dresses.
OR Penny and Sue Jones *like* (past tense) to wear pretty colored dresses.

c A surface phrase represented by a single word in which the OR does not change the grammatical function regardless of the grammatical filler.

ER *Coyotes* run away.
OR *Wolves* run away.

ER *She* said.
OR *Susan* said.

ER He ran *home*.
OR He ran *rapidly*.

ER He went *in*.
OR He went *home*.

ER Give me two *pencils*.
OR Give me two *reds*.

d Shifts in number (singular ←→ plural) or tense (present ←→ past, etc.) which don't cause other structural changes in the phrase or within categories where no transformation has been marked (adj → noun adjunct, adjunct → verb derived adj).

ER I leaned on the baby bed.
OR I leaned on the baby beds.

ER They impress my mind better that way.
OR They impressed my mind better that way.

ER He was a *criminal* lawyer.
OR He was a *busy* lawyer.

1 *A substitution is involved at the phrase level.* This can involve a change in phrase structure or the substitution of one phrase structure for another.

ER The *yellow* dog . . .
OR the dog . . .

ER . . . started *toward* the rimrock.
OR . . . started *to work* the rimrock.

ER ... is quite a *businessman.*
OR ... is quite a *busy man.*

ER I haven't...
OR I have not...

ER I was not...
OR I wasn't...

ER The sight of his pet *frightened* Billy, for Lightfoot was off Winnebago land.
OR The sight of his pet *frightening* Billy, for Lightfoot was off Winnebago land.

The noun phrase changes from *The sight of his pet* to *The sight of his pet frightening Billy.*

2 *An insertion is involved at the phrase level.* This must be the introduction of a phrase structure which was not present in the ER.

ER She was little more than...
OR She was little, more than...

ER Knew I mustn't move.
OR *I* knew I mustn't move.

ER "Quickly Timber, *but* take your shoes off."
OR "Quickly Timber, *you* take your shoes off."

3 *An omission is involved at the phrase level.* This must be the loss of a phrase structure which was in the ER.

ER ... that grew under *water, snails,* and...
OR ... that grew *underwater snails,* and...

ER But *first* he wanted to buy a present for his mother.
OR But he wanted to buy a present for his mother.

First is a proadverb for the deep structure phrase *in the first instance.*

4 *A reversal is involved at the phrase level.* This must involve the movement from one clause to another of either a phrase or an element from a phrase.

ER He was speaking more slowly than ever *now and* so softly I had to lean close to hear him.
OR He was speaking more slowly than ever *and now* so softly I had to lean close to hear him.

ER Mr. Miller sighed. "*Seriously,* Tinker, sometimes I wish you didn't want to be a scientist."
OR Mr. Miller sighed *curiously.* "Sometimes I wish you didn't want to be a scientist."

16 CLAUSE

The surface structure of a sentence can be composed of varying combinations of independent, dependent and embedded clauses. At the deep structure level, a clause is considered to be composed of a noun phrase and a verb phrase. At the surface level, a clause might retain both its noun and verb phrases or might be represented by any one or several of its constituents.

the *yellow* dog (surface structure)

Adjectives embedded within noun phrases represent deep structure clauses.

The dog. *The dog is yellow.* (deep structure)

The boy *walking down the street* is my brother. (surface structure)

The boy is walking down the street. The boy is my brother. (deep structure)

0 *The clause level is not involved in the miscue.*

a The miscue involves phonemic, bound morpheme, free morpheme, word, or phrase level changes which do not cause changes in clausal relationships.

ER It was fully dark when the alert ears of the *larger* dog caught the sound of a sharp whistle.
OR It was fully dark when the alert ears of the *large* dog caught the sound of a sharp whistle.

ER I was only washing the doll *to* make it look like new.
OR I was only washing the doll *and* make it look like new.

ER We could have a contest and pick a baby out of all *the* babies in town.
OR We could have a contest and pick a baby out of all babies in town.

b The miscue involves an OR word for which a grammatical function can not be found.

ER ... I said, "*It* helps me to remember the ..."
OR ... I said, "*to* helps me to remember the ..."

to could be either a verb marker or a preposition.

c If either the ER or the OR does not progress as far as the verb, we do *not* mark the clause level.

Ⓒ Then
Take it away.

Ⓒ though
I could feel it through my pajamas, moving on my stomach.

1 *A substitution is involved at the clause level.* This involves surface level variations for the same deep structure, the substitution of one deep structure for another, as well as moves between active and passive, declarative and question, positive and negative.

ER The book *which* you gave me was exciting.
OR The book you gave me was exciting.

ER Where did it bite you?
OR A bite?

ER This baby isn't typical.
OR This baby isn't typical?

ER I approached the gates ... (active)
OR I was approached ... (passive)

2 *An insertion is involved at the clause level.* This can be a surface level word insertion which represents a deep level clause, or the insertion of a surface level clause.

ER The flowers were for the party.
OR The *yellow* flowers were for the party.

ER ... quite a *businessman.*
OR ... quite a *busy man.*

ER I would like to win one *of* those.
OR I would like to win one *if* those.

ER Mr. *Vine* was excited when he saw the picture of the crow.
OR Mr. *Vine's* was excited when he saw the picture of the crow.

3 *An omission is involved at the clause level.* This can be a surface level word omission which represents a deep level clause or, the omission of a surface level clause.

ER As a matter of fact it wasn't *a* surprising thing for a krait to do.
OR As a matter of fact it wasn't surprising , thing for a krait to do.

The way to attach the final clause to the sentence is lost.

ER Such wishful thinking arises from the preconception that maturity will force the young to stop fighting for a future they want and begin to accept a future they can get.
OR Such wishful thinking arises from the preconception that maturity will force the young to stop fighting for a future . they want and begin to accept a future they can get.

The way to attach the final clauses to the sentence is lost.

ER They took pictures of *their* mother wearing her party clothes.
OR They took pictures of mother wearing her party clothes.

ER The *frantic* bleating became less frequent.
OR The bleating became less frequent.

4 *A reversal is involved at the clause level.* It is a resequencing or reorganizing of existing elements without a change in clause dependency.

5 *Clause dependency is altered within the sentence.* Only one ER sentence should be involved in the miscue.

ER When I arrived he was there.
OR I arrived when he was there.

ER He was wearing a pair of pajamas with blue, brown and white stripes.
OR He was wearing a pair of pajamas, blue and brown with white stripes.

Blue and *brown* represent embedded clauses which move in dependency from stripes to *pajamas.*

ER I was only washing the doll *to* make it look like new.
OR I was only washing the doll *and* make it look like new.

The deep structure for the ER and OR remain the same—*I was washing the doll, I will make it look like new.*—the dependency changes.

ER "Our Kitten!" the Jones children said.
OR "Our Kitten Jones!" children said.

6 *Clause dependency is altered across sentences.* Two ER sentences should be involved in the miscue.

ER "Ganderbai's coming. He said for you to lie still."
OR "Ganderbai's coming," he said. for you to lie still.

ER But his hands were steady *and* I noticed that his eyes were watching.
OR But his hands were steady. I noticed that his eyes were watching.

ER As he was eating, Freddie decided to fix the clock.
OR He was eating. Freddie decided to fix the clock.

ER I found her with the camera. *I* thought she was just playing.
OR I found her with the camera *and* thought she was just playing.

17 GRAMMATICAL CATEGORY AND SURFACE STRUCTURE OF OBSERVED RESPONSE

Researchers face a problem in dealing with the grammatical structure of language passages. Traditional, Latin based grammars are incomplete and inappropriate for describing English because they incorporate many misconceptions. Grammatical systems based on descriptive linguistics are better, but they fail to explore fully all aspects of grammar and are inadequate for dealing with language process. Generative transformational models are better suited to process, but do not fully explain surface structures, their relationships to deep structures, and the rules used for generating them.

For our research on reading miscues—unexpected oral responses to printed texts—a system is required that can be used to assign a grammatical function to each and every text word of a piece of prose. In our studies we are comparing the writer's surface structure with one regenerated by the reader.

Such a need immediately forces us to deal with phenomena beyond those which linguists have yet explored. At times it is necessary to make arbitrary distinctions in "grey areas" so that we can achieve consistency even though our system "leaks."

There are two reasons for lack of information about some aspects of English grammar:

- a Modern insights have not been applied yet to many phenomena.
- b Linguists have done little recent work that goes beyond sentences to connected discourse.

Our grammatical system has been organized by augmenting a descriptive grammar developed by Fries with the use of transformational analysis.

The system has five general categories—noun, verb, noun modifier, verb modifier, and function word. Two additional categories are used for words of indeterminate grammatical function and for contractions. Nouns, verbs, adjectives, and adverbs are additionally marked for filler and function aspects.

The canary lived in *space*.

category — noun
filler — common noun
function — noun in prepositional phrase

Function words are marked by type (noun marker, verb marker, verb particle, etc.). And, contractions are marked according to the functions of their left and right components. As we have not yet found a consistent way of handling numerals and initials they are treated as place holders and coded zero.

F.B.I. S.S.T. H.E.W.
He lives at *942* Main Street.
Mary read Part *B*.

Blank *This category is not appropriate.* The miscue involves:

a A phrase level miscue which cannot be broken into word level submiscues.
b Any one of the following allologs:
contraction/full
full/contraction
contraction not represented in print
long and short forms, or syllable deletion/insertion
misarticulation
c A phonemic level dialect miscue.
d An inflectional dialect miscue which involves an alternate surface form for the ER grammatical structure.

ER He walk(ed) home.

Walk is being keyed as dialect involved past tense form and so category 17 will be blank.

1__ **Noun Category.** Nouns are words that have concrete or abstract referents. They are things or ideas, entities which function as subjects, objects or in related ways.

Noun Filler

10_ *indeterminate*

11_ *common noun.* It is simplest to say that all nouns that aren't otherwise designated are common.

117
"He's a pretty good brother," I said.

12_ *proper noun.* Included are all names of specific people or places.

John Chicago Cherokee Mary England

Each of the words in two-word names are coded separately as proper nouns.

12_ 12_ 12_ 12_ 12_ 12_ 12_ 12_
John Smith Detroit River Kansas City Boston University

Where phrases have been turned into names or when the name has a direct semantic descriptive tied to the person or place "noun phrasal" unit is marked. (See 15_).

13_ *pronoun.* Included are any nominative, reflexive, or objective forms which take the place of a noun or phrase or clause acting as a noun in subsequent text occurrences.

everything, he, I, she, they, you, him, it, me, them
I want a red *one.*
This is mine.
We beat *ourselves.*
I want *some.*

14_ *verb derived noun.* These are nouns that are derived directly from a verb in a deep structure clause. At the surface level the word looks like a gerund or other verbal.

141
The fighting was severe.
(Someone was fighting. That was severe.)
141
Jogging can be invigorating.
(Someone is jogging. That can be invigorating.)

When more than the verb has been retained from the deep structure clause then the word is coded as a verb.

221
Fighting the Vietcong is difficult.
(Someone is fighting the Vietcong. That is difficult.)

15_ *phrasal unit noun.* Phrases can be turned into names. The original grammatical relationships of the words in the phrase are lost and the phrase operates as a unitary element in the deep structure. Two types of phrasal unit are possible: a hyphenated word sequence which is inflected at the end like a noun

15_ 15_
brother-in-law dog-catcher

or, a phrase which has become a proper name.

15_ 15_ 15_ 15_ 15_ 15_ 15_ 15_
New York City Candy Man Air Force One

Old Mill Road Michigan State University

16_ *word as word name.* Any word may be used as a noun when it is the name of the word.

164 164
The words "corral" and "boss" meant something to the dog.

162
He spelled "philosophical" correctly.

These word names must not be confused with words out of context. (See 62_)

17_ *quantifier or ordinal as noun.* Quantifiers and ordinals may appear in noun positions when the noun they introduce has been deleted from the surface structure.

At last (the last time). At first (the first time).

I want the third (thing).

Another (ship) was due any day.

Few (people) were available.

Three (something) of them came home.

18_ *noun modifier as noun.* Noun modifiers may sometimes be the remnants of deep structure noun phrases.

He flew off into the blue (sky).

You took mine. (my something)

She has a new convertible. (car)

He knew that his (something) was a serious case.

"Excuse me, mister (someone)," I said.

Noun Function

1_0 *indeterminate*

1_1 *subject.* Sentence subjects exist at two different levels: deep structure and surface structure levels. At either level, the relationship of the subject to the rest of the sentence is that of head noun in the noun phrase immediately dominated by *S.* The surface level manifestation of the subject may or may not be the same, then, as the deep structure subject. For instance:

a imperative transformations result in deleted subject, *you,*

Get out! (*You* get out)

b passive transformations result in an objectified subject,

Tom was hit by the ball. (The ball hit Tom)

c embedding transformations can result in a deleted subject or a subject that is replaced by a clause marker.

> The boys, having chosen up sides, decided to play baseball. (The boys chose sides. The boys decided to play baseball.)

For our purposes, nouns are coded as *surface level subjects* when they are the head nouns of noun phrases immediately dominated by *S.* (Jacobson & Rosenbaum, *English Transformational Grammar).* Each sentence needs at least one subject but may have as many as there are deep structure verbs. Some clauses may not have surface subjects.

151 151
The Detroit River is not wide.

151 151
Kitten Jones was her pet.

131 131
He knew that she would win.

Nouns may retain a subject function even though the verb is deleted from the surface structure.

111 111
The moon is bigger than the biggest mountain. (is big)

111 111
After the show (was over) the boys walked to Fifth Street.

There and *it* can occur as function words (rather than as verb modifier and pronoun, respectively). When these words occur as function words at the beginning of a NP, the deep structure subject of the sentence is coded as the subject.*

5(11)0 111
There is going to be a big show.

A big show is the subject in the deep structure and determines agreement of subject and verb at the surface level. *Show*, then, is coded as the subject of the sentence.

But in:

5(11)0 241
It is going to rain.

To rain, an infinitive verb form, is the deep structure subject, though not coded as subject. *It* is coded as a function word. *It* is not a pronoun since it represents no antecedent noun phrase.

Since the subject is in a particular relational position in the sentence, phrase and clause units can serve the subject function. These units are not coded as subject phrases. The words within them are coded according to their function within the embedded phrase or clause.

---

*Numbering systems for function words (5__), verbs (2__), etc. may be found further on in this section.—Ed.

221 112
Playing tennis is strenuous.
550 131 221
What he wanted was a drink.
530 241
To win was his ambition.

1_2 *direct object.* The direct object's relationship to the rest of the sentence can be described as that of the NP (excluding prepositional phrase) immediately dominated by the main verb in the verb phrase.

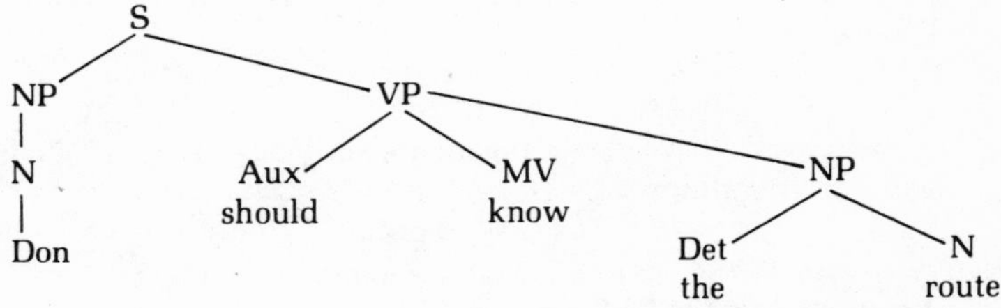

The direct object can be made the subject of a passive form of the sentence: *The route should be known by Don.* but can not have a preposition or phrase marker as an optional surface structure marker. *Don should know to the route.*

In some surface structures the direct object can occur between the verb and the verb particle.

221 112 530
Don put the fire out.

An adverbial element is also part of the verb phrase but holds a different relationship to the rest of the sentence structure. It can not be made the subject of a passive sentence.

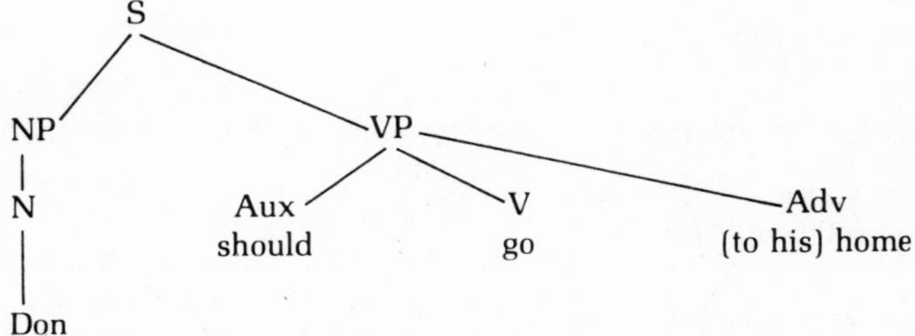

Cross references: transitive verbs (22_), verb particles (53_), indirect object (1_3), intransitive verb (23_).

1_3 *indirect object.* This function is the head noun in a noun phrase immediately dominated by the verb phrase. It is distinguished from the direct object by the feature + preposition. The preposition (usually *to* or *for*) is absent from the surface structure when the noun is coded as 1_3:

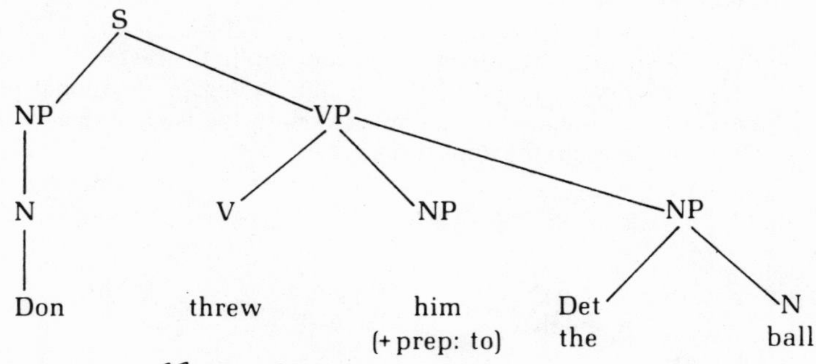

Don threw him the ball.

Don threw the ball to him.

A direct object may not always accompany an indirect object in the surface structure. Verbs such as *pay*, *promise*, *tell*, *ask*, *allow*, *let* have indirect objects with omitted direct objects:

He paid him. (He paid something to him.)

He asked Don. (He asked something of Don.)

1_4 *appositive.* This function involves the restatement of a noun for purposes of identification. The noun in the appositive position follows its noun equivalent in the surface structure.

John, the barber, worked quickly.

My mother, the telephone operator, cooks well.

The appositive is a surface structure manifestation of a deep structure subject complement:

John is the barber.

John worked quickly.

This function includes a deep structure predicate nominative that is transformed via embedding and reduction to a position following the head noun of a clause or phrase.

It is possible, then, to insert a dependent clause beginning with *who is* before the noun functioning as an appositive and retain an acceptable sentence structure:

John (who is) the barber, worked quickly.
My mother (who is) the telephone operator, cooks well.
We (who are) the boys will go in.

In children's speech, the appositive sometimes changes position:

121 134
Jim, he ran away. (he = Jim)

Rather than:

131 124
He, Jim, ran away.
114 131
The men over there, they are coaches.
114 131
Us boys, we are going.

Cross references: address (1_5), object complement (3_3), subject complement (3_3), subject complement (3_1).

Owen P. Thomas in *Transformational Grammar and the Teacher of English* (Holt, Rinehart & Winston, 1965) calls an appositive a noun modifier position (p. 95). We call it an equivalent form.

1_5 *address.* The noun in this function serves as an attention getter, director or organizer. It can occur in various positions in a sentence, and in fact is not part of the basic structure. It appears to be an optional element in dialogue.

125
John, where is the hammer?
125
"Come, Peggy. Let's go."
125
"Here, Peggy, old girl," he said.
125 125
Jimmy! Jimmy!
125
Look, Sally, look.
115
Boys, we will go in.

Nouns in the address function sometimes look like appositives if preceded or followed by a pronoun.

125 131
John, you are to stay here.
131 125
You, John, are to stay here.

1_6 *noun in prepositional phrase.* This function is that of object or head noun in a phrasal unit begun by function words called phrase markers (prepositions). Or, the noun may be in an adverbial phrase consisting of noun marker or adverbial noun modifier with the phrase marker deleted from the surface structure.

411 560 560 510 116
He fell down out of the tree.

560 156 156 156 560
The shallow basin of Salt Creek Wash became a gathering pool of dark-
116 560 116 560 116
ness where a band of eight hundred sheep with their lambs were bedding
530 560 116
down for night.

560 116
She sniffed the cool air of the late spring drifting down the wash.

560 176
At first the flowers failed to bloom.
560 176
At last the war was ended.

560 176
The call was returned at once.

510 116
(On, During) That night the storm hit.

382 116
(On, During) Last night he completed the task.

372 116
(On, During) Tomorrow night . . .

510 116
(On, During) One day . . . (Here, *one* is not a quantifier, but is comparable to *that* or *the*.)

510 116
(On, During) Some day . . .

116
She had eaten mutton (during) many times.

Note: It is possible to have a compound phrase marker or a compound verb particle, but not a compound adverb. (Proadverb: See 41_, below.)

1_7 *subject complement*. This function might also be labeled predicate noun. The noun follows a form of the verb *be* or *become*, *remain* or *stay* (special cases of copulative verbs). Generally, the subject complement can be regarded as an equivalent statement and can be interchanged with the subject.

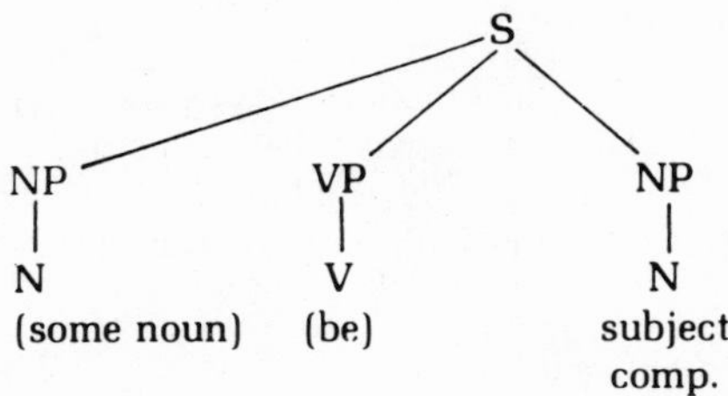

131 117
He remained a blacksmith all his life.
131 117
They would become easy prey to the coyotes.
131 117
It was a house of fine architectural design.
131 127
He was Mr. Big in the industry.

Function word place holders must be distinguished from the subject of the sentence in determining subject complements.

511 570 171
There was nothing more to eat.

Note: Forms of *be* can be substituted for *become*, *remain* and *stay* when they are followed by a subject complement.

1_8 *object complement*. This function co-occurs with and is an equivalent statement for the direct object. Transitive verbs such as *name*, *elect*, *appoint*, *make* often are followed by object complements. The surface structure is a result of embedding and deleting.

They appointed Fred.
Fred is President.
They appointed Fred President.

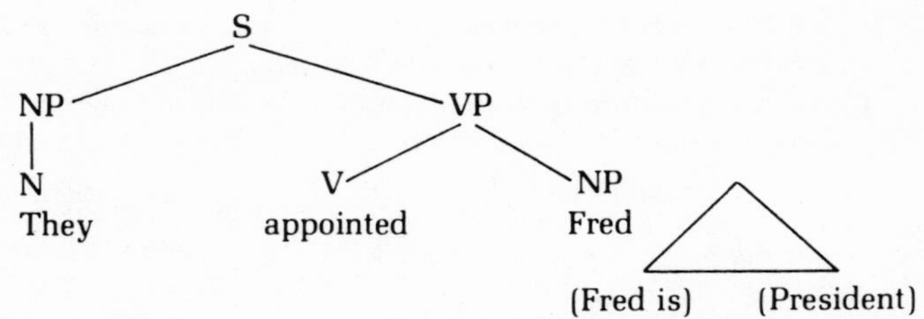

The object complement can generally be preceded by *to be.*

They appointed Fred (to be) President.
They elected Don (to be) senator.
They named him (to be) Don.

Cross references: appositive (1_4), address (1_5), subject complement (1_7), transitive verb (22_), direct object (1_2).

1_9 *noun in a phrase of intensification.* The intensifier function qualifies or indicates degree with respect to adverbials and adjectives.

He is very happy.
He lives far down the river.

The two examples above are function word intensifiers. Nouns can serve a similar kind of function.

We're two days out from the corrals and a day late on the drive.
A coyote emerged from the edge of the sage not fifty feet away.
A star is many many times bigger than yòu are.
All night long she cried.

Cross references: intensifier (57_), adverb (42_).

2__ Verb Category

Verb Filler

20_ *indeterminate*

21_ *"be" form.* This includes forms of *be* used as the main verb in a sentence, but does not include forms of *be* used as (auxiliary) verb markers. Some sentences contain both uses of *be.*

520 211
He is being helpful.

211
Sally was the victor.

Cross reference: function word (5__).

22_ *transitive verb.* These verbs can be followed by one or two NP's. Generally, transitive verbs are characterized as (1) those head verbs whose VP's have in their surface structures NP's immediately dominated by the VP, (2) verbs which can undergo the passive transformation. However, this definition must be augmented by noting:

1 The direct object NP can be eliminated from the surface structure.

He pays (to) him (something).
He asks (of) him (something).
He promises (to) him (something).
He sold (to) him (a bill of goods).
He smokes (something).
He sings (something).
He plays (something).

2 Some transitive verbs can not undergo the passive transformation. Gleason calls these pseudotransitive, Owen Thomas calls them middle verbs.

It *cost* ten dollars.
The trip *took* two days.

Cross references: indirect object (1_3), direct object (1_2), verb markers (52_).

23_ *intransitive verb.* These verbs do not have a passive form and have adverbial or adjectival phrases in the VP rather than NP's functioning as direct and indirect objects.

231
He was working hard.

231
She sat very still in her chair.

The category includes verbs such as *seem, remain, stay* and *become* which can be replaced by a form of *be.*

231 211
He became frightened. He was frightened.

231 211
He remained at home. He was at home.

231 211
He seems talented. He is talented.

Some verb forms traditionally labeled gerunds are coded as verbs.

231 231
They sat talking on the fence.

231 231
He went fishing in the river.

231 231
He came running down the road.

231 231
He went hunting in the woods.

The sentences can be restated as:

They sat and (they) talked on the fence.
They went and (they) fished in the river.
He came (down the road) (and he was) running down the road.
He went (in the woods) (and he was) hunting in the woods.

Subject complements can be distinguished from verbs by attempting to insert an intensifier.

331
He was (very) interesting.

311
He was (very) capable.

331
They seemed (very) ashamed.

Cross references: verb marker (5_2, noun modifier (18_).

24_ *infinitive.* A sequence of the verb particle *to* + verb generally signals the presence of the infinitive form of the verb:

530 520 241
He wanted it to be done.

530 241
He wanted to do it.

In some sentences, the element *to* is omitted from the surface structure:

241 He had him come.	530 241 (He had him to come.)
241 Let him go.	(Let him to go.)
241 Let go of it.	((You) let it to go.)

See Spot run. (See Spot to run.)

An infinitive form represents a deep structure clause:

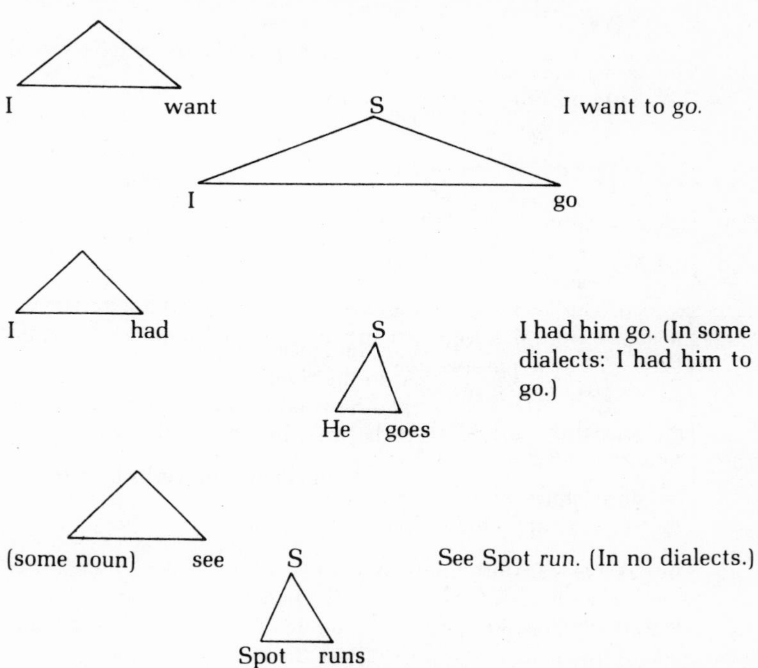

Note: Martin Joos, *The English Verb: Form and Meanings* (University of Wisconsin, 1968), recognizes the infinitive only when it is preceded by the marker *to*; the other form—minus the marker—he calls a presentative. (p.16)

25_ *proverbs.* These verbs function much as do the elements traditionally identified as pronouns; i.e., they are an abbreviated surface structure representation of an entire phrase, in this case, the verb phrase. They are the first elements in the verb phrase.

Sam was going to buy candy.

John wished he could too.

The deep structure VP includes *buy candy*, but the VP is reduced to include only the modal in the surface structure.

A proverb may also be a verb of duration (see verb marker under function word) that is not followed by the main verb.

Stop, Dick, stop.

This is the surface representation of *Stop pushing the merry-go-round, Dick, stop pushing the merry-go-round.*

Verb Function

2_0 *indeterminate*

2_1 *active*

2_2 *passive.* Traditional grammar identifies the verb characteristic voice. In the active voice the deep structure and the surface structure subject are identical. In the passive voice the deep structure subject becomes the surface structure agent.

John kissed the girl. (active)
The girl was kissed by John. (passive)

The storm uprooted the tree. (active)
The tree was uprooted by the storm. (passive)

The passive transformation involves (1) the inversion of the first NP in a sentence with one of the other NP's immediately dominated by the VP, (2) the inclusion of *be* or *get* prior to the verb markers and/or main verb, and (3) the inclusion of *by* + NP, at the end of the clause.

Passive verb forms can be identified in the surface structure by the presence of *be* or *get* as verb markers along with the agentive VP phrase begun with *by* + (some noun or noun phrase). Often the *by* or agentive phrase is missing from the surface structure.

The girl was kissed (by someone).
The girl got kissed (by someone).

Note: *Most* transitive verbs but *no* intransitive verbs function in the passive voice.

2_3 *imperative.* The imperative most often is incompletely characterized as the presence of the main verb at the beginning of a clause and the absence of a subject NP in the surface structure. Traditional grammar characterizes the imperative verb form as having as a deleted subject *you*, which is "understood." The tag question transformation lends validity to the idea that *you* is the subject.

223
Check the parking meter.

can be transformed to:

223
Check the parking meter, will you.

223
You will check the parking meter.

223
You check the parking meter.

The imperative is characterized by a syntactic context including (1) a second person pronoun for a subject which may or may not be in the surface structure, (2) *will* as the one and only auxiliary which is present in the surface structure when the pronoun subject is present, and (3) the present tense.

213
Be on time.

223
If you can, come at six.

223 530
Look at that car!

2_4 *subjunctive.* Conditional status is indicated by the subjunctive verb. It is marked by a dependent clause begun with *if* and the subjunctive verb forms *be* or *were*. The subjunctive is becoming archaic in speech though it is present in writing.

214
If he be king . . .

214
If I were you . . .

234
If Nixon were elected . . .

3__ **Noun Modifier Category**

Noun Modifier Filler

30_ *indeterminate*

31_ *adjective.* An adjective qualifies as a noun. The test for adjectives is:

111 311
The ______________ is ______________.

The new wagon arrived.

111 311
The wagon is new.

The lively kitten played with twine.

111 311
The kitten is lively.

Some adjectives can be easily confused with proper noun and noun adjunct:

312
The oak trees are beautiful.

311
The trees are oak.

117
The trees are oaks.

187
The tree is *an* oak. (tree)

312
The Cherokee boy arrived.

311
He is Cherokee.

131 127
He is a Cherokee.

127
They are Cherokees.

312 127
The American boy arrived. The boys are Americans.

111 311
The boy is American.

127
The boy is *an* American.

311
The boys are American.

32_ *noun adjunct.* A noun adjunct is a noun functioning in an adjective position.

circus tent *criminal* lawyer *ice-cream* man *fire* hydrant

A noun adjunct must fit one of the following tests.

1 It may be transformed to the noun in a prepositional phrase.

the tent *for the circus*
the lawyer *for criminals*
the hydrant *for the fire department*

2 It may be the direct object of an embedded, deleted sentence.

the man (the man sells ice-cream)
the man (who sells ice-cream)
the ice-cream man

3 It may be the subject complement of an embedded, deleted sentence.

the teacher (the teacher is a student)
the teacher (who is a student)
the student teacher

33_ *verb derived modifier*. This includes verbs which are placed in a modifying position prior to a noun.

The painted fence is new.
Running water is available.

The test for verb derived modifiers:

The ____________ is ____________.
noun verb

The fence is painted (by me).

The water is running.

34_ *possessive noun*

35_ *possessive pronoun*. These are nouns and pronouns of the following sort:

Mr. Green's car arrived.
His car was green.

Some pronouns have two possessive forms—one to use in embedded position and the other as subject complement or noun substitute.

Embedded:	Her car arrived.
Subject complement:	The car is hers.
Noun substitute:	Hers is new.

Note: Embedded possessives have a double function since they replace the noun marker when they are embedded.

The car is green. The car is his. His car is green.

We choose to classify possessives as noun modifiers only since handling both functions carries our analysis to another level of complexity.

36_ *titles.* Titles occur with proper nouns.

Mr., Mrs. Grandfather Grandmother Uncle, Aunt Doctor General President King, Queen	+ proper noun

Some of these items may exist by themselves with no proper noun or phrasal unit attached. If so, they are coded as proper nouns.

12_
The President of the United States
362 12_
King George
362 12_
Grandfather Eastman

Cross references: nominal phrasal unit (15_), proper noun (12_).

37_ *adverbial.* Adverbs which are placed in a modifying position prior to a noun. These modifiers qualify nouns with respect to time and place and seem to be remnants of embedded adverbial phrases.

372
tomorrow night . . .
(the night of tomorrow . . .)
372
yesterday morning . . .
(the morning of yesterday . . .)
37_
front yard . . .
(the yard in the front . . .)
37_
side lot . . .
(the lot at the side . . .)
37_
top floor . . .
(the floor at the top . . .)

Cross references: noun modifier (3__), ordinal number (38_), adjective (31_).

38_ *ordinal number.* This grouping indicates sequence.

382 121
Next Monday is the parade.

382 116
He went home last week.

382 111
The third game was lost.

39_ *phrasal unit.* This includes both hyphenated and unhyphenated noun phrasal units placed in a modifying position prior to a noun. The unit, not each word, is the modifier.

392 392
the dining room table.

392 392
an internal combustion engine

392
a mother-in-law phobia

Noun Modifier Function

3_1 *subject complement.* This function might also be labeled predicate adjective. The noun modifier follows a form of *be* or of *become, remain, stay,* or *feel* for which some form of *be* can be substituted.

371
He was late.

311
He is young.

311
He remained alert.
(He was alert.)

311
He stays awake.
(He is awake.)

311
They felt happy.
(They were happy.)

Sometimes a subject complement begins a sentence and is the only remaining element of a deep structure sentence:

311
Desperate, he ducked into a dark passageway.

311
(He was) desperate, (and) he ducked into a dark passageway.

3_2 *embedded.* Noun modifiers which precede the element modified are surface structure representations of embedded clauses.

312 312 11_
the new red wagon . . .
(the wagon is new)
(the wagon is red)
382 392 392 11_
the first dog catcher truck . . .
(the truck is the first)
(the truck is for the dog catcher)
312 362 12_
little Miss Muffet . . .
(Muffet is little)
(Muffet is a Miss)

3_3 *object complement.* In sentences such as *He painted the fence green.*, the noun modifier, *green*, is the remains of an embedded clause. It modifies the head noun in a noun phrase immediately dominated by the verb phrase.

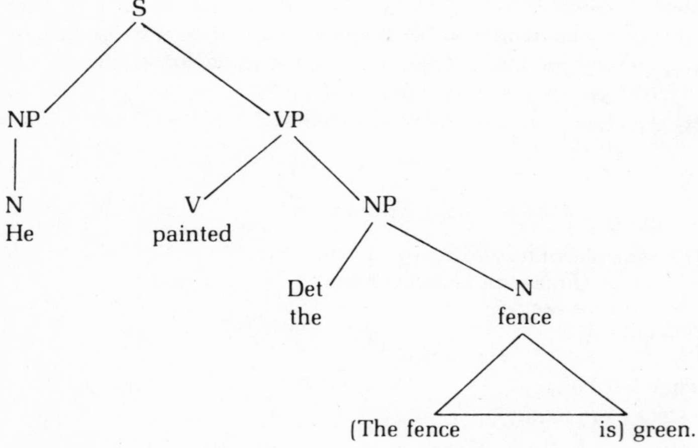

4__ **Verb Modifier**

Verb Modifier Filler

40_ *indeterminate*

41_ *proadverb.* A proadverb functions much as do proverbs and the elements traditionally labeled pronouns. A proadverb stands for an entire adverbial phrase which is not present in the surface structure. Proadverbs include: (1) the first element of a compound phrase marker; (2) the phrase marker without a following noun phrase.

411
He went back.

560 560
(He went back to someplace).

411
He ran out.

560 560
(He ran out of someplace).

A proadverb will be only the first of any sequence of phrase markers. Proadverbs can not exist in compound or consecutive sequences.

411
He fell down.

560 560 560
He fell down out of the tree.

Cross references: verb particle (53_), noun in adverbial phrase (1_6), adverb (42_), phrase marker (56_).

42_ *adverb.* Single words which qualify the head verb in the verb phrase with respect to time, place, manner or any "other" way and which are, themselves, immediately dominated by VP are coded as adverbs. They are frequently marked morphologically by the *-ly* suffix, but this is not true in all dialects.

422
. . . he tied the tubing tight with a knot.

43_ *noun form.* Nouns which are the remaining elements of a deep structure adverbial phrase are included here.

431
He went home. He went {back home. / to his home.}

431
There is Dick. {Over / Down} there is Dick.

431
Come here. Come {over / in} here.

He should be here (by) now.

That was (on) yesterday.

Cross references: noun in adverbial or other prepositional phrase (1_6), adverb (42_), proadverb (41_).

Verb Modifier Function

4_0 *indeterminate*

4_1 *place.* Verb modifiers will indicate where the verb operates.

He ate there.

Most frequently, adverbials of place are prepositional phrases. Where they are not, they frequently are proverbs with the preposition left in the surface structure and noun deleted.

He waited outside (the door).

Or nouns as verb modifiers with prepositions deleted.

He went (to) home. He went (to) there.

4_2 *manner.* Verb modifiers will indicate how the verb operates.

He ran rapidly.

4_3 *time.* Verb modifiers will indicate when (or for how long) the verb operates.

Please come now.

Adverbials of time will often be prepositional phrases or transformed phrases that result in nouns remaining after preposition deletions.

He came (on) yesterday. (On) Monday he went home.

It lasted (for) weeks.

4_4 *reason.* Adverbials of reason add reason to the verb's operation. They are generally prepositional phrases.

He did it purposely.

4_5 *other.* A small collection including *too*, *also*, etc.

Note: All words in prepositional phrases are separately coded regardless of the function of the whole phrase.

126
I'm going on next Monday.

When only the preposition is deleted the coding remains the same.

126
I'm going next Monday.

But when only the noun remains, then it is coded as a verb modifier.

433
I'm going Monday.

5__ **Function Word Category** *

Function Word Filler

50_ *indeterminate*

51_ *noun marker.* Words which signal the presence of nouns and which have little concrete or abstract meaning are noun markers.

One day . . .
Some day . . .

That, this, these, those, the, followed by a noun are noun markers.

Noun markers—with the exception of *the* and *a*—can also function as pronouns.

Cross references: pronoun (13_), quantifier (5(10)_).

52_ *verb marker.* These include auxiliary verbs in the verb phrase. The modals, *have* and *be* can be verb markers when the main verb is included in the surface structure.

520 520
He should have come.

520
He is coming.

Do is also a verb marker when the main verb is present in the surface structure.

520
He did arrive late.

---

* In the 5_ (Function Word) Category, the third element, designating function, becomes redundant and is represented by an underline (_) in the list, by (0) over examples.—Ed.

520
Did he get home?

Verb markers can occur in multiple sequences:

520 520
He should have been here.
520 520 530 520 530 240
Jane is going to have to go to Paris.
520 520 530 241
Tom will have to mow the lawn.

There are verb markers which seem to indicate duration of time: keep + on, go + on, went + on, stop, continue.

520 530
He went on walking.
520
He kept (on) walking.

Other examples which might be noted.

520
He ought to do it.
520
He must do it.
520
He has to do it.

Going is often used as a tense marker. In speech, *going* is the future tense marker more often than is *will* or *shall*.

520
I'm going to go.
520
I will go.
(I shall go).

Get and its alternate forms can also be verb markers.

520
He got going.
520
She gets started early.

They are particularly common as passive markers.

520
He got hit by the ball.
520
She gets kissed often (by men).

Cross references: verbs, transitive (22_) and intransitive (23_).

53_ *verb particle.* Verb particles are words that can look like prepositions or adverbs but which are essential to the full meaning of the verb. For example, in the sentence *He turned off the light.* The separable element *off* is essential to the meaning of the verb *turn.* If *off* is left out of the sentence, the meaning is significantly changed: *He turned the light.*

There is a sequence of tests which can be used to judge verb particles.

Semantic

1 A synonym seems to be a possible equivalent for the two-word verbal.

He *turned* the lights *off.*
(He *extinguished* the lights.)

2 The particle seems to go with the main verb and, in fact, seems essential to its meaning.

Syntactic

1 Are the verb and following element separable?

He *turned off* the lights.
He *turned* the lights *off.*

He put up his bike.
He *put* his bike *up.*

Note: When a pronoun is present, a noun needs to be substituted:

He put it up.
*He put up it (the bike).

2 If the particle and main verb are not separable, can the sentence be transformed into a *semantically similar* and *acceptable "how"* or *"where"* question *without* the use of the particle? For example:

particle needed	The car (ran into) the store. (hit, struck) What did the car run into? Answer: the store.
prepositional phrase not necessary to form question	The boy (ran into) the store. (entered) Where did the boy run? Answer: into the store.

3 Can the main verb and particle be transformed into a passive sentence?

He was watching for the police.
(The police were being watched for by him.)

But the same words can have a different deep structure.

He was watching for the police.
(The police asked him to watch something.)

No passive possible.

4 Does the main verb have a latinate prefix which duplicates the meaning of the separate element?

He *de*parted *from* . . . He *con*tracted *with* . . .
He *en*tered *into* . . . She *dis*pensed *with* . . .

Notice that the syntactic question has been whether the NP dominated by the VP is the object of the verb (including particle) or the object of a preposition.

Problems arise in both the semantic and syntactic realms when one attempts to identify a category of separable verbs exclusive of large numbers of exceptions and special cases.

The *to* marking infinitive verb forms is coded as a verb particle.

530 241
Tom will have to mow the lawn.

530 241
"I was only washing the doll to make it look like new," Freddie explained.

54_ *question marker.* Question patterns are generally indicated in two ways: (1) the inversion of auxiliary + tense and the noun phrase; (2) the inclusion of one of a group of question words at the beginning of the sentence. These question words include: *what, when, which, why, where, how.*

540
Which chair is ready to ship?
540
How do you play chess?

But notice that when a question is embedded in a larger structure and functions as a dependent clause, the question marker function is superseded by the clause marker function (see below).

550
Do you know which chair is ready to ship?

Does anyone know how you turn on the air conditioner?
(In some dialects this would be: Anybody know how do you turn on the air conditioner?)

Do you know why he is leaving the company?

55_ *clause marker*. Clause markers begin dependent clauses and join them to the independent clauses.

He knew that the car was new.

The news that the plane was late wasn't startling.

The play which John wrote was performed.

Ted is bigger than John. (is big)

He ran as fast as he could.

After the show (was over), the boys went to the drive-in.

In the last three examples above, the verb phrase of the relative clause is incomplete or absent. The last two examples above show that words traditionally labeled prepositions can also be clause markers. In the last example, the verb phrase is missing completely from the surface structure.

56_ *phrase marker*. These are words which introduce an adverbial or other prepositional phrase. These may occur in a series.

His home is *by the expressway*.

The hat *on his head* fell *over his eyes*.

Sam ran *down the road*.

Ted fell *down out of the tree*. (In some dialects: Ted fell *down out the tree*.)

I'm going *over to Judy's*.

Cross references: proadverb (41_), verb particle (53_), adverb (42_), adverb (42_), adverb particle (5(12)_), clause marker (55_).

57_ *intensifier.* Intensifiers indicate amount or degree with respect to *adjectives* and *adverbs.* Adjectives and adverbs are *intensified*; noun forms are *quantified.* They can modify either single words or phrases.

570 420
Very well.

570 311
He is indeed clever.

570 422
The doctor moved very quickly.

570 311
The bottle was { almost full. / 570 half / 570 quite / 570 barely }

570 423
Just then, he arrived.

570 331
He was very tired.

570 560 186 560 136
Put it right on top of this.

570 311
John was { hardly happy. / 570 completely }

570 560 510 116
{ Precisely / 570 Right } at that moment, he arrived.

Intensifiers may occur in two word sequences.

570 570 423
All too soon it was time to go.

570 570 311
A ladybug is very, very small.

Cross references: noun in intensification (1_9), quantifiers (5(10)_).

58_ *conjunction.* Words which conjoin clauses or phrases or elements within clauses or phrases are conjunctions. Only parallel and equal elements may be conjoined.

580
John and Sue arrived.

580 580
He wanted neither red nor white.

580
The dish is broken, therefore, she'll buy another.

580 580
He knew what to do and so he began.

59_ *negative.* Both *no* and *not* are included in this category. When *not* occurs in a contraction, it is coded as part of the contraction (see contractions).

510_ *quantifier.* Nouns are quantified, adjectives and adverbs are intensified.

5(10)0
What fun this is.

5(10)0
Few people came.

5(10)0 510 119 311
The water is half a foot deep.

5(10)0 119 371
They are three days late.

Negative quantifiers include:

He is { 5(10)0 scarcely an athlete.
590 5(10)0 not exactly
5(10)0 hardly }

511_ *other*. This category contains special instances of *it* and *there*.

5(11)0
It is raining.

5(11)0
There is a good restaurant in the Union.

Here is included when its "place" reference is diminished from a specific *in this place* to a general, idiomatic usage.

5(11)0
Here you are.

5(11)0
Here is my idea.

5(11)0
Now see here.

Yes is included in this category. Actually *yes* is a special case. It is included here to avoid creating a special category for one word.

512_ *adverb particle*. These elements may look like prepositions but do not mark the beginning of a phrase; rather, they are pattern completers which add little to meaning.

425 5(12)0
He is better off.

423 5(12)0
We'll discuss it later on.

423 5(12)0
Earlier on they'd discussed it.

425 5(12)0
Right on!

6__ Indeterminate Category

Indeterminate Filler

60_ *indeterminate*

61_ *interjection*

Hell! Oh! Well! Indeed! Gracious! Damn! (in the nominal sense of *damnation*)

62_ *words out of syntactic context.* When an isolated word or a list of words occurs inside quotation marks, then the word is coded as lacking its usual syntactic contexts. Included, too, are full mailing addresses and signs.

620
"Philosophical," he said.

620 620 620
"Savage: wild, not tamed."

620 620 620 620
"Sinewy: stringy, strong or powerful."

620 620 620
Mr. J. Johns

000 620 620
224 Park Street

620 620 620 620
New York, New York

Note: Numbers and alphabetic initials are not coded, since they involve another system and do not elicit any single, correct, expected response.

116 000
He lives in apartment 3A.

116 000
He ran toward number 749.

63_ *defies classification/ambiguous.* This category is used in the rare case that some tentative assignment to another category can not be made.

64_ *greetings.* This category includes all *one*-word greetings and *two*-word greetings such as *good morning.* Greetings such as *How do you do?* are treated literally.

7__ **Contraction Category.** This category allows us to code both parts of either an ER or OR contraction.

Left Part of Contraction

71_ *pronoun.* All words coded as pronouns which appear as left parts of contractions.

711
He's coming.
712
That's mine.

72_ *verb marker.* All words coded as verb markers which appear as left parts of contractions. *Be, have* and *do* forms are differentiated from their verb marker counterparts.

724
He isn't coming.

724
They don't see us.

73_ *be forms.* All *be* forms in copula position. Note that *be* forms also appear as right parts of contractions.

734
He isn't here.

734
They aren't happy.

74_ *let.* This verb as a contraction appears only with the pronoun *us.*

745
Let's go.

75_ *question marker/clause marker.* All words which are normally coded question or clause markers.

752
What's his name?
751
How've you been?
751
Where're we going?
751
The house that's falling down.
751
That's the boy who's crying?

76_ *it/there/here.* These three words are coded here, when they would normally be coded *511–other* under function word if they appeared separately.

762
Here's a job for you.
761
It's raining.
761
There'll be a hot time tonight.

77_ *adverb.* Words such as *here* and *there* used as adverbs.

772
Here's mine.

772
There's the man.

78_ *noun.* All words (other than pronouns) coded as nouns.

781
Tom's leaving.

781
Mary'll come too.

782
Bob's happy now.

79_ *transitive verb* (have). Forms of *have* may appear as transitive verbs in left parts. Rarely, they also appear in right parts (see 7_3).

794
He hasn't any money.

794
They haven't any food.

Note: Avoid confusing *has* forms used as verb markers.

724
He hasn't left yet.

Right Part of Contraction. A smaller number of possibilities may be right parts of contractions. One example is given with each possible left part. Obviously many combinations are not possible in English.

7_1 *verb marker.* All words normally coded verb markers which occur as right parts.

711
He's coming.

761
It's raining.

781
Mary's got it.

751
He is the one who'll try.

7_2 *be forms.* In copula position as right part.

712
It's here.

752
Who's home?

772
Here's the place.
782
Mary's home now.

7_3 *have* (transitive verb). Rarely, forms of *have* may occur in American English as right parts.

713
They've a new car.

7_4 *negative*. Always appears as *n't*.

724
They aren't coming.

734
They aren't here.

744
They haven't any.

7_5 *pronoun*(us). Some pronouns appear to be contracted, such as *him* and *them*, but are not written as contractions. They are not normally counted as miscues.

795
Let's go.

Additional Notes:

Idioms. Idioms are treated literally, e.g.:

221 510 112 560 510 116
She's had a heck of a time.

This procedure is followed despite the probability that idioms exist as single lexical entries in deep structure.

Partial Sentences. Syntactic structures preceding and following the sentence fragment are reviewed, and grammatical functions assigned in accordance with prior and subsequent occurrences, e.g.:

421
I want to go outside.
421
Outside! It's too cold out there.

18 OBSERVED RESPONSE IN VISUAL PERIPHERY

The possibility exists that any substitution or insertion miscue which a reader makes has been partially cued by an item in the reader's visual peripheral field—that as the reader scans the text, what he reads can be influenced by text items in the periphery of his vision.

This category is limited to word level substitution and insertion miscues and to consideration of the five text lines immediately surrounding the miscue.

Mother looked at Freddie.
She said, "You are too little
to help Father and Jack. } near } extended
You are not too little to help me.
Here is something you can do."

Blank *This category is inappropriate.* An omission, nonword substitution, or phrase level miscue is involved.

0 *The visual periphery are not involved in the miscue.* The OR item can not be found within the surrounding five lines of text.

Mother looked at Freddie.
She said, "You are too little
work
to help Father and Jack.
You are not too little to help me.
Here is something you can do."

1 *The OR can be found in the near visual periphery.* The OR can be found in the text within the three lines surrounding the miscue.

Mother looked at Freddie.
She said, "You are too little
said
to help Father and Jack. } near
You are not too little to help me.
Here is something you can do."

2 *The OR can be found in the extended visual periphery.* The OR can be found in the text within the second line before or after the line containing the miscue.

Mother looked at Freddie.
She said "You are too little
Mother
to help Father and Jack. } extended
You are not too little to help me.
Here is something you can do."

9 *It is doubtful whether the visual periphery were involved in the miscue.* The OR can be found within the visual periphery but there is an unusual amount of intervening space caused either by paragraphing or the use of double columns of print.

Developing a Comprehension Rating

Editor's Note: The data basis for miscue analysis is an audio tape recording of a student's oral reading and retelling of a story. After a short conversation to put the student at ease, the researcher asks the student to read an entire story aloud without assistance or interference from the researcher, and, after finishing the story, to close the book and retell the researcher as much of the story as can be remembered. After the student relates as much as he or she can, the researcher asks further questions which are designed to elicit all possible remembered information, but these questions do not refer to anything the student has not already mentioned. If, for example, the student does not mention a character, the researcher can ask, "Was there anyone else in the story?" but may not ask, "Who was ________?"

Guide Questions to Aid Story Retelling

1 Now, would you tell me everything you remember about the story you just read?
(Do not interrupt or interject any questions until the child has completed this retelling. Keep in mind the Story Comprehension form. Then, ask any of the following kinds of questions to elicit responses in areas the child either failed to cover or was ambiguous about.)

2 Can you think of anything else that happened? (events)

3 Who else was in the story? (character recall) Tell me about them.

4 What happened that's funny, exciting or sad in the story? (subtleties)

5 What do you think the story was telling you? (theme)

6 Where did the story take place? (setting)

7 Tell me more about (key character). (character development)

8 Tell me why (key event) happened. (plot)

Additional Instructions

1 If the child seems to grope for words or stops, the researcher may pick up a question or comment from the child's final statement (#1 above) to encourage further response.

2 Inserting questions such as "What happened next?", "How did that happen?", etc. may also encourage further response.

3 If the child's response has left it unclear whether or not he knows the plot, etc., then additional specific questions are in order. The unique organization of some stories might necessitate preparing such questions prior to the taping.

4 When using any of the suggestions provided above, no specific information may be used in a question if the child has not already provided that information.

5 Always check the reader's comprehension of any unusual key words from the text.

Story Outline

A content outline should be developed for each piece of reading material, with one hundred points being distributed across the items within each of the categories.

Character recall (list characters)	15
Character development (modifying statements)	15
Theme	20
Plot	20
Events (list occurrences)	30

Information Outline

Major concept(s)	30
Generalization(s)	30
Specific points or examples	40

The reader's retelling is compared to the outline and points are deducted from the total of one hundred for missing or confused information.

INDEX